Development is Back

Edited by

Jorge Braga de Macedo, Colm Foy and Charles P. Oman

OECD

DEVELOPMENT CENTRE OF THE ORGANISATION
FOR ECONOMIC CO-OPERATION AND DEVELOPMENT

ORGANISATION FOR ECONOMIC CO-OPERATION AND DEVELOPMENT

Pursuant to Article 1 of the Convention signed in Paris on 14th December 1960, and which came into force on 30th September 1961, the Organisation for Economic Co-operation and Development (OECD) shall promote policies designed:

- to achieve the highest sustainable economic growth and employment and a rising standard of living in Member countries, while maintaining financial stability, and thus to contribute to the development of the world economy;
- to contribute to sound economic expansion in Member as well as non-member countries in the process of economic development; and
- to contribute to the expansion of world trade on a multilateral, non-discriminatory basis in accordance with international obligations.

The original Member countries of the OECD are Austria, Belgium, Canada, Denmark, France, Germany, Greece, Iceland, Ireland, Italy, Luxembourg, the Netherlands, Norway, Portugal, Spain, Sweden, Switzerland, Turkey, the United Kingdom and the United States. The following countries became Members subsequently through accession at the dates indicated hereafter: Japan (28th April 1964), Finland (28th January 1969), Australia (7th June 1971), New Zealand (29th May 1973), Mexico (18th May 1994), the Czech Republic (21st December 1995), Hungary (7th May 1996), Poland (22nd November 1996), Korea (12th December 1996) and the Slovak Republic (14th December 2000). The Commission of the European Communities takes part in the work of the OECD (Article 13 of the OECD Convention).

The Development Centre of the Organisation for Economic Co-operation and Development was established by decision of the OECD Council on 23rd October 1962 and comprises twenty-two Member countries of the OECD: Austria, Belgium, Canada, the Czech Republic, Denmark, Finland, France, Germany, Greece, Iceland, Ireland, Italy, Korea, Luxembourg, Mexico, the Netherlands, Norway, Portugal, Slovak Republic, Spain, Sweden, Switzerland, as well as Argentina and Brazil from March 1994, Chile since November 1998 and India since February 2001. The Commission of the European Communities also takes part in the Centre's Advisory Board.

The purpose of the Centre is to bring together the knowledge and experience available in Member countries of both economic development and the formulation and execution of general economic policies; to adapt such knowledge and experience to the actual needs of countries or regions in the process of development and to put the results at the disposal of the countries by appropriate means.

 THE OPINIONS EXPRESSED AND ARGUMENTS EMPLOYED IN THIS PUBLICATION ARE THE SOLE RESPONSIBILITY OF THE AUTHORS AND DO NOT NECESSARILY REFLECT THOSE OF THE OECD, THE DEVELOPMENT CENTRE OR THE GOVERNMENTS OF THEIR MEMBER COUNTRIES.

*
* *

Publié en français sous le titre :
Retour sur le développement

Foreword

It is a pleasure and an honour to be asked to contribute the Foreword to this book marking the 40th Anniversary of the creation of the OECD Development Centre.

Until recently, I was not aware that the idea for the Centre was first expressed by President John F. Kennedy before the Parliament of Canada in May 1961. I did not hear that speech, not becoming a Member of Parliament until some 17 years later, but that very day I watched the President lay a wreath at the Canadian War Memorial, and then walk on foot with the Prime Minister to Parliament to deliver his address.

I relate this personal anecdote because development issues were very much on my mind at the time, having participated in the World University Service Seminar in West Africa just four years before. A co-participant was later to become one of Canada's most outstanding prime ministers, Pierre Elliot Trudeau, a man for whom "development" was a life-long pursuit.

As I pen these remarks, it is difficult for me to believe that 41 years have elapsed since that day when President Kennedy proposed the Development Centre. Perhaps my memory of the day is so "vivid" because it was the first and last time that I actually saw JFK.

Indeed, it was an appropriate moment and an appropriate place for such a suggestion. We were, in what Angus Maddison in this book describes as the "West", perplexed about our relations with the developing world, and we, the West, were, as now, particularly concerned about the fate of the poorer countries. Concern, however, is not enough, if, as I wrote in the OECD Observer's May 2002 issue, it results in aid as "conscience money" and produces the dismal record we have seen in sub-Saharan Africa where per capita incomes are barely higher than they were in 1960. Aid has to be partnered by knowledge and experience, otherwise good intentions can have the perverse effect of inducing laxity and wastage into aid policies, punishing the poor first and most.

This is another reason why I am pleased to have been asked by the Centre's President, Jorge Braga de Macedo, to contribute to this volume. The OECD Development Centre has worked and evolved over these last four decades to improve our knowledge of development issues within the OECD family. As the OECD has integrated development more and more into its programmes, we have become aware of the benefits of explaining the principles which have guided our own development — peer pressure, democracy and good governance — to non-member countries. We are not here attempting to dictate "OECD solutions" to other countries in the style of the Cold War, but to point out that there is much they can learn from our experience.

As the OECD Development Centre enters its fifth decade, I am sure its expertise, as demonstrated in these pages, will continue to nourish our knowledge of the problems of development. It will continue to reinforce our efforts to help — in an effective way — those countries and peoples less well off than ourselves.

Sadly, we will never know whether the Centre fulfilled JFK's expectations, but we all hope that it has.

Donald J. Johnston
Secretary–General of the OECD

Table of Contents

PART TWO: PERSONAL PERSPECTIVES

Preface

Globalisation has generalised knowledge about the challenges facing developing countries, and emphasised the need for good governance and institutional change. When globalisation and governance interact positively, notably through national and international peer pressure, reform can be sustained along the entire development path from aid–dependence to political and financial freedom.

The OECD Development Centre's most recent work programme has been on the interactions between globalisation and governance. It thus appears natural to mark our 40th anniversary by identifying responses to the many development challenges still facing us today from the perspective of the "reformers' club" that is the OECD. Looking back can help us to move forward by reminding us of solutions that may have been forgotten. Hence our title, *Development Redux,* which — at the insistence of the publisher — we translated into *Development is Back.*

The interaction between the international and the domestic and regional environments is crucial to understanding why some policies failed and others worked. This has led the OECD to examine the problems of development on the basis of its own, unique expertise. In consequence a development element now finds its way into most, if not all the Organisation's work programmes; this process represents a major challenge for the Centre and other units in the development "cluster" (see Postscriptum towards the end of this volume).

The principles guiding the interaction among OECD countries and the modes of governance that they enjoy go a long way to explaining their adaptive capacity and resistance to shocks. The challenge consists in finding means of adapting the institutional and policy framework in which developed countries operate to each developing country's capacities and ambition.

The principle of peer pressure helps to take into account diverse development experiences and expectations. Originally conceived of to co–ordinate implementation of the Marshall Plan, peer pressure installs informal controls on the behaviour of Member states and encourages a learning process between nations. The system epitomises "unity with diversity", as different aspects of mutual surveillance apply to diverse circumstances.

Also core to the framework is the principle of proximity, enshrined in the European Union's founding articles. This recognises the efficiency and political responsiveness of citizen–based governance, even in a context of supra–national institutions. Proximity of institutions to the citizen also helps to provide an environment conducive to enterprise and the creation of wealth.

Part One of this book is concerned with the aspects of economic policy which can contribute to growth and increasing prosperity in the poorer countries. Starting with an update on the celebrated "millennial perspective on the world economy", the reasons for the observed growth patterns between developed and developing countries are identified. Potential routes to economic policy solutions available to developing countries themselves are then offered, before dealing with such topics as sustainable development, poverty, the firm, privatisation, trade and investment, finance and civil society. The introductory chapter and the contributions to Part Two report how each decade in the life of the Centre brought its particular challenges and responses.

The idea of looking back to move forward, first presented on 25 October 2000 at the meeting of Centre's Advisory Board by the Swiss Ambassador, turned into project *Redux*. As President of the Board, the French Ambassador supported the project. Thanks are due to her and to Don Johnston, who recorded his own impressions of the Centre's origin.

When my term began — one year to the day before the Swiss initiative — I was already convinced that comparative development analysis and policy dialogue at the OECD derive enhanced credibility from the Organisation's brand name as a "reformers' club". The Development Centre contributes to this brand name, a fact which, in the light of the Organisation's ongoing reform, has been recognised in the co–ordination by Seiichi Kondo. Unity with diversity brings hope in development.

I am grateful to the contributors, colleagues and friends associated with project *Redux* including those who would have wished but were unable to contribute to this volume. Ulrich Hiemenz and Catherine Duport deserve thanks for their support in managing the project, Colm Foy, Charles Oman and Véronique Sauvat for their support in editing the volume. Morag Soranna researched and tabulated systematic information on the Centre's associates and visitors (available together with publications at www.oecd.org/dev/redux). Sheila Lionet turned the project into this book.

Development is Back will help root OECD development work in the "reformers' club" perspective. It should moreover suggest to readers that all of those people listed at the end of the volume agreed with Fernando Pessoa's message:

> "It is worth while, all,   *(Tudo vale a pena*
> if the soul is not small" *se a alma não é pequena.)*

Jorge Braga de Macedo
President
OECD Development Centre
September 2002

Chapter 1

The Development of the Centre

Véronique Sauvat

Introduction

The 40th anniversary of the founding of the Development Centre of the Organisation for Economic Co–operation and Development offers an opportunity to take stock of the experience accumulated over an already long history. Such a review allows a balanced assessment of the Centre's role, in terms of theoretical progress in development economics, research methods, influence over policies that have actually been implemented, and network building.

This chapter outlines the stages in the institutional life of the Development Centre, its main activities and how they have changed, and its participation in a dense network of contacts and partners (see Box 1). In addition, this "logbook", of 40 years of existence within a multilateral organisation built upon co–operation among its own Member countries, places the Centre's activities within the changing international context. The Centre's research, its publications (over 500) and its "dialogues" — mechanisms for co–operation and transfer of experience — reflect the approaches taken by the Centre and the Organisation to development economics and to the economic policy recommendations made to governments.

No institution exists in isolation from the context in which it operates, or which it purports to influence. The OECD Development Centre, for its part, has been involved in international relations running the gamut from solidarity to confrontation. Its creation in the early 1960s took place in a context of the emergence of a so–called North–South divide, corresponding to the antagonism between rich and poor countries. Forty years later, the world has become much more diversified. The end of the East–West conflict, the differing paths of the three large continents making up the "Third World", globalisation, and the internationalisation of the major economic, political and cultural challenges have *de facto* given rise to reappraisals and changes in the positioning of the Centre and the Organisation. An overview of this institution's history thus affords an

Box 1. **Research Capacity Building in Developing Countries**

Since its establishment, the Development Centre has regarded the support of researchers in developing countries and the strengthening of research capacity for policy advice as an important objective of its activities. As early as the 1960s, the Centre undertook a series of joint seminars, particularly in African countries (*séminaires itinérants*), to initiate policy dialogue and help researchers in these countries to engage in policy design. Throughout its existence, the Centre has also sought to delegate field research to researchers in developing countries to benefit from their local expertise but also to improve their analytical capabilities and familiarity with the international development debate. In the same vein, staff of the Centre trained researchers in developing countries in the use of modern analytical tools such as computable general equilibrium models to allow them to undertake their own policy simulations. Over the decades, the Centre has thus been able to create an international network of researchers active in development which allowed a cross–fertilisation of ideas and facilitated policy dialogue.

With this mutually beneficial nature of international networking in mind, the Centre became a founding member of the European Association of Development Research and Training Institutes (EADI) which was established in 1975 and co–operates closely with research networks in Latin America and Asia. In recent years, the Centre has played an important role in exploiting the options created by modern communication technologies to add new dimensions to its international networking. One example was the launch of the EU–LDC network in 1999 in which I participated in my capacity as the Director for Co–ordination of the Centre subsequently to become one of the three elected members of the network's Management Board. It seeks to address all researchers interested in EU relations to developing countries on the basis of an interactive website and an annual conference. The objectives are to provide easy access to relevant information regarding EU procedures and events, to engage researchers in discussion fora on new topics, and to encourage joint research among participants from developing countries and the EU. For the Centre, this network provides an outlet for work on Africa and intensifies contact with African researchers, in particular.

Another example is the Global Development Network (GDN) where I have represented Europe on its Governing Body since 2000. The GDN focuses on building social science research capacity in developing countries by organising and financing global as well as regional research competitions through its seven regional hubs in developing countries. The regional hubs in OECD countries, such as the EU DN with its secretariat in Bonn, Germany, provide research advisors and project evaluations for these competitions while promoting development–related activities in their respective regions, such as summer workshops, exchanges of PhD students and joint research meetings. As one of the initial members of the Governing Body and a founding member of EU DN, I was able to bring the Centre's longstanding experience to bear on the discussions on how to shape the network in order to strengthen participation and ownership by researchers in developing countries. The Centre, in turn, benefits from direct access to research undertaken under the umbrella of this network, particularly in the context of the global project on "Bridging Research and Policy".

Ulrich Hiemenz

opportunity to reflect on the relevance of the concept of development for the future, as well as on the future forms of both development co-operation and constructive management of differences of interest at the national and regional levels.

1962–72: The Formative Years

The Creation and Mandate of the OECD Development Centre

In the early 1960s, the Organisation for European Economic Co-operation (OEEC), which had been created after the Second World War to administer Marshall aid and establish procedures for co-operation among the European states, became the Organisation for Economic Co-operation and Development (OECD). In the process, it became not merely European but transatlantic in scope, and its mission was broadened to include the economic growth of non-member countries as well as Member countries (see Chapter 14).

At the time, the decolonisation process was nearing completion, and the South was asserting itself as a Third World, standing alongside the East and West (the Bandung conference; a majority at the United Nations). The OECD established its position with respect to these countries, known as developing countries, by creating two bodies: the Development Assistance Committee (DAC), which manages aid flows and co-ordinates the policies of Member countries *vis-à-vis* less developed countries; and the Development Centre, which is tasked with enhancing knowledge and understanding of the development of non-member countries (Council, 1962).

The Centre was granted special status within the OECD (not bound to seek a consensus and permitted to receive voluntary contributions made for a specific purpose) and charged with the following mandate: to collect information on the economic policies of Member countries at the time of their reconstruction and growth; to adapt this information to the less developed countries; to analyse the policies of developing countries; and to inform Member countries of the needs of non-member countries as expressed by the latter.

The International Environment: Catching Up and Development Co-operation

For the Western countries, the decade 1962–72 marked the end of the long post-war phase of robust economic growth. This period brought the spotlight to bear on the efforts of developing countries (whether newly independent or not) to imitate the development of the industrialised countries: to copy their growth and their industrialisation processes, and catch up to their standards of living.

11

In the economic sphere, developing countries did not challenge the foundations of the international economic system originating in the Bretton Woods Agreement (1944) and the GATT (1947). In contrast to what was happening politically (and what was to happen in the following decade), their economic strategies were not aggressive towards the rest of the world, nor even based on demands for redress. Rather, these strategies were adaptive: the idea was that growth is primarily the result of investment in physical capital and that the main constraint on such investment is the problem of access to financial resources.

The development strategies of these countries were also interventionist. Instead of trusting in the free play of market mechanisms, they viewed planning as the key to growth and successful development. This conviction was supported by the apparent success of the Soviet model, by the prestige of India's experience and the ambitions of China. Attention was focused on income growth, and not on the problem of how this income was to be distributed. The prevailing ideology favoured inward–looking policies of national development inspired either by the socialist model or by import–substitution industrialisation theory (developed in particular in the structuralist work of the United Nations Economic Commission for Latin America and the Caribbean, or ECLAC; this body of theory was summarised by Oman and Wignaraja, 1991, on the occasion of the Development Centre's 25th anniversary). These policies took the form of high levels of protection on national output, with exports playing a minor role. India, most of the Latin American countries, Algeria, Tunisia and many African countries implemented national development policies of this type.

Bilateral colonial relationships immediately gave way to what was to be called "development co–operation". Most of the newly independent countries maintained close links with their former colonial powers. Through official development assistance, the wealthy countries, which moreover were confident of the virtues of their own models of economic progress, provided a considerable volume of funding for the economic development of the former colonies.

The development policies followed up to that time, however, had already led to some failures. The concept of development planning (whether mandatory, indicative or selective) and the aid policies that support it were subjected to critical assessment, and this led the United Nations in 1964 to hold the first UNCTAD conference on the theme of "trade, not aid". This shift in stance influenced the work of the Development Centre, which became involved in assessing the aid policies of Member countries, in the transfer of technical skills, and in the issues of capital formation and mobilisation in developing countries. The work of the World Bank's Pearson Commission (whose report was published in 1969) followed the same trend.

Starting Up Activities

The first management team under President Robert Buron (1962–66), took the view that although the Centre's work should be of some interest to OECD Member countries, it was primarily intended for developing countries. This view was expressed in three guiding principles:

1) establishing dialogue with elite groups in newly independent countries to help them formulate their development policies. This led to roving seminars and policy dialogues in Côte d'Ivoire, Cameroon, Guinea, Ecuador, Peru and Iran (see Chapter 15), and to productivity experts' missions;

2) gathering and disseminating the available information on development and accumulating fresh information by means of a question–and–answer service (SVP–Développement), as well as by collecting and developing statistical data;

3) encouraging collaboration among development research and training institutes in different continents (network building, Norway meeting in 1966).

Raymond Goldsmith, vice–president of the Development Centre from 1962 to 1966, was the moving force behind the first research programme. The work undertaken was intended not to be of direct operational value but to produce thorough analyses of the policies followed in developing countries. The methodology specified at that time was to remain a characteristic of the Centre: systematic use of comparative methods, and involvement of research institutes or academics from the countries concerned. Ian Little, who held the vice–presidency in 1966 and 1967 after serving initially as head of research, further expanded the Centre's research activities (see Chapter 16).

From 1962 to 1972, the main areas of research were demography, employment, aid, financial systems, project analysis, industrialisation, foreign trade and technical progress in agriculture.

Research on demography provides a good illustration of the interaction between the Centre's autonomous status and its ability to undertake pioneering work on innovative topics. When some countries opposed the DAC's studying birth control issues, it was the Development Centre that took on this subject of capital importance for developing countries. A first report on population control and economic growth (Ohlin, 1967) was followed by many studies that provided material for annual conferences and subsequently contributed to the preparations for the major United Nations conference on population (1974). Another avenue of research involved preparing for the UNCTAD meeting on regional economic integration. Agricultural modernisation issues were handled jointly with the DAC, and a series of studies on private foreign investment was produced.

During this period, the Centre helped to revitalise economic thought, particularly through its studies of industrial project analysis and industrialisation. Little and Mirrlees (1968, 1969) published a manual of industrial project analysis, the methodology of which is in part based on a more sophisticated treatment of conventional cost–benefit analysis and on the calculation of shadow prices and shadow wages. Their theoretical findings were then applied to a series of case studies. Of over 500 works published by the Centre since its foundation, that of Little and Mirrlees has probably been cited most often. In addition, the Centre was the first to undertake critical analysis of the import–substitution industrialisation model in vogue in many developing countries. Industry and Trade in Some Developing Countries, by Little, Scitovsky and Scott (1970), highlights the inefficiencies of ISI strategies in six countries (Brazil, India, Mexico, Pakistan, the Philippines and Chinese Taipei) and recommends greater reliance on market mechanisms and the encouragement of production for export.

Social concerns were also well represented, particularly employment and rural development. The research programme on employment — a topic not often addressed at the time — was launched by André Philip (president from 1967 to 1970) and Montagu Yudelman (vice–president, then interim president, from 1967 to 1972) and brought to completion by David Turnham. The resulting volume emphasised the phenomenon of under–employment in informal activities, a more intractable problem than unemployment. This study (Turnham, 1971) subsequently inspired the surveys and publications of the International Labour Office (ILO) on the informal sector, as well as an entire work programme.

During the same period, the Centre began to gather basic statistics, an activity which continued into the 1990s. It collected national accounting data for countries using different economic systems and harmonised them in order to allow comparison. This empirical work of data collection and gradual improvement of economic and social indicators made it possible subsequently to test the validity of theory (see Chapter 15).

In addition, the Centre brought together 250 research institutes in support of South–South co–operation, compiled a directory of development banks in developing countries and devised a list of descriptors that would become the Macrothesaurus, a standard classification system for information on development. In 1972, the SVP–Développement service was transferred to a US–based NGO, the Society for International Development (SID).

Conclusion: The Centre's activities fall into three categories: research, both theoretical and applied; conferences, with publication of the proceedings; compilation of catalogues of institutes and programmes in the development field. It quickly built up an international reputation for its advanced scientific work. The research carried out over this period is remarkable both for the variety of the fields covered and for the quality of the authors (A. Lewis and J.A. Mirrlees won

Nobel Prizes, and several others today have prestigious reputations in the field). Dialogue with the governing elites of the South was kept up via experience–sharing seminars and experts' missions. The question–and–answer service met a genuine need by collecting and organising information on development (including academic literature) and making it available to development stakeholders as quickly as possible. The diversity of these activities brought the Centre into a network of development actors ranging from academic circles to policy makers and development associations.

A first review of the Centre's activities was conducted shortly before the end of André Philip's presidency (Council, 1968). The Council of the OECD renewed its mandate but expressed a desire that research results be of more direct interest to the rest of the Organisation. The vice–president's position was eliminated at that time and the Advisory Board formed shortly thereafter (Council, 1971).

1973–82: A Bridge between North and South

A Decade of Strained North–South Relations

The oil crises of 1973 and 1979 raised the level of tension in North–South relations. This led to the creation of a North–South group on the OECD Council to co–ordinate the negotiating positions of group B (OECD Member countries) with respect to group C (Third World countries, with group A being the socialist countries) in the United Nations.

In 1974, some developing countries called for the creation of a New International Economic Order (NIEO) which would enable them to obtain a more equitable share of the benefits of world growth.

In 1975, the OECD adopted a declaration on its relations with developing countries. The ministers expressed their determination to give developing countries a stronger position in the world economy and, working together with these countries, to examine the issues facing them, giving special emphasis to food production, energy, commodities and development aid. The second policy laid down by the Council was to participate in a constructive manner in the United Nations' efforts to formulate a strategy for the second decade of development and, later, in the preparations for UNCTAD meetings (the 1974 conference had to do with an integrated commodities programme). The Organisation would henceforth take a holistic, interdisciplinary approach to development problems, instead of considering them solely from the standpoint of aid. The Centre took an active part in the debates of the DAC and the UN.

The Role of the Centre

In this new context, the role of the Centre as a conduit for messages from the Southern countries to the OECD became more complex, shifting towards that of a "facilitator of dialogue" between the countries that finance the Centre and those with which it was intended to work. It endeavoured, through its intellectual contributions, to participate constructively in changing attitudes on both sides. At the same time, the Centre's presidents and directors (Paul–Marc Henry, 1973–77, and director Friedrich Kahnert; followed by Louis Sabourin, 1978–82, and director Yves Berthelot) launched a policy of "all–out" diplomacy that continued in the early 1980s with the proliferation of high–level meetings between political leaders and development experts (Chapter 17).

To facilitate this dialogue, the Centre undertook a detailed census of development research organisations, both in the South and in the industrialised countries, and another of OECD–based NGOs involved in international co-operation. Giulio Fossi's group helped to organise networks in developing regions and in Europe (creation of the Inter–regional Coordinating Committee of Development Associations, or ICCDA, and the European Association of Development Institutes, or EADI mentioned in Box 1). The Centre collaborated with the three regional associations of research and training institutes — the Latin American Social Science Council (CLACSO), the Association of Development Research and Training Institutes of Asia and the Pacific (ADIPA) and the Council for the Development of Economic and Social Research in Africa (CODESRIA) — thus serving as a forum for communication in the pre–Internet era.

Without abandoning macroeconomics, the Centre turned towards more structural and microeconomic research topics that were likely to find direct applications in the field. Examples include its research on appropriate technologies and methods for modernising agriculture in developing countries, which helped to identify the causes of famines and measured the consequences of food aid, and its work on industrialisation technologies in a context of rising energy prices. The Centre also worked on migration (subsequently incorporated into the OECD's Continuous Reporting System on Migration, or SOPEMI), on the status and role of women, and joint research projects with the Mediterranean Council of Regional Economies (in 1977, the Centre supported the creation of the Association of Arab Institutes and Centres for Economic and Social Development Research — AICARDES). The Centre began a series of studies on development financing, giving particular attention to the possibilities for three–sided co-operation between oil–producing countries, developing countries and OECD countries, as well as on new forms of investment.

From 1973, the Centre was concerned with the living conditions of the poorest, initiating studies that led in 1976 to the notion of "basic needs". The studies were concerned with, among other things, the definition of basic food needs, the government actions required to satisfy these needs and improved production, processing and marketing of staple food products.

Maintaining the Link

During these years, some of the Centre's initiatives were aimed at establishing close collaborative relationships with research institutes in the South and launching consultations with a view to global negotiations (on the feasibility of an NIEO in particular) in order to reduce tension.

At the same time, however, the Centre broadened its traditionally "personal" contacts with academics and decision makers to include industrialists and the business community generally, as well as NGOs. In particular, it launched a major project to catalogue the NGOs working in the development field, which led to the publication of several standard directories, an activity that continued until 1998.

In its search for the causes of changes in the relations between the industrialised and developing countries, the Centre adopted a new work programme that explicitly placed the future of development in the context of global interdependence. This new issue was approached from several angles. Attempts were made to measure the effects of external shocks on countries' balance of payments (e.g. for the non–oil–producing developing countries facing the sudden rise in oil prices) and to assess the measures taken to address the problem. More generally, consideration was given to the influence of external factors on countries' choice of development models and on the policies implemented. To this end, the Centre studied the capacity of developing countries to satisfy the food needs of their populations and the consequences of variations in international food prices for local producers.

Another manifestation of interdependence was the internationalisation of banking activity. This trend was analysed from the standpoint of the contribution that private banks might make to development aid. In addition, the proliferation of foreign investments in developing countries, particularly in duty–free zones, led the Centre's researchers to investigate the spillover effects on the rest of the economy, the benefits of the technology transfers associated with such investments and any dangers they may represent (see Chapter 7). The economic role of knowledge, particularly technical knowledge, was also explored.

This initial work on interdependence was subsequently extended through investigation of the respective responsibilities of domestic factors (poor management, inappropriate policies) and external factors (the inequalities intrinsic to the world trading system) in maintaining under–development. The Centre also worked on problems specific to the least developed countries, which were the subject of an international conference in Paris in 1981.

Research on the raw materials processing sector, vital in many developing countries, was also conducted: technical factors related to project size, problems of returns to scale, spillover effects on the national economy as a whole, etc. On this occasion, a sizeable database was compiled in collaboration with the World Bank, and medium–term forecasts of output, consumption, trade and investment were produced. Several other projects to develop statistical resources were later conducted jointly with the World Bank.

The Centre actively pursued its external collaborative activities, notably by promoting an inter–regional organisation (for Africa, Asia and Latin America) so as to strengthen South–South co–operation. Within the OECD, it worked with the DAC on the difficulties experienced by developing countries in making efficient use of aid resources granted for population control measures. For the first time, the Centre organised a seminar bringing together decision makers and academics from both OECD countries and developing countries to discuss the trend towards interdependence (the Dourdan and Rolleboise meetings). This type of dialogue was to become one of the distinctive features of the Centre's work.

Conclusion: The 1970s saw radical changes in the situation of both Third World countries and wealthy countries. The events of this period mark the beginning of transformations whose effects are still being felt today. The decade clearly revealed the differences of interest between developing countries and OECD countries, which were reflected in considerable tension in international negotiations. In most cases, the positions taken by the Centre supported those of developing countries, provoking criticism from the Centre's member countries. The result was an institutional crisis in the early 1980s that ended in budget cuts and a reoriented work programme.

The decade nevertheless showed the Centre's ability to address problems of current interest, while anticipating future problems in economic relations on a global scale, as was demonstrated by its work, both general and specific, on global interdependence. The future and the growth prospects of all parties were now inextricably linked, and recognition of this fact opened the way for new forms of international co–operation. In this context, the Centre endeavoured to rise above the tensions of the moment in order to facilitate negotiations and fully play its role as a bridge between North and South.

1983–92: Interdependence and Divergent Paths

Increasing Disparities

Whereas the preceding decades had been characterised by sustained progress and an interventionist view of development, the 1980s saw the end of the illusion of linear growth and of the notion that the less advanced countries would automatically catch up with the industrialised ones. Not only did international tension persist, but a series of monetary crises occurred. The recycling of petrodollars and lending policies that financed the growth of public spending and unprofitable investment led many developing countries, particularly in Latin America, to situations of overindebtedness. The financial difficulties of developing countries were so great that they induced the World Bank and the IMF to introduce structural adjustment programmes. These programmes, which were aimed at re-establishing budget balances, entailed high social costs and cutbacks in education and health spending.

During this decade, the "global negotiations" between North and South came up against new bottlenecks related to the global economic situation, but also to a new geopolitical scene that radically changed the terms of North–South relations. The collapse of the Soviet system put an end to the East–West confrontation and induced a shift in the co–operation priorities of the industrialised countries towards the so–called transition countries. Third World arguments that the North was responsible for under–development were contested by a series of studies pointing to the deadlocked situations of Southern political regimes, errors in development strategies, infringements of human rights, oversized bureaucracies etc. At the same time, the responsibility of the Southern countries in maintaining under–development was underlined. Aid policies were called into question. Lastly, whereas growth and, in some cases, per capita income, were clearly falling in Africa and Latin America, the newly industrialised economies of Asia continued to grow and develop. The heterogeneity of and cleavages among the Southern countries, which were already considerable, grew steadily worse over the course of the decade.

In the Front Lines

This new context was accompanied by changes in the OECD's relations with non–member countries, which entailed a *de facto* repositioning of the Centre. Dialogue was initiated with the dynamic Asian economies, and a Centre for Co–operation with the Economies in Transition (CCET) was created in 1990.

The Centre began to disseminate the results of its work more widely within the OECD, so as to bring them more into the mainstream. Finding itself in a situation of potential competition within the Organisation, however, it focused on countries like China and Viet Nam, with which it had longstanding relationships (studies on the special economic zones as early as 1981, on the reconversion of the Chinese military industry, etc.). It also supported the countries sharing a border with South Africa in their efforts to achieve regional integration (Southern African Development Community — SADC). This period saw the confirmation of the Centre's role as a ground–breaker devoted to working on "emerging issues".

In this context, the President of the Development Centre, Just Faaland (1983–85; director Jean Bonvin, 1983–92) took the initiative of organising meetings between political figures and academics from both South and North, with the involvement of the OECD General Secretariat. The chairpersons of important committees, such as the Trade and Industry Committees, also participated. These confidential meetings at ministerial level allowed the participants to set out their respective positions, and enabled movement on sensitive issues, such as debt management by creditor and debtor countries, the role of private foreign investment and preparation for the next round of trade negotiations. The meetings were intended to ease North–South tensions by promoting informal but substantive dialogue. As part of the EADI work programme, the Centre initiated comparative research on developing countries' experiences with regional integration. It took an active part in organising the fourth conference of this network.

Other work addressed the issue of the role of women, with a view to preparing for the first major United Nations conference that explicitly recognised the function of women in society and in development (Mexico, 1985). Research activities were organised under two heads: one on the internal problems of developing countries, and the other on the interdependence between developing countries and OECD countries. Studies of rural development pointed to the positive role of export–oriented agricultural policies, and this work was supplemented by a study of the advantages and limitations of aid projects in favour of rural development. This study of aid efficiency also gave consideration to the problems involved in co–ordinating aid procedures and sectoral initiatives. Along with research on knowledge and continuing education, work on financial intermediation, foreign direct investment and debt was continued using a prospective approach (Chapter 18).

New Directions for Research

The next president, Louis Emmerij (1986–92), launched a five–point research programme with the aim of providing some response to the debt crisis and structural adjustment programmes.

—   Development financing. In the 1980s, the growth prospects of developing countries seemed to be compromised and the adjustment programmes recommended by the international organisations (reduction of public spending) coincided with a decline in official development assistance. Research revealed that debt, taxation/budgetary policy and exchange–rate management are tightly intertwined. Financing long–term development thus calls for a rebalancing of the roles of the public and private sectors, and in particular for reform of the financial sector in developing countries, mobilisation of domestic savings and promotion of foreign direct investment (Oman, 1984).

—   New technologies and shifts in comparative advantage. The Centre showed its ability to anticipate problems by raising questions at this time as to developing countries' capacity to embrace the new information technologies and as to the role of these technologies in industrial development and integration into the world economy (Antonelli, 1991).

—   Adjustment and equity, the political feasibility of structural adjustment. The Centre undertook a series of studies on IMF and the World Bank adjustment programmes for developing countries. These showed, apart from longer–term positive effects, risks of serious social unrest if tensions are not anticipated and forestalled by compensatory measures (Morrisson, 1991).

—   With the worsening of unemployment problems, notably in sub–Saharan Africa, owing to the gap between population growth rates and the increase in job offers, research on employment was redirected towards the opportunities offered by the informal sector. A volume summarising this work became a benchmark in the field (Turnham, 1993).

The 25th anniversary of the Development Centre, celebrated in 1989, served as an occasion to bring together people from many developing countries — decision makers and high officials, academics, business executives — for joint reflection on interdependence in a two–speed, multi–polar world economy. The discussions were summarised in a volume entitled *One World or Several?* (Emmerij, 1989; see also Oman and Wignaraja, 1991). However, taking advantage of the fact that OECD Member countries may choose not to be members of the Centre, Australia withdrew in 1987 and Turkey in 1988.

In addition to its contributions to the work of the DAC, the Centre undertook prospective research on the new Asian economies, and in particular on the place of China in the world economy. The 1990–92 research programme combined the terms "globalisation" and "regionalisation" for the first time.

Apart from research, emphasis was given to disseminating the work of the Centre more effectively and to arranging conferences involving the managers of major corporations. The principle of testing different points of view against each other was broadened to include all economic actors.

Conclusion: The appearance of "several worlds" moving at different speeds, was the primary concern of the Centre during this period. From the standpoint of research methodologies, the economic approach was broadened to take account of the political, institutional, social and cultural dimensions of development policies.

Over this period, the Centre's independence in setting its work programme gave rise to occasional controversy and tension with a few Member countries, but the Centre's existence and its role within the OECD were not called into question.

1992–2002: Crises and Reform

Ideological Consensus and Financial Crises

The fall of the Berlin Wall marked the beginning of a decisive change in policy stance. A consensus had formed in favour of the market economy and democracy, and ideological feuds had given way to a more pragmatic spirit. In particular, the role of the state was completely rethought, with the aim of reducing it and making it more efficient.

The phenomenon of economic globalisation — driven by corporate internationalisation strategies, the gradual liberalisation of goods and services markets, the integration of financial markets — is not new, as Angus Maddison showed in his economic history of the last millennium (updated in Chapter 2). But it picked up speed as from the 1980s. It brought new opportunities: *i)* owing to the faster flow of goods, capital, people, ideas and technologies; *ii)* because it helped to support economic growth; and, *iii)* because it allowed nearly 2 billion people, mostly in Asia, to catch up economically to some degree. Globalisation also brought new risks: economic and financial shocks; social inequalities and the tension that they bring; threats to the environment; public health hazards; expansion of international crime; cultural domination; and risks to the stability and integrity of the international financial system.

During this period, the levers of control over the economy passed from the hands of policy makers towards the financial markets. The volatility of capital flows was one of the instigating factors of several major crises in the emerging economies (notably in Mexico in 1994 and in Asia in 1997–98) and the spreading of these crises from region to region. The need for international regulation, and in particular for reform of the international financial system, became generally accepted.

In this context, where problems were taking on an international dimension, development economics as a specific discipline was called into question. Where trade, employment, financial flows and new technologies were concerned, the strategies of North and South had become closely intertwined. Does this mean that the economic development of developing countries has no distinctive features? This was the opinion of some schools of economic thought, which obliged the Centre and the Organisation to make adjustments with a view to increasing the coherence of their activities.

The Debate over the Role of the Centre and Opening Up to Emerging Countries

In the context of globalisation, the Member countries of the OECD once again focused on strengthening dialogue with developing countries and sought to include the "development" dimension in the cross–disciplinary working themes of the Organisation. Under the presidencies of Jean Bonvin (1993–99) and Jorge Braga de Macedo (1999–) and the directorship of Ulrich Hiemenz (1993–), the positioning of the Centre within the Organisation was again called into question on a number of occasions. This led to tighter integration of the Centre within the OECD, with the aim of making it more relevant for its users (Council, 2000). This strengthening of synergies was reflected in particular in the Centre's co–ordination of a major cross–disciplinary study on global interdependence (*Linkages*). During this period, the Centre was one of the sectors of the Organisation that were deeply involved in such cross–disciplinary work (ageing, sustainable development, corporate governance, etc.).

As the logical result of decades of dialogue and openness to emerging countries on the part of the OECD, the Development Centre admitted Korea in 1992; Argentina, Brazil and Mexico in 1994; Chile in 1998; and India in 2001. Mexico also became a full Member of the OECD as from 1994; the Czech Republic in 1995; Hungary, Poland and Korea in 1996 (Hungary chose not to become a member of the Centre); followed by the Slovak Republic in 2000. However, the United Kingdom withdrew from the Centre in 1996, the United States in 1997, Japan in 1999 and Poland in 2001, for budgetary reasons. The growing disparity between the Member countries of the OECD and of the Development Centre was one of the reasons for the reform of the development architecture undertaken as from 2000 (Council, 2000; Advisory Board, 2000a, 2001).

Globalisation has by no means resolved the problem of stalled development in the poorest countries. It is even revealing certain contradictions in the policies adopted by the OECD countries: their policies on trade, environmental protection and investment are not always compatible with the development of poor countries. Developing countries have their own needs and interests which must be taken into consideration if they are to become fully–fledged actors in the world economy. It is recognised that the Centre still has a role to play in this respect.

New Working Methods, New Approaches

Where Africa is concerned, the Centre is one of the development actors that have refused to throw in the towel: the subjects of conflict prevention, the fight against corruption and rent–seeking behaviour, and the feasibility of reforms are all studied because of their possible contribution to Africa's growth. The Centre is also participating, through its work on emerging Africa, in the DAC's Partnership Strategy for the 21st Century, the aim of which is to reduce poverty in a sustainable manner.

The changes occurring in the world economy led the Centre to change the scale of its analyses. In addition to comparison of national policies, it studies phenomena such as decentralisation (Brazil, China, India) and regional co–operation (studies of Mercosur, APEC, ASEAN and SARC). The organisation of annual "economic perspectives" fora with the regional development banks is also in keeping with this regional approach to problems (the forum with the Inter–American Development Bank was launched in 1990, that with the Asian Development Bank in 1995 and that with the African Development Bank in 2000). Furthermore, efforts have been made to strike a balance between one–off studies (e.g. the enormous project conducted in co–operation with the Chinese authorities on the conversion of military industries to civilian production, the study on privatisation in India) and long–term studies (prospective study on interdependence — OECD, 1995). Lastly, the Centre is still working to broaden both its audience and its range of partners to include civil society (research on the participatory dimension of development) and the business community (the role of the private sector in fighting corruption; see Chapter 19).

The Centre has left its mark on this decade through its work on a few themes where the findings have caught the attention of the stakeholders concerned; these themes are addressed in detail in the following chapters of this volume. These chapters also constitute an overview of the results of the 2001/2002 work programme on globalisation and governance (Advisory Board, 2000b) and a look ahead to the 2003/2004 work programme on the integration effects of globalisation and adaptation capability (Advisory Board, 2002).

Financial liberalisation: The financial crises that shook the emerging economies during the 1990s had been anticipated in a number of the Centre's studies of financial market liberalisation. These studies put the spotlight on the risks associated with financial liberalisation and the need to make liberalisation conditional on the establishment of domestic rules aimed at protecting the national financial system (establishment of a regulatory framework). After the outbreak of the crises, the Centre's research efforts were directed to identifying the causes (external shocks, volatility of short–term capital flows, excessive exposure to risks, the appearance of speculative bubbles, etc.); searching for political and financial solutions to help the affected countries bounce back; and thinking more broadly about how the international financial architecture should be reformed to reduce the risk of further crises (Chapter 10).

International Trade: In the early 1990s, Goldin and van der Mensbrugghe (1992) undertook to measure the growth benefits that participating countries would derive from the liberalisation of trade in agricultural products, in a context of a deadlock in the multilateral negotiations under the Uruguay Round (GATT). An econometric model (Rural–Urban/North–South, or RUNS) was used to construct various scenarios of the overall effects of trade liberalisation. This work attracted a great deal of attention and helped to get the negotiations started again on a new and more solid basis (Chapter 9).

Environment and Sustainable Development: The Centre's work in the 1980s had already pointed to indications of global interdependence where the environment is concerned. Over the 1990–92 period, the Centre, in partnership with the Economic Affairs Department of the OECD, developed a general equilibrium econometric model on a global scale, known as GREEN. The model is used, particularly where the energy sector is concerned, to measure the impact of the use of natural resources on the environment and climate change. It is also used to assess the economic impact of policies to reduce greenhouse gas emissions. After being managed for several years by the Centre, this model was transferred to several developing countries and used as a decision support tool for environmental policies (Dessus *et al.*, 1994). Research on sustainable development continued in the form of a series of studies on climate change, particularly in large developing countries (China and India). These studies enabled the Centre to propose ways of measuring the fringe benefits of greenhouse gas reduction policies, notably for health, as well as providing material for the OECD's cross–disciplinary activities on sustainable development (Chapter 5).

Social and Institutional Dimensions of Development: Purely economic analyses were supplemented by consideration of the institutional factors that influence growth: the role of the public and private sectors in combating corruption, the impact of conflicts on the national economy, ways of improving political governance. Earlier work on income distribution was pursued and deepened, in particular through the involvement of the "forgotten people" of globalisation in both research and dialogue (Chapter 6).

Conclusion: Despite a number of difficulties, experience since 2000 has confirmed the Centre's continued ability to anticipate trends and draw decision makers' attention to the factors that cause crises well before they actually break out. The debate over the proper place of the Development Centre within the OECD continued, while the departure of several influential countries weakened the Centre and strengthened calls for its work to be better integrated into the activities of the OECD. From 1999 to 2002, the Council of the OECD re–examined the

Centre's mandate on several occasions and, while confirming the importance of this specialised entity, established procedures for more precise co–ordination of the activities of the entire Organisation (Council, 1999a). The note on strategic goals drafted by the OECD Secretary–General states that: "The OECD cannot offer its Members the best analysis and the best policy options unless it takes into account developments in important countries beyond its current membership" (Council, 1999b).

An external assessment carried out in 2000 showed that the Centre's role as a protector of diversity is better understood outside the Organisation than within it (Advisory Board, 2000a). It is now up to the Centre to manage its intellectual heritage with due consideration for diversity, occupying a position midway between the OECD Member countries and the rest of the world (Advisory Board, 2001). Its specific mission remains that of studying the policies applicable to developing countries, basing its assessments on its own research, on its activities to foster dialogue and on the experience of the OECD.

With due regard for efforts to reform the Organisation, particularly the work of the "Development Group" and the desire of the Member states to see greater coherence in this area, the Centre is making great efforts to work even more closely with the OECD Secretariat, notably by contributing to cross–disciplinary projects and to discussions on policy coherence. The context is now one of establishing partnerships between Northern and Southern countries so as to favour the integrating effect of globalisation, both between countries and within countries. The reform thus reflects recognition of the importance of development issues as well as their gradual integration into the Organisation's other sectors of activity.

Although the very concept of the Third World has been challenged, with some observers expressing doubts as to the usefulness of analysing development, recent trends show that, far from being obsolete, this body of thought is now spreading outward to touch all issues related to the functioning of economic and social systems.

Note

1.   Upon his taking up office in 1999, Development Centre President Jorge Braga de Macedo asked for a comprehensive report on the Centre's activities since its foundation (Fossi et al., 2000). The present chapter is based on this work, on the external assessment of the Centre conducted in 2000 and on information and commentary provided by Ulrich Hiemenz, Director for Co–ordination. The opinions expressed are nonetheless those of the author alone.

Bibliography

ANTONELLI, C. (1991), *The Diffusion of Advanced Telecommunications in Developing Countries*, Development Centre Studies, OECD, Paris.

BRAGA DE MACEDO, J. (2001), "Globalisation and Institutional Change: A Development Perspective", paper presented to the Annual Meeting of the Vatican's Pontifical Academy of Social Science, *in* E. MALINVAUD AND L. SABOURIN (eds.).

DESSUS, S., D. ROLAND–HOLST AND D. VAN DER MENSBRUGGHE (1994), *Input–based Pollution Estimates for Environmental Assessment in Developing Countries*, Technical Papers No. 101, OECD Development Centre, Paris.

EMMERIJ, L. (1989), *One World or Several?*, OECD Development Centre, Paris.

FOSSI, G., WITH J. BONVIN, C. MORRISSON AND T. THOMAS (2000), "Tenir parole. Une brève histoire du Centre de Développement (1962–2000)", mimeo, OECD Development Centre, Paris.

GOLDIN, I. AND D. VAN DER MENSBRUGGHE (1992), *Trade Liberalisation: What's at Stake?*, Policy Brief No. 5, OECD Development Centre, Paris.

LITTLE, I.M.D. AND J.A. MIRRLEES (1968, 1969), *Manual of Industrial Project Analysis in Developing Countries*, 2 vols, OECD Development Centre, Paris.

LITTLE, I.M.D., T. SCITOVSKY AND M.F.G. SCOTT (1970), *Industry and Trade in Some Developing Countries*, Oxford University Press for the OECD Development Centre, London.

MALINVAUD, E. AND L. SABOURIN (2001), *Globalization: Ethical and Institutional Concerns*, Pontifical Academy of Social Sciences, Vatican City.

MORRISSON, C. (1991), *Adjustment and Equity in Morocco*, Development Centre Studies, OECD, Paris.

OECD (1995), *Linkages: OECD and Major Developing Economies*, Study and synthesis, OECD, Paris.

OHLIN, G. (1967), *Population Control and Economic Development*, Development Centre Studies, OECD, Paris.

OMAN, C. (1984), *New Forms of International Investment in Developing Countries*, Development Centre Studies, OECD, Paris.

OMAN, C., WITH F. CHESNAIS, J. PELZMAN AND R. RAMA (1989), *New Forms of Investment in Developing Country Industries: Mining, Petrochemicals, Automobiles, Textile, Food*, Development Centre Studies, OECD, Paris.

OMAN, C. AND G. WIGNARAJA (1991), *The Postwar Evolution of Development Thinking*, Development Centre Studies, OECD, Paris.

TURNHAM, D. (1993), *Employment and Development: A New Review of Evidence*, Development Centre Studies, OECD, Paris.

TURNHAM, D. (assisted by I. JAEGER) (1971), *The Employment Problem in Less Developed Countries: A Review of Evidence*, Development Centre Studies, OECD, Paris.

Official OECD Documents

ADVISORY BOARD OF THE DEVELOPMENT CENTRE (2002), Work Programme 2003/2004.

ADVISORY BOARD OF THE DEVELOPMENT CENTRE (2001), *Managing User Diversity at the Development Centre*, Note by the OECD Development Centre, CD/AB(2001)1, 20 April.

ADVISORY BOARD OF THE DEVELOPMENT CENTRE (2000a), *Report of the Task Force on the External Evaluation of the OECD Development Centre*, CD/AB(2000)6.

ADVISORY BOARD OF THE DEVELOPMENT CENTRE (2000b), Work Programme 2001/2002.

COUNCIL (2000), *The OECD Development Centre: Users' Guide (for Members and non-members)*, Note by the President of the OECD Development Centre, C(2000)14/REV1, 20 April 2000.

COUNCIL (1999a), Meeting of the Development Centre Advisory Board, 8 July 1999 (Summary note by the Chairman, Ambassador Valaskakis), C(99)124.

COUNCIL (1999b), *OECD: Challenges and Strategic Objectives*, 1999/2000, C(99)165.

COUNCIL (1971), Council Resolution dated 12 October 1971 C(71)191.

COUNCIL (1968), Council Resolution dated 11 June 1968, C(68)70(Final).

COUNCIL (1962), Council Decision dated 23 October 1962, C(62)144(Final).

PART ONE

ANALYTICAL TOPICS

Chapter 2

The West and the Rest in the International Economic Order

Angus Maddison

On the occasion of the Development Centre's 40th birthday, it is useful to survey what happened in the world economy in the past five decades and to speculate on future prospects. My tables quantify the picture since 1950, but they also show performance since the founding of the Centre in 1962.

In 1962, we usually divided the world into three regions. The advanced capitalist group was then known as the developed world. The second was the "Sino–Soviet bloc". Countries "in course of development" were the Third World. The China–USSR split occurred in the early 1960s; most of the communist regimes collapsed around 1990, and the hostility of the Cold War has largely faded away. The income gap between the former communist countries and the advanced capitalist group has become very much wider than it was. For this reason, a tripartite division of the world economy is no longer appropriate.

For rough comparisons, it now useful to divide the world in two and compare developments in the advanced capitalist group with the aggregate for lower–income countries — designated as the "West" and the "Rest" in our tables. On average, the West increased its income per head fourfold from 1950 to 2001 — a growth rate of 2.8 per cent a year. In the rest of the world there was a threefold increase — a growth rate of 2.2 per cent a year. In both cases this was much better than earlier performance. From 1820 to 1950, income grew 1.3 per cent a year in the West and 0.6 per cent in the Rest. Though the gap in income level was still increasing, the acceleration in performance was bigger in the Rest.

Population of the West rose by half from 1950 to 2001 (0.8 per cent a year), about the same pace as in 1820–1950. In the Rest, the situation was very different. Population grew by 2.0 per cent a year, compared with 0.6 per cent in the earlier

31

period. This reflected a major improvement in welfare as mortality declined and life expectancy rose from 44 years in 1950 to 65 in 2001 — much faster than in the West. In the past two decades birth rates have fallen rapidly — a demographic transition which happened earlier in the West.

Total output grew faster in the Rest. Their GDP rose by 4.1 per cent a year in the five decades following 1950 compared with 3.3 per cent in the West. Their share of world output rose from 40 to 48 per cent; their share of world population from 78 to 86 per cent.

The West is now a relatively homogeneous group in terms of living standards, growth performance, economic institutions and modes of governance. Over the past five decades there has also been significant convergence in most of these respects. This is not true of the Rest. There are more than 180 countries in this group. They have nearly all increased their income levels significantly since 1950, but the degree of success has varied enormously. It is not possible to look at individual country experience in the space of a short article (for country detail, see Maddison, 2001), but there is some degree of homogeneity within different regional groups. Most of Asia is experiencing fast per capita income growth. Most African countries are fairly stagnant. Most Latin American countries found it very difficult to keep a steady trajectory of advance in the 1980s and 1990s. Population growth is fastest in Africa, a good deal slower in Latin America and slower still in Asia. Life expectancy and levels of education are lowest in Africa, better in Latin America, and better still in Asia.

Between 1950 and 2001, the Asian group increased per capita income fivefold and narrowed the relative gap between its incomes and the West. In other regions there was no convergence. Latin American income rose more than twofold, in the former command economies of Eastern Europe and the USSR less than twofold and Africa about two–thirds.

The divergence was even more striking in 1990–2001. In this period the Western group increased its income by a fifth, the Asian group by half, Latin America by a sixth, Africa stagnated and in the former communist countries per capita income fell by a quarter.

The Impact of the West on the World Economy

Free Trade Imperialism, 1850–1914

The Western group was the most dynamic part of the world economy from 1500 to 1850. From then to 1914 its growth and the absence of major wars had a stimulating effect on the Rest in spite of various types of colonialism in most of Asia and Africa and neocolonialism in Latin America. Technical progress was fast in shipping and opened new opportunities for international trade which were reinforced by the creation of the Suez and Panama canals. The leading capitalist country, the United Kingdom followed a policy of zero tariffs, which it imposed in its imperial possessions and in places where it had political leverage (the Ottoman Empire, China and Persia). It opened its economy to agricultural imports and cheerfully accepted the collapse of farm employment. The British economist Stanley Jevons (1865) published a lyrical assessment of its gains from free trade: "the plains of North America and Russia are our cornfields; Chicago and Odessa our granaries: Canada and the Baltic are our timber forests; Australasia contains our sheep–farms; the Hindus and the Chinese grow tea for us, and our coffee, sugar and spice plantations are in all the Indies". The stimulus from British free trade imperialism was biased towards the Western offshoots, but some trickled down to Asia, Africa and Latin America. Foreign investment was another vector by which growth was transmitted. In the decade before 1914, British foreign investment was as big as domestic investment, and in 1914, its foreign assets were 1.5 times as big as GDP. Other West European countries contributed to this capital outflow. In 1914, the stock of foreign capital invested in developing countries was 32 per cent of their GDP, compared with 22 per cent in 1998.

Defensive Autarchy, 1914–50

This liberal world order disappeared in the first world war, which crippled the major European economies and sparked off the Russian revolution. The economy of the leading capitalist country, the United States, collapsed in 1929 and sparked a world depression which led to a proliferation of trade barriers, widespread debt default, and collapse of international investment. The United Kingdom abandoned free trade in 1931. Japan and the European imperial powers (mainly Britain and France) created protectionist inward–looking trading systems which extended to their empires. The democratic political systems of Germany, Italy, Portugal and Spain were replaced by fascist dictatorships with even more autarchic trade policies. Developing countries suffered major declines in GDP and worse terms of trade than the colonial powers. In the politically independent countries of Latin America the old landlord oligarchies were toppled in favour of populist regimes which defaulted on debt, switched to import–substituting industrialisation, high tariffs, exchange controls and bilateral trade and payments deals of the type pioneered by Dr. Schacht in Germany. The Second World War was much more damaging than the first to the economies of East Asia and North Africa which were involved in armed conflict. When colonialism ended in Asia, the new political leadership had no nostalgia for the liberal order. Their commercial policies were inward–looking. They were very suspicious of foreign capital and many were attracted to the dirigiste policies and state enterprise of the Soviet Union which were perceived (in India and China) as a workable alternative to forces of the market.

Emergence of a Neoliberal World Order, 1950–2001

In the immediate postwar years most of Western Europe (with the exception of Ludwig Erhard's Germany) was also deeply suspicious of market forces and the liberal order. Attitudes were changed by the Marshall Plan, which was the most benign outcome of the Cold War. Between 1947 and 1952 the United States provided $12 billion (about 1 per cent of its GDP) in aid to Western Europe, most of it in grants. It was given on condition that Western Europe get rid of quantitative barriers to trade and establish mutual consultation to avoid the beggar–your–neighbour policies of pre–war years. As a result, the west European economy experienced a secular investment boom and recovered quickly from the effects of the war and the wastes of the 1930s. Surprisingly the boom continued until the early 1970s with relatively low inflation and very high rates of employment. The Cold War had similar repercussions in East Asia, where the United States provided substantial economic assistance to Japan, Korea and Chinese Taipei which helped to put them on a fast growth trajectory. The extraordinarily fast growth of the advanced capitalist economies (GDP increasing nearly 5 per cent a year from 1950–73) gave a major stimulus to world economic growth which was greatly reinforced by trade liberalisation.

Trade

West European countries became much keener on building a liberal world economy by the 1960s. They and the United States pushed for lower trade barriers on a worldwide basis through successive rounds of negotiation in GATT (the Dillon, Kennedy, Tokyo and Uruguay rounds between 1960 and 1994) and the creation of the WTO. As a result of this, rapid progress in shipping technology and the momentum imparted by Western growth, world trade volume rose 22–fold from 1950 to 2001. The ratio of exports to world GDP rose from 5.5 per cent in 1950 to about 18 per cent in 2001. The expansion in exports of the Rest was almost as fast as in the West, but there was a big difference between the experience of Asia and Africa. Asian export volume rose by 7.5 per cent a year, African by 3.5 per cent. There was also a huge increase in international travel, communications and other service transactions. The improved international division of labour facilitated the diffusion of ideas and technology, and improved resource allocation.

Nevertheless, things could have been better. The advanced capitalist countries favour "fair" trade not free trade. The European Union and the United States haggle over bananas, steel and textiles. Their trade union pressure groups regard low wages in the poorer countries as unfair competition. Protectionist policies for agriculture involve a major waste of resources for the West, and a serious obstacle to faster growth in the Rest. Transfers associated with agricultural policies are much larger than the flow of aid to the Rest. They were estimated by OECD to cost about $300 billion in the year 2000 (see OECD, 2001). Free trade imperialism was more liberal.

34

Aid

In the early 1960s the United States urged the European countries and Japan to increase their aid to developing countries. In 1962 the net flow of bilateral and multilateral aid from DAC countries was around $6.7 billion — about 0.6 per cent of the total GDP of OECD Member countries at current exchange rates. Nearly 60 per cent of the flow came from the United States. In real terms the net flow of aid peaked in the early 1990s at a level about 50 per cent higher than in 1962, but it fell after the Cold War ended; by 2001 it had fallen back to its 1962 level in real terms. At the end of the 1990s the flow was only 0.2 per cent of OECD GDP and the US share had fallen to about a sixth of the total (see DAC reports and provisional figures for 2001 in World Bank, 2002). The size of the aid effort and its impact have clearly been smaller than the Marshall Plan.

Private Capital Flows

Private capital flows to developing countries were about $2.2 billion in 1962, about a third of official aid flows. By the 1980s they were generally larger than the aid flow, and they rocketed upwards in the 1990s, peaking around $300 billion in 1997. The most useful from the viewpoint of development was direct investment which was drawn particularly to Asia by the dynamism of its growth, and the availability of skilled labour at much lower wages than in the West. By 1998, the total stock of foreign direct investment in the Rest was $1.3 trillion, about $248 per head of population. This investment supplemented domestic saving but was more important in transferring technology, skills and competitiveness of exports. However, such investment was much bigger within the West, where the stock was $2.8 trillion in 1998, $3 266 per head of population. A large part of the private financial flow was speculative and rose rapidly after payments restrictions were ended in Western Europe, Asia and Latin America in the 1990s. The Asian and Russian crises of 1997–98 sparked off large reverse flows of short–term capital. The provisional IMF estimate for 2001 shows a net flow of $160 million, a huge drop from the $300 million peak of 1997. The volatility of these flows prompted Joseph Stiglitz (2002), former chief economist of the World Bank and Nobel laureate, to suggest that liberalisation of financial flows had gone too far, that IMF bailouts give excessive protection to foreign investors, and that borrowers in difficulty should have more scope for bankruptcy and debt default (as they had in the 1930s and earlier).

Migration

In the period 1870–1914, there was large–scale migration from Western and Eastern Europe to the United States, other Western offshoots, Argentina and Brazil. Net migration of this type totalled about 20 million. There was also a significant, but much smaller migration from Asian countries to these destinations.

Between 1914 and 1949, the flow was very much smaller, but the origins and destinations were similar. Between 1950 and 1998 the net flow to the United States and other Western offshoots was bigger (about 34 million), but a much larger proportion of the migrants were from Asia, Africa and Latin America. In Western Europe there was a complete transformation. In 1950–98, there was net **immigration** of more than 20 million. A large proportion were from Africa or Asia. Because of the large fall in the real cost of international transport and communication, migrants now maintain closer links with their countries of origin. There is therefore a flow of emigrants' remittances from the advanced capitalist countries to the rest of the world. There has also been a transmission of skills and know–how. Within the total flow there have been a significant number who came to study and have gone back with skills and qualifications which have accelerated the development process. One notable example of this is the information technology industry in Asia, which benefited from a return flow of skills and entrepreneurship.

Slowdown in the Momentum of Western Growth ,1973–2001

From the 1970s onwards the pace of economic advance slowed significantly in Western Europe and Japan. To some extent the deceleration was warranted as once–for–all opportunities for catch–up had already been seized and the rate of growth of technical progress in the lead country (the United States) had moderated. But Western Europe has been operating below potential with very high levels of unemployment. In 1994–8 it averaged nearly 11 per cent of the labour force. This is higher than in the depressed years of the 1930s. Unemployment on this scale would have created a major depression if the unemployed had not received substantial income support from social security. The major reason for the rise was a change in macro–policy objectives.

The early 1970s were a time of inflationary pressure, when expectations of accelerating inflation were greatly augmented by the first OPEC shock. It was feared that any accommodation of inflation would lead to hyperinflation. The objectives of full employment and economic growth were jettisoned, and the major policy emphasis switched to achieving price stability. By the early 1990s these policies were successful in reducing the pace of inflation to modest levels, but deflationary policies were prolonged for a decade by a new policy objective monetary union.

The path to monetary union was not smooth, but the determination to succeed was very strong, particularly in countries which had historically had the biggest problems of inflation and exchange rate instability. They were willing to prolong the period of high unemployment to satisfy the "convergence" obligations of membership. The new monetary regime started in 1999, with establishment of the European Central Bank (ECB) and freezing of exchange rates. The Euro currency was successfully inaugurated in 2002. However, ECB policy has continued to be deflationary, concerned only with price stability, not with unemployment or economic growth.

Emphasis on closer integration within the European Union also involved long delay in helping East European countries to fulfil their aspirations for integration with the West. The EU made large transfer payments to Greece, Ireland, Portugal and Spain and there have been huge transfers within Germany from the west to the new Länder. Liberalisation of capital movements led to a large outflow of European investment to the United States. Financial flows to Eastern economies in transition have been modest.

The slowdown in Japanese growth in the 1990s has been much sharper than in Western Europe. In 2001, per capita income was below its level six years earlier, stock market capitalisation is less than half its 1989 level, consumer demand is very sluggish, and unemployment has risen continuously. Here again there were large capital outflows, some to the East Asian economies but a larger movement to the United States

American policy since 1973 has been much more successful than that of Western Europe and Japan in realising potential for income growth. The incidence of unemployment is now about half of that in Western Europe, whereas in 1950– 73 it was usually double the European rate. Labour force participation increased, with employment expanding from 41 per cent of the population in 1973 to 49 per cent in 1998, compared with an average European rise from 42 to 44 per cent. The percentage drop in working hours per person was half of that in Western Europe. These high levels of activity were achieved with a rate of inflation which was generally more modest than in Western Europe.

US policy makers have been less inhibited in operating at high levels of demand than their European counterparts. Having the world's major reserve currency, and long used to freedom of international capital movements, they generally treated exchange rate fluctuations with benign neglect. The Reagan administration made major tax cuts, and carried out significant measures of deregulation in the expectation that they would provoke a positive supply response that would outweigh potential inflationary consequences. The United States operated with more flexible labour markets. Its capital market was better equipped to supply venture funds to innovators. Its economy was as big as Western Europe but much more closely integrated. Demand buoyancy was sustained by a stock market boom in the 1990s.

The United States was a major gainer from the globalisation of international capital markets. In the postwar period until 1988, US foreign assets always exceeded liabilities, but thereafter its net foreign asset position moved from around zero to minus $1.5 trillion (more than 20 per cent of GDP). Thus the rest of the world helped to sustain the long American boom and financed the large US payments deficit.

Future Prospects

Table 1 provides a quantification of growth performance of eight major regions of the world economy and some very tentative projections for development up to the year 2015.

Table 1. **Levels of Per Capita GDP, Population and GDP: World and Major Regions, 1950-2015**

	1950	1962	1973	1990	2001	2015
GDP per capita (1990 international $)						
Western Europe	4 594	7 512	11 534	15 988	19 196	24 226
Western Offshoots	9 288	11 537	16 172	22 356	27 892	36 400
Japan	1 926	4 778	11 439	18 789	20 722	23 472
"West"	**5 663**	**8 466**	**13 141**	**18 798**	**22 832**	**29 156**
Eastern Europe	2 120	3 250	4 985	5 437	5 875	8 886
Former USSR	2 834	4 130	6 058	6 871	4 634	6 450
Latin America	2 554	3 268	4 531	5 055	5 815	7 163
Asia (excluding Japan)	635	837	1 231	2 117	3 219	5 487
Africa	852	1 038	1 365	1 385	1 410	1 620
"Rest"	**1 091**	**1 478**	**2 073**	**2 707**	**3 339**	**5 101**
World	2 114	2 921	4 104	5 154	6 043	8 100
Population (million)						
	1950	1962	1973	1990	2001	2015
Western Europe	305	332	358	377	391	397
Western Offshoots	176	218	251	298	333	369
Japan	84	96	109	124	127	126
"West"	**565**	**646**	**718**	**799**	**851**	**892**
Eastern Europe	87	101	110	122	121	120
Former USSR	180	222	250	289	290	295
Latin America	166	230	308	443	529	631
Asia (excluding Japan)	1 296	1 637	2 139	2 979	3 534	4 138
Africa	228	296	388	621	811	1 078
"Rest"	**1 960**	**2 485**	**3 196**	**4 454**	**5 285**	**6 262**
World	2 525	3 132	3 913	5 253	6 136	7 154
GDP (billion international $)						
	1950	1962	1973	1990	2001	2015
Western Europe	1 402	2 497	4 134	6 032	7 506	9 618
Western Offshoots	1 635	2 519	4 058	6 666	9 288	13 432
Japan	161	458	1 243	2 321	2 636	2 957
"West"	**3 198**	**5 474**	**9 435**	**15 020**	**19 430**	**26 007**
Eastern Europe	185	328	551	663	711	1 066
Former USSR	510	915	1 513	1 988	1 343	1 903
Latin America	424	753	1 398	2 239	3 076	4 520
Asia (excluding Japan)	825	1 370	2 633	6 307	11 375	22 705
Africa	195	307	529	860	1 144	1 746
"Rest"	**2 138**	**3 674**	**6 624**	**12 057**	**17 649**	**31 940**
World	5 336	9 147	16 059	27 076	37 079	57 947

The demographic projections are those of the United Nations Population Division, and indicate a continuing decline in the rate of population growth in virtually all parts of the world (see Table 2). Nevertheless there would still be a very striking difference between the advanced capitalist group and Africa. At 0.33 per cent a year it would take 210 years to double population in first group. In Africa it is likely to happen within 32 years.

Table 2. **Growth Momentum: Per Capita GDP and Population,**
World and Major Regions: 1950-2015

	1950–73	1973–90	1990–2001	2001–15
	Growth of GDP per Capita (annual average compound rate)			
Western Europe	4.08	1.94	1.68	1.68
Western Offshoots	2.44	1.92	2.03	1.92
Japan	8.05	2.96	0.89	0.89
"West"	3.73	2.13	1.78	1.76
Eastern Europe	3.79	0.51	0.71	3.00
Former USSR	3.36	0.74	−3.52	2.40
Latin America	2.52	0.65	1.28	1.50
Asia (excluding Japan)	2.92	3.24	3.88	3.88
Africa	2.07	0.09	0.16	1.00
"Rest"	2.83	1.58	1.93	3.07
World	2.93	1.35	1.46	2.11
	Growth of Population (annual average compound rate)			
Western Europe	0.70	0.30	0.33	0.11
Western Offshoots	1.55	1.02	1.00	0.73
Japan	1.15	0.76	0.27	−0.06
"West"	1.05	0.63	0.58	0.33
Eastern Europe	1.03	0.58	−0.07	−0.07
Former USSR	1.43	0.87	0.02	0.12
Latin America	2.73	2.15	1.63	1.27
Asia (excluding Japan)	2.19	1.97	1.56	1.13
Africa	2.33	2.81	2.47	2.21
"Rest"	2.15	1.97	1.57	1.22
World	1.92	1.75	1.42	1.10

Source: 1950–98 from Maddison (2001), Appendix C.
GDP updated to 2001 from IMF, *World Economic Outlook,* April 2002. Population 2001–2015 (medium variant) from UN Population Division, *World Population Prospects, 1998 Revision,* New York, 1999. Per capita growth rates 2001–2015 in Western Europe and Japan assumed to be at the same pace as in 1990–2001; some slowdown assumed in United States; Asia excluding Japan assumed to be at the same pace as in 1990–2001; for other regions, see text. The GDP projections are derivative.

In making per capita GDP projections, I assumed a continuance of 1990–2001 rates of performance in Western Europe and Japan and mild slowdown in the United States, where the information technology bubble of the 1990s has burst, and where the capital inflow which financed its trade deficit seems likely to slacken substantially. Aggregate per capita growth in the "West" seems unlikely to slow down very significantly, but combined with the demographic slowdown, it means that aggregate GDP growth would be about 2 per cent a year. This pace would be similar to that in 1913–50. Growth momentum transmitted by the "West" is likely to be more modest than in 1870–1913 and 1973–2001.

Asia (excluding Japan)

The most buoyant part of the world economy since the early 1970s has been Asia (excluding Japan). These economies have grown faster than those of the West and their buoyancy has been sustained in great part by their own policies. Their weight in the world economy is much larger than any other non–western region. I assumed that their per capita growth 2001–15 would be at the same pace as in 1990–2001. In 2001 they produced 31 per cent of world GDP and by 2015 the projections imply that this will rise to 39 per cent. By contrast, the "West's" share would fall from 52 to 45 per cent.

These economies are catching up with the West and are still at a level of development where "opportunities of backwardness" are unlikely to erode. The combination of high investment rates and rapid GDP growth means that their physical capital stock has been growing more rapidly than in other parts of the world. The East Asian economies also have a high ratio of employment to population. This is due to falling fertility and a rising share of population of working age, but also reflects the traditionally high labour–mobilisation of multi–cropping rice economies. In all cases which are documented they had high rates of improvement in education and the quality of human capital. Equally striking was the rapid growth of exports, the high ratio of exports to GDP, and a willingness to attract foreign direct investment as a vehicle for assimilation of foreign technology. These characteristics of China, South Korea and Chinese Taipei have made for super–growth, but there is a second tier of countries whose growth is accelerating rapidly. The most notable case is India which has the potential to join the super–growth club. There are other economies where prospects are more problematic, but these are only a sixth of the Asian total. The projections assume no substantial change in their performance.

Latin America

Latin America is the second largest non–western region with about 8 per cent of world product and a slightly bigger share of world population. Until the 1970s, economic policy was different from that in the advanced capitalist group. Most countries never seriously tried to observe the fixed rate discipline of Bretton Woods. National currencies were repeatedly devalued, IMF advocacy of fiscal and monetary rectitude was frequently rebuffed, high rates of inflation became endemic. Most countries reacted with insouciance to the worldwide explosion of prices, and governments felt that they could accommodate high rates of inflation. They were able to borrow on a large scale at negative real interest rates to cover external deficits incurred as a result of expansionary policies.

40

However, the basic parameters had changed by the early 1980s. By then, the OECD countries were pushing anti–inflationary policy very vigorously. The change to restrictive monetary policy initiated by the United States Federal Reserve pushed up interest rates suddenly and sharply. Between 1973 and 1982 external debt increased sevenfold and the creditworthiness of Latin America as a whole was grievously damaged by Mexico's debt delinquency in 1982. The flow of voluntary private lending stopped abruptly, and created a massive need for retrenchment in economies teetering on the edge of hyperinflation and fiscal crisis. In most countries resource allocation was distorted by subsidies, controls, widespread commitments to government enterprise and detailed interventionism. Most of them also had serious social tension, and several had unsavoury political regimes.

In the 1930s, most Latin American countries resorted to debt default, but it was not a very attractive option in the 1980s. World trade had not collapsed, international private lending continued on a large scale. The IMF and World Bank had substantial facilities to mitigate the situation, and leverage to pressure Western banks to make involuntary loans and legitimate a substantial degree of delinquency.

In the course of the 1980s, the attempts to resolve these problems brought major changes in economic policy. But in most countries, changes were made reluctantly. After experiments with heterodox policy options in Argentina and Brazil, most countries eventually embraced the neoliberal policy mix pioneered by Chile. They moved towards greater openness to international markets, reduced government intervention, trade liberalisation, less distorted exchange rates, better fiscal equilibrium and establishment of more democratic political systems.

The cost of this transition was a decade of falling per capita income in the 1980s. After 1990, economic growth revived substantially but the process was interrupted by contagious episodes of capital flight.

I assumed in the projections for Latin America, that there will be some modest improvement in per capita performance in 2001–15.

Africa

Africa has nearly 13 per cent of world population, but only 3 per cent of world GDP. It is the world's poorest region, with a per capita income less than 5 per cent of that in the United States. Its population is growing seven times as fast as in Western Europe. Per capita income in 2001 was 5 per cent below its 1980 peak. African economies are more volatile than most others because export earnings are concentrated on a few primary commodities, and extremes of weather (droughts and floods) are more severe and have a heavy impact.

As a result of rapid population growth, age structure is very different from that in Western Europe. In Europe more than two–thirds are of working age, in Africa little more than half. Almost half the adult population are illiterate. They have had a high incidence of infectious and parasitic disease (malaria, sleeping sickness, hookworm, river blindness, yellow fever). Over two–thirds of HIV infected people live in Africa. As a result the quantity and quality of labour input per head of population is much lower than in other parts of the world. Until late in the 19th century, most of the continent was unknown and unexplored, occupied by hunter–gatherers, pastoralists or practitioners of subsistence agriculture. Levels of education and technology were primitive. Land was relatively abundant, was allocated by traditional chiefs, without Western–style property rights. The only territorial units which resembled those of today were Egypt, Ethiopia, Liberia, Morocco and South Africa. The European powers became interested in grabbing Africa in the 1880s. France and Britain were the most successful. Twenty two countries eventually emerged from French colonisation, 21 from British, five from Portuguese, three from Belgian, two from Spanish. Germany lost its colonies after the First World War, Italy after the Second. The colonialists created boundaries to suit their own convenience, with little regard to local traditions or ethnicity. European law and property rights were introduced with little regard to traditional forms of land allocation. Hence European colonists often got the best land and most of the benefits from exploitation of mineral rights and plantation agriculture. African incomes were kept low by forced labour or apartheid practices. Little was done to build a transport infrastructure or to cater for popular education.

European colonisers withdrew between 1956 and 1974. In South Africa, the mass of the population did not get political rights until 1994. Independence brought many serious challenges. The political leadership had to try to create elements of national solidarity and stability more or less from scratch. The new national entities were in most cases a creation of colonial rule. There was great ethnic diversity with no tradition or indigenous institutions of nationhood. The linguistic vehicle of administration and education was generally French, English or Portuguese rather than the languages most used by the mass of the population.

Africa became a focus of international rivalry during the Cold War. China, the USSR, Cuba and East European countries supplied economic and military aid to new countries viewed as proxies in a world–wide conflict of interest. Western countries, Israel and Chinese Taipei were more generous in supplying aid and less fastidious in its allocation than they might otherwise have been. As a result, Africa accumulated large external debts which had a meagre developmental pay–off.

There was a great scarcity of people with education or administrative experience. Suddenly these countries had to create a political elite, staff a national bureaucracy, establish a judiciary, create a police force and armed forces, send out dozens of diplomats. The first big wave of job opportunities strengthened the role of patronage and rent—seeking, and reduced the attractions of entrepreneurship. The existing stock of graduates was too thin to meet the demands and there was heavy dependence on foreign personnel.

The process of state creation involved armed struggle in many cases. In Algeria, Angola, Mozambique, Sudan, Zaire and Zimbabwe, the struggle for independence involved war with the colonial power or the white settler population. Burundi, Eritrea, Ethiopia, Liberia, Nigeria, Rwanda, Sierra Leone, Uganda and Zaire have all suffered from civil wars and bloody dictators. These wars were a major impediment to development.

In many African states, rulers have sought to keep their positions for life. In most states, rulers relied for support on a narrow group who shared the spoils of office. Corruption became widespread, property rights insecure, business decisions risky. Collier and Gunning (1999) suggest that nearly two—fifths of African private wealth now consists of assets held abroad (compared with 10 per cent in Latin America and 6 per cent in East Asia). Such estimates are necessarily rough, but with presidents like Mobutu in Zaire or Abacha in Nigeria, it is not difficult to believe that the proportion is high.

A major factor in the slowdown since 1980 has been external debt. As the Cold War faded from the mid—1980s, foreign aid levelled off, and net lending to Africa fell. Although the flow of foreign direct investment has risen it has not offset the fall in other financial flows

The challenges to development in Africa are greater than in any other continent, the deficiencies in health, education and nutrition the most extreme. It is the continent with the greatest need for financial aid and technical assistance. The per capita GDP projections assume that these kinds of aid will be increased and that per capita growth will be positive. However, it is unlikely that African countries will, by 2015, be able to establish a trajectory of rapid catch—up such as Asian economies have achieved.

Eastern Europe

In Eastern Europe, the economic system was similar to that in the USSR from 1948 to the end of the 1980s, and so was economic performance. In 1950–73, per capita growth more or less kept pace with that of Western Europe, but faltered badly as the economic and political system began to crumble. From 1973–90, it grew at 0.5 per cent a year compared with 1.9 per cent in Western Europe.

The transition from a command to a market economy was difficult in all of the countries. The easiest part was freeing prices and opening of trade with the West. This ended shortages and queueing, improved the quality of goods and services and increased consumer welfare. However, much of the old capital stock became junk; the labour force needed to acquire new skills and work habits; the legal and administrative systems and the tax/social benefit structure had to be transformed; the distributive and banking networks to be rebuilt from scratch. The travails of transition led to a fall in average per capita income for the group from 1990 to 1993, but it rose by over 3 per cent a year from then to 2001. The projection assumes that this pace of advance can be maintained at least until 2015. In fact, these countries can probably do better than this if they can be integrated into the European Union with better access to its goods, labour and capital markets, its regional and other subsidies, than they have thus far enjoyed. Present real income levels are only a third of those in Western Europe. Wages are also much lower, but the disparity in skills is much less. The Eastern economies are therefore capable of mounting a catch–up dynamic similar to that of Asia if the integration takes place.

Successor States of Former USSR

Fifteen successor states emerged from the collapse of the Soviet Union in 1991. In all of them, there was already a very marked deceleration of economic growth in 1973–90. There was colossal inefficiency in resource allocation, a very heavy burden of military expenditure and associated spending, depletion and destruction of natural resources.

Average and incremental capital/output ratios were higher than in capitalist countries. Materials were used wastefully as they were supplied below cost. Shortages created a chronic tendency to hoard inventories. The steel consumption/GDP ratio was four times as high as in the United States, the ratio of industrial value added to gross output much lower than in Western countries. In the USSR, the average industrial firm had 814 workers in 1987 compared with an average of 30 in Germany and the United Kingdom. Transfer of technology from the West was hindered by trade restrictions, lack of foreign direct investment and very restricted access to foreign technicians and scholars. Work incentives were poor, malingering on the job was commonplace.

The quality of consumer goods was poor. Retail outlets and service industries were few. Prices bore little relation to cost. Consumers wasted time queueing, bartering or sometimes bribing their way to the goods and services they wanted. There was an active black market, and special shops for the *nomenklatura*. There was increasing cynicism, frustration, growing alcoholism and a decline in life expectancy.

Soviet spending on its military and space effort was around 15 per cent of GDP in the 1970s and 1980s, nearly three times the US ratio and five times as high as in Western Europe. There were significant associated commitments to Afghanistan, Cuba, Mongolia, North Korea, Viet Nam and Soviet client states in Africa.

44

In the 1950s a good deal of agricultural expansion was in virgin soil areas, where fertility was quickly exhausted. Most of the Aral sea was transformed into a salty desert. Exploitation of mineral and energy resources in Siberia and Central Asia required bigger infrastructure costs than in European Russia. The Chernobyl nuclear accident had a disastrously polluting effect on a large area of Ukraine.

In 1985–91 Gorbachev established a remarkable degree of political freedom and liberated Eastern Europe but had no coherent economic policy. From then to end 1999, Yeltsin broke up the Soviet Union, destroyed its economic and political system and moved towards a "market" economy. The economic outcome was a downward spiral of real income for the mass of the population. On average, GDP was 43 per cent lower in 1998 in the 15 ex–republics than in 1990. Fixed investment and military spending fell dramatically, so the drop in private consumption was milder. There were very big changes in income distribution. Under the old system, basic necessities (bread, housing, education, health, crèches and social services) had been highly subsidised by the government or provided free by state enterprises to their workers. These all became relatively more expensive, the real value of wages and pensions was reduced by hyperinflation, and the value of popular savings was destroyed. There were major gains in the income of a new oligarchy.

The new "market" economy is grossly inefficient and unfair in allocating resources. There has been legislation to establish Western style property rights, but in practice accountancy is opaque and government interpretation of property rights is arbitrary. Many businesses are subject to criminal pressure. Property owners such as shareholders or investors are uncertain whether their rights will be honoured. Workers are not sure their wages will be paid.

Between the rouble devaluation of 1998 and 2001, the economy had three years of rapid growth, with per capita GDP rising nearly 6 per cent a year. This is too brief a period to be used as a basis for projection. I assumed that the economies of the former USSR would have somewhat slower growth of per capita GDP than Eastern Europe.

Bibliography

COLLIER, P. AND J.W. GUNNING (1999), "Explaining African Performance", *Journal of Economic Literature,* March, pp. 64–111.

IMF (2002), *World Economic Outlook*, Washington D.C., April

JEVONS, W.S. (1865), *The Coal Question*, Kelley Reprint, New York, 1965.

MADDISON, A. (2001), *The World Economy: A Millennial Perspective*, Development Centre Studies, OECD, Paris.

OECD (2001), *Agricultural Policies in OECD Countries: Monitoring and Evaluation*, Paris.

STIGLITZ, J.E. (2002), *Globalization and its Discontents,* Norton, New York.

UN POPULATION DIVISION (1999), *World Population Prospects,* 1998 revision, New York.

WORLD BANK (2002), *Global Development Finance*, Washington, D.C.

Chapter 3

Growth in Theory and in Practice

Daniel Cohen

Introduction

The income disparities between the richest and the poorest countries have widened steadily over the last two centuries. In 1820, India's per capita income was $531 (1990 dollars; data from Maddison, 1995), making India at that time (already) poorer than the United States by a factor of 2.5. By 1910, India's per capita income amounted to $688: the country had become seven times as poor as the United States. In 1990, it had reached a per capita income of $1 316, bringing it (at last) to the level where the United States had been in 1820, but making it poorer than the contemporary United States by a factor of 16! India is a fascinating example in that it epitomises the fate of countries that are still "developing" today: it participated in the British free–trade area in the 19th century, then succumbed to the protectionist temptation in the 20th, but in both cases, the gap between India and the rich countries grew ever wider. The fierce debates in economic growth theory have largely turned on the interpretation of these gaps. How is it possible for the income disparities between countries to increase? In the words of Robert Lucas (one of the first to revive this debate), once you begin to ask these questions, there are few others that really matter.

Over the last 20 years, considerable progress has been made in understanding these phenomena. Fresh data have enabled economists to measure wealth differentials between countries over long periods. Thanks to the work of Maddison (1995), the Development Centre played a leading role in this respect. Together with the equally well–known work of Summers and Heston, Maddison's data (the source for the above comparisons between India and the United States) made it possible to assess the growing gaps between the richest and the poorest countries over the very long term. In contradiction to previous data, notably from Bairoch, it seems not to be true, first of all, that on the eve of the industrial revolution of the late 18th century, the European countries had approximately the same levels of income as the countries known today as developing countries. The cumulative process by which wealth goes to the wealthiest thus seems to be at work as early as the 18th century. According to Maddison, when the cumulative growth process that characterises the last two centuries began, Europe was already twice as rich as today's developing countries. Figure 1 presents data covering the 20th century, with the abscissa representing the country's income in 1913 and the ordinate its growth rate over the 20th century. Nothing indicates that the countries which were poorest initially grew faster than the wealthy countries; in fact, the correlation observed is just the opposite: the gap widened, as in the comparison between India and the United States.

The same result is reached if we use data for the period after 1950. One explanation that comes to mind for this cumulative phenomenon is that national economies are subject to economies of scale, which allow the most advanced to be more productive than the others and thus to engender a cumulative effect to their advantage. This is the message of "endogenous growth" theories, which were the first to present growth data in the form used in Figure 1[1]. The idea of a world subject to increasing returns to scale (the richer a country, the more productive it is) is good news for overall economic growth. It shows that there is no reason to fear an end to growth, the "stationary state" defined by John Stuart Mill in which growth necessarily runs out of steam in the end. It leads one to regard globalisation as a process of market enlargement, which as such is favourable to world growth.

This idea is alarming, however, where the rising inequality between nations is concerned: if the poorest country grows poorer with respect to the wealthy, the wealth disparities may rapidly become unbearable. However, closer examination of the growth conditions of poor countries, while obviously not cancelling out the historical facts, nevertheless offers a more encouraging message. It seems possible, depending on a number of factors, for a poor country to catch up with the rich countries. To borrow a figure of speech used by Paul Krugman, what poor countries need is more perspiration than inspiration. To catch up with the rich countries, they must first accumulate the same production factors as rich countries: physical capital and human capital. We will first gauge the extent of their handicap in this respect, and subsequently address the reasons why it seems so difficult to overcome.

Figure 1. **Growth and Initial Income, 1913-90**

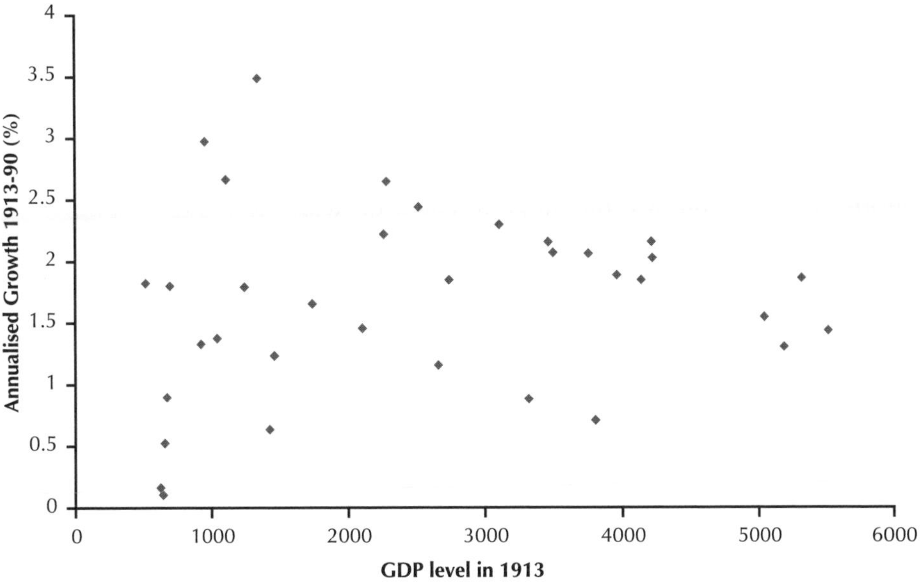

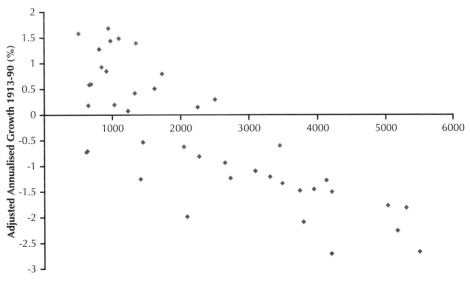

Source: Maddison (1995).

Figure 2. **Conditional Convergence, 1913-90**

Source: OECD Development Centre.

49

The Wealth of Nations

Conditional Convergence

Barro's (1991) article played a vital role in challenging the radical pessimism stemming from examination of growth over the course of the 20th century, because it showed that developing countries are liable to experience, if not a process of outright convergence, at least a process of "conditional convergence" (see Chapter 4). The idea is that countries may hope to catch up with the richest countries on condition that, among other things, they are as well educated as rich countries. In the first version of Barro's work, the simplest interpretation of this result is to say that within a given class of countries having the same level of education, a convergence "process" is at work: the poorest countries grow faster than the wealthiest. This conditional convergence process is illustrated in Figure 2, where we reproduce OECD Development Centre data compiled by Maddison (1995) for per capita income and by Cohen and Soto (2001) for human capital.

This notion of "conditional convergence" must be interpreted with caution. First of all, it does not mean that within a given class of countries having the same level of education (regarding educational level as fixed for the moment) the poorest countries will catch up with the richest. It is perfectly possible for the rich country to remain at a stable level of 100 (without growth) while the poor country converges towards the level of 50 (recording positive growth).

Moreover, nothing indicates that educational levels will remain unchanged in rich countries. On the contrary, everything indicates that they will rise at least as fast in well–endowed countries as elsewhere. This is in fact the reason why conditional convergence does not imply absolute convergence. Table 1 presents the figures obtained.

Table 1. **Number of Years of Education**

Year	Latin America	Other developing countries	Rich countries	United States
1913	2.9	1.4	5.6	7.0
1960	3.8	1.9	7.8	10.2
1970	4.6	2.5	8.9	11.3
1980	5.5	3.4	9.9	12.2
1990	6.6	4.4	10.6	12.6
2000	7.3	5.3	11.3	12.6
2010	8.0	6.0	11.8	13.2

Source: Cohen and Soto (2001).

A first difficulty appears. The human capital of the poorest countries, measured in terms of the number of years of education, seems to grow much faster than that of rich countries. From 1913 to 1990, the human capital of Latin America grew by 175 per cent, and that of the United States by 88 per cent. If human capital is the crucial variable of the convergence process, then convergence should have been observed. The results are even more striking for the other developing countries, where the number of years of schooling grew by 328 per cent, nearly four times as fast as in the United States! This is the gist of the analysis presented by Benhabib and Spiegel (1994), who conclude their remarkable article by challenging the idea that human capital is a determining factor of growth. We see things in a different light, however, if we compare the differences in *levels* of education. The increase in the number of years of schooling was 5.1 years in Latin America and 6.2 years in the United States: there is thus no convergence whatsoever in level (even though there is convergence in growth rates). The same is true for the other poor countries, where the number of years of schooling rose less quickly, by only 4.6 years. The point is that, in the standard formulation first developed by Mincer (1974) and used the most often thereafter (on this subject, see Mincer's studies conducted at the World Bank under the supervision of François Bourguignon), it is in fact the absolute difference in educational levels that explains the relative difference between the incomes of two persons and (by aggregation) between those of two countries. The apparent paradox presented by Benhabib and Spiegel is therefore resolved: despite appearances, there has in fact been no convergence of human capital between rich and poor countries, which allows us to understand why human capital has not been a factor allowing the latter to catch up with the former.

Inspiration and Perspiration

The spectacular work of Young (1995) on Singapore showed that this country, whose income rose from a level comparable to that of India in 1950 to a level equal to that of the United Kingdom in 1990, owes all of this income growth to the investment in people and machinery that it undertook over this period. Singapore recorded an average investment rate of over 30 per cent of GDP during the 1960s and 1970s, and doubled the average number of years of schooling of the population between 1960 and 2000. The testing scores of lower secondary students in Singapore today are among the highest in the world. Obviously, it is extremely difficult to mobilise resources on this scale, and unshakable confidence in the dividends of such a policy is needed to launch a country on this path. As Paul Krugman (1994) put it, the example of Singapore illustrates the merits of "perspiration over inspiration". The fact is that throughout the years of rapid growth Singapore made virtually no progress in total factor productivity, which measures the contribution made by technical efficiency to a country's wealth, above and beyond the accumulation of physical and human capital. The lesson to be drawn from Singapore is, in some respects, a hopeful message: it shows that a growth strategy can succeed, although it requires huge investment outlays.

To sum up the nature of this debate, it is helpful to follow the formulation of Mankiw et al. (1992). In the basic neo–classical model used — Solow's model — there are three production factors, capital, labour and technical progress, with per capita income depending only on the capital stock per capita and on technical progress. In this model, a country is poor with respect to another only if its capital stock per capita is low, as technical progress itself is assumed to be shared by all. In their synthesis of Solow's model and the facts enumerated by Barro (1991), Mankiw et al. (1992) put forward an "augmented" neo–classical model in which human capital is added to capital and technical progress. This breakdown makes it possible to isolate the contributions of physical capital, of human capital and of technical progress to economic growth. In their Development Centre Study, Cohen and Soto (2002) suggest the following breakdown. Income per capita is written as the product of three terms: human capital (per capita), physical capital per unit of human capital (with an exponent reflecting the contribution of capital to growth, i.e. 1/3), and a third, "residual" term, namely total factor productivity, which is generally associated with technical progress. This yields the following results.

Table 2 is to be interpreted as follows. The first column is the product of the three subsequent columns, with rich countries being taken as the numéraire. It can thus be seen that poor countries outside of Africa have human capital (per capita) worth 58 per cent of that of rich countries, that their deficit of physical capital per unit of human capital reduces their income to 65 per cent of that of the rich countries and lastly that their total productivity is also lower, which similarly pulls down their income to 65 per cent of that of rich countries. To simplify, we will say that they are one–third less well endowed than rich countries in each of the three terms that determine the wealth of a country. Overall, the product of these three terms explains why the incomes of poor countries outside of Africa amount to a quarter of rich countries' incomes. The result is even more striking in the case of Africa. Each of the three components of Africa's wealth is worth about 40 per cent of the level of the richest countries, but when multiplied together they explain why Africa's income stands at only 6 per cent of the level of rich countries.

It can thus be seen that the poverty of nations may be interpreted as the product of a series of handicaps, in terms of resources and of total productivity. Each of these handicaps is in fact "moderate", in the sense that individually, neither human capital, physical capital nor technical progress would suffice to explain the poverty of developing countries. It is the fact that they are combined that makes them extremely difficult to overcome, so difficult that it is tempting to use the term "under–development trap" to convey what is at stake in growth policies. It also becomes understandable why the "perspiration" strategy of Singapore can succeed. By tackling each of these handicaps, a country can rise out of poverty. But if it wishes to tackle them all, immense sacrifices will be required.

Table 2. **Per Capita Income and Its Causes**

	Income/ per capita	Human capital	Contribution of physical/human capital	Total factor productivity
	(1)	(2)	(3)	(4)
Rich countries	1	1	1	1
Poor countries excluding Africa	0.25	0.58	0.65	0.65
Africa	0.06	0.38	0.38	0.41

Note: (1) = (2)*(3)*(4)
Source: Cohen and Soto (2002).

Globalisation and Governance

In addition to the individual efforts a country can make to escape from under–development, its international environment plays a vital role (see Berthélemy's analysis of convergence clubs in Chapter 4). What hopes can emerging countries place in "globalisation", and what position can they hope to occupy in the new international division of labour? This is an essential question, and one to which the answers given vary considerably in space and time.

From One Wave of Globalisation to Another

The current process of globalisation is not the first of its kind (see Oman, 1994, 1996). Over the course of the 19th century, a first "globalisation" had taken place owing to the exceptional reduction in transport costs. Railroads, steamboats and the invention of refrigeration were all factors that suddenly eliminated the distances between countries. As Bairoch (1971) put it, the trade policy of countries at the time consisted solely in offsetting the fall in transport costs through tariff barriers. Those which did not manage to do so — usually because the rich countries forbade them to — suffered irreversible damage as a result. Throughout the 19th century, the countries which over this period became the Third World were subjected to such fierce competition from the industrialised countries, mainly England, that it brought about the eradication of their craft activities, which could have served as a basis for their industrialisation. At the beginning of the 19th century, for example, India was an exporter of high–quality silk goods and textiles; at the end of the century, it had to import the bulk of its domestic consumption. Over the 19th century, the countries of the South suffered from the effects of the law of comparative advantage: industry went to the advanced countries, while the others were left with agricultural and tropical products that excluded them from the beneficial effects of industrialisation. The impact on income distribution was substantial.

In imitation of what the United States did after the Civil War and what European countries such as France and Germany did to protect themselves against England, most Third World countries opted of their own volition for firmly protectionist development strategies when they acceded to independence. The history of the 20th century, however, was still harsher with respect to these strategies than the history of the 19th century had been with respect to free trade. The reason is that protectionism deprived poor countries of access to the major technological innovations of the 20th century. European countries could easily copy the innovations of their neighbours (France copied England, Germany copied both England and France), since the industrial revolution, whose impact was felt throughout the 19th century, was relatively easy to imitate. Bairoch (1971) tells the humorous story of how Marc Seguin bought a locomotive, set it up in the middle of his workshop and had his workers copy it. This method proved less fruitful in the 20th century. A few countries, such as Japan and Korea, succeeded in striking a delicate balance by protecting their domestic markets and expanding their exports, but no country that was totally cut off from world markets managed to catch up with the rich countries.

As from the mid–1970s, the former USSR, China and India began to recognise that inward–looking development did not suffice. In the short period from the death of Mao to the fall of the Berlin Wall, developing countries changed their perception of the effect of the global market on their growth strategies. They grasped that the world market was the force driving their industrialisation, that the structure of comparative advantage had changed since the 19th century. A fundamental qualitative change took place: the share of manufactured products in the exports of developing countries rose from 20 per cent in 1970 to 70 per cent today. Although in the North globalisation is currently quickening the pace of de–industrialisation, in the South it is a factor that can promote industrialisation. The question is whether it can become a factor of growth and convergence (see also Chapter 7).

Globalisation Today

Sachs and Warner (1995) present important results that tend to prove the positive effect of openness on a country's economic growth. They show that over the 1970–95 period, the group of "open" economies grew at a rate of 4.5 per cent annually, whereas the "closed" economies grew by 0.7 per cent per year. Within the group of open economies, the emerging economies grew faster by two percentage points than the rich economies; among the closed economies, there are no such differences. Trade openness thus seems to be conducive to convergence. According to Sachs and Warner, in fact, the results are conclusive: all of the countries that chose an open trade policy grew more rapidly.

54

The "openness" variable selected by Sachs and Warner has been considered in many subsequent studies. According to Sachs and Warner's classification, 78 emerging countries (excluding the former Soviet bloc) opted for a protectionist development policy of one form or another. Of these countries, 43 had altered their strategies at least once. For the 15 countries that ventured to try openness to trade and subsequently closed their economies again, Sachs and Warner find that growth during the closed period was in every case lower than during the open period. The definition they used has nevertheless been criticised, notably by Rodriguez and Rodrik (2000), on the grounds that it included many aspects other than international trade. In their careful review of the tests applied to the notion that trade is a factor of growth, Rodriguez and Rodrik show that the variable which mainly explains Sachs and Warner's results is the exchange rate discount on the black market. The interpretation of this variable suggested by Sachs and Warner is that it represents a tax on trade, since exporters must (in general) sell their foreign exchange at the official rate, while importers (at the margin, at least) must buy it on the black market. Of course, many macroeconomic policy variables other than trade policy are correlated with the black market — financial repression, inflation, the debt crisis and so on — which makes it extremely difficult to resolve the question of whether the observed effect is really due to trade barriers.

Later studies sought to demonstrate that trade was indeed the issue. Noting that a country's geography favours trade to varying degrees (depending on the country's access to the sea, the distance separating the main commercial centres, etc.), Frankel and Romer (1999) show that these "exogenous" factors did indeed have a significant influence on the economic growth of a country. In their critique of this article, Rodriguez and Rodrik (2000) show that these "geographical" variables can have a direct impact on a country's productivity, through many other channels than trade in the narrow sense. As Dornbusch astutely noted in his commentary on Sachs and Warner's article (1995), "...openness, broadly defined; contributes to growth through the exchange of ideas, technology and factors of production. But merchandise trade is only a marginally important part of the openness that provides these benefits."

Cohen (2001) shows, for instance, that the Sachs–Warner variable is significant mainly when it is combined with a country's education variable. An "open" economy in the sense of Sachs and Warner considerably increases the return on human capital: in practice, everything happens as if openness increased the productive use of the knowledge available in a country. One possible interpretation, however, along the lines of the analysis put forward by Krueger (1974), is that closed economies do not make productive use of their human capital, but employ it in unproductive activities that siphon off wealth (on this point, see also Berthélemy et al., 1997).

55

Institutions

The criticisms of Rodriguez and Rodrik highlight a fact that in itself is not easily disputable: trade openness is rarely an isolated phenomenon, but is almost always combined with a number of other domestic factors. Hall and Jones (1999) endeavour to take account of the "quality" of institutions, or what they call social infrastructure, whose adherence to the "rule of law" is a vital characteristic.

The role played by the rule of law has already been considered in economic analyses of growth. For example, Kormendi and McGuire (1985), a study not cited by Hall and Jones, showed the explanatory power of such an index. Among later studies, Knack and Keefer (1995) also drew up an index that is used in the publications of the International Country Risk Guide, a rating agency that ranks countries with respect to 24 categories, including respect for law and order, bureaucratic quality, the risk of expropriation, repudiation of contracts and corruption. Hall and Jones make use of this index, combining it with that of Sachs and Warner (1995), which in this context does indeed seem to be a piece of the puzzle. The argument here is that an "open" country will have "probably fewer degrees of freedom to engage in predatory activities". The resulting social infrastructure index gives the highest ranking to Switzerland and the United States, and the lowest to Zaire, Haiti and Bangladesh. By itself, it explains a considerable part of the disparities in total factor productivity, whose importance was discussed above.

Other works have highlighted the role of good governance in economic growth. The Development Centre's work programme "Globalisation and Governance" is part of this line of research. For example, Bonaglia et al. (2001) studied the impact of good governance (measured on the basis of indices similar to those of Hall and Jones) on direct investment. Similarly, Wei (2000) emphasises the incidence of governance on international trade. We should also mention the research conducted at the Development Centre by Hors (2001), which pointed up the factors best able to reduce corruption (the role of public opinion, of an entrepreneurial class free of government control, of simplified legislation etc.).

These studies recall the insights of Nobel prize–winner Douglass North. Economic activity, explains North, is always torn between value creation and value diversion. The balance between warriors and farmers, between pirates and seamen, is among the foremost reasons why the state almost invariably emerges. But the state itself is very often an actor that siphons off wealth. The quality of a social institution is measured, in North's terms, by the extent to which it reconciles the private returns and the social returns to economic activity. North and Thomas, in their famous work *The Rise of the Western World* (1973), explain that the West, in contrast to other civilisations, managed to create what would subsequently come to resemble a state of law, which gradually reined in wealth–diverting activities. Getting the private and social returns to productive activities into phase seems indeed to be an important issue for emerging capitalism in many developing countries. Globalisation is probably as crucial from this perspective as it is from the more traditional, but no less important, standpoint of promoting the importation of technical progress.

Conclusion

For poor countries, new technologies and globalisation constitute both a fresh challenge and a source of convergence with rich countries. Far from being able to count on a miracle solution, such as opening up their economies or stringing telephone lines, poor countries must compensate simultaneously for a series of mutually reinforcing handicaps. The analysis of the African case provided here is particularly instructive in this respect. Africa's total factor productivity stands at 40 per cent of the level in rich countries, as do its capital stock and its level of education. Individually, none of these terms provides a sufficient explanation for the extreme destitution of Africa, but when multiplied together term by term, they do suffice: 40 per cent cubed explains why Africa's income is only 6 per cent that of rich countries. It is easy to understand the disappointment of politicians who have by turns given priority to only one of these factors at a time. The task is immense, as it requires policies to promote the transmission of technical progress, savings and human capital formation and to develop an institutional framework that is conducive to all of these factors. But the counter–examples to the trap of under–development — Japan yesterday, Singapore today — are so many messages of hope.

Note

1.   One of the authors who has helped to rethink the theory of economic growth is the economist Paul Romer, a disciple of Robert Lucas at Chicago and currently a professor at the Stanford Business School. Romer's starting point was to understand which endogenous factors determine technical progress. The conventional approach to economic growth, which we owe to Solow, holds that technical progress is exogenous and given for all, which makes it impossible to understand both what determines the long-term growth of an economy, and what allows some poor countries, but apparently not all, to gain access to these factors. Romer's (1986) most fundamental insight — which partly builds on the argument of Dixit and Stiglitz (1977) and some of Helpman and Krugman's (1985) ideas on international trade — is that technical progress is the result of a specified economic activity, namely research and development, the intensity of which will vary with the size of the market to which it is applied. This idea was subsequently taken up and developed by Aghion and Howitt (1998) using a Schumpeterian approach to growth and extended to the case of world trade by Grossman and Helpman (1991).

Bibliography

AGHION, P. AND P. HOWITT (1998), *Endogenous Growth Theory*, MIT Press, Cambridge, Mass.

BAIROCH, P. (1971; nouvelle édition 1992), *Le Tiers Monde dans l'impasse*, Gallimard, Paris.

BARRO, R. (1991), "Economic Growth in a Cross Section of Countries", *Quarterly Journal of Economics*, 56 (2), 407–444.

BARRO, R. AND J.-W. LEE (1993), "International Comparisons of Educational Attainment", *Journal of Monetary Economics*, 32 (3).

BENHABIB, J. AND M.M. SPIEGEL (1994), "The Role of Human Capital in Economic Development: Evidence from Aggregate Cross–country Data", *Journal of Monetary Economics*, 34, 143–173.

BERTHÉLEMY, J.-C. (2002), "Convergence Clubs and Underdevelopment Traps", Chapter 4 in this volume.

BERTHÉLEMY, J.-C., S. DESSUS AND A. VAROUDAKIS (1997), *Capital Humain, ouverture extérieure et croissance : estimation sur données de panel d'un modèle à coefficients variables*, Documents techniques No. 121, OECD Development Centre, Paris.

BILS, M. AND P. KLENOW (2000), "Does Schooling Cause Growth?", *American Economic Review* 90 (5), 1160–83.

BONAGLIA F., J. BRAGA DE MACEDO AND M. BUSSOLO (2001), "How Globalization Improves Governance", CEPR Discussion Paper No. 2992, Centre for Economic Policy Research, London.

BOURGUIGNON, F. *et al.* (1999), "Research Project on the Microeconomics of Income Distribution Dynamics", The World Bank and the Inter–American Development Bank, Washington, D.C.

COE, D., E. HELPMAN AND A. HOFFMAISTER (1997), "North–South R&D Spillovers", *Economic Journal* 107, 134–139.

COHEN, D. (1996), "Tests of the Convergence Hypothesis: Some Further Results", *Journal of Economic Growth* 1 (3), 351–361.

COHEN, D. (2001), "Fear of Globalization : The Human Capital Nexus", Annual Bank Conference on Development Economics, 2002, World Bank, Washington, D.C.

COHEN, D. AND M. SOTO (2001), *Human Capital and Growth: Good Data, Good Results*, Technical Papers No. 179, OECD Development Centre, Paris.

COHEN, D. ET M. SOTO (2002), *Why Are Some Countries So Poor: Another Look at the Evidence and a Message of Hope*, Technical Papers No. 197, OECD Development Centre, Paris.

DE LA FUENTE, A. AND R. DOMÉNECH (2000), "Human Capital in Growth Regressions: How Much Difference Does Quality Data Make?", CEPR Discussion Paper 2466, Centre for Economic Policy Research, London.

DIXIT, A.K. AND J.E. STIGLITZ (1977), "Monopolistic Competition and Optimum Product Diversity", *American Economic Review* 67(3), 297–308.

EASTERLY, W. AND R. LEVINE (1997), "Africa's Growth Tragedy: Policies and Ethnic Divisions", *Quarterly Journal of Economics*, 112 (4), 1203–1250.

FRANKEL, J.A. AND D. ROMER (1999), "Does Trade Cause Growth?", *American Economic Review*, June, 89 (3), 379–399.

GROSSMAN, G.M. ET E. HELPMAN (1991), *Innovation and Growth in the Global Economy*, MIT Press, Cambridge, Mass.

HALL, R. AND C. JONES (1999), "Why Do Some Countries Produce So Much More Output per Worker than Others?", *Quarterly Journal of Economics*, 114 (1), 84–116.

HECKMAN, J. AND P. KLENOW (1997), "Human Capital Policy", University of Chicago, Department of Economics.

HELPMAN, E. ET P. KRUGMAN (1985), *Market Structure And Foreign Trade: Increasing Returns, Imperfect Competition, and the International Economy*, MIT Press, Cambridge, Mass.

HORS, I. (2001), *Fighting Corruption in Customs Administration: What Can We Learn from Recent Experiences?*, Technical Papers No. 175, OECD Development Centre, Paris.

KNACK, S. AND P. KEEFER (1995), "Institutions and Economic Performance", *Economics and Politics* (1995), VII, 207–227.

KORMENDI, R. AND P. MCGUIRE (1985), "Macroeconomic Determinants of Growth: Cross–country Evidence", *Journal of Monetary Economics*, 16 (2).

KRUEGER, A. (1974), "Political Economy of the Rent Seeking Society", *American Economic Review*, 64, 291–303.

KRUGMAN, P. (1994), "The Myth of Asia's Miracle", *Foreign Affairs*, November.

LUCAS, R. (1998), "On the Mechanics of Economic Development", *Journal of Monetary Economics* 22 (1), 3–42.

MADDISON, A. (1995), *Monitoring the World Economy 1820–1992: Analysis and Statistics*, Development Centre Studies, OECD, Paris.

MANKIW, N.G., D. ROMER AND D.N. WEIL (1992), "A Contribution to the Empirics of Economic Growth", *Quarterly Journal of Economics* 107 (May), 402–37.

MINCER, J. (1974), *Schooling, Experience, and Earnings*, Columbia University Press, New York.

NORTH, D. (1981), *Structure and Change in Economic History*, Norton, New York.

NORTH, D. AND R. THOMAS (1973), *The Rise of the Western World*, Cambridge University Press.

OMAN, C. (1996), *The Policy Challenges of Globalisation and Regionalisation*, Policy Brief No. 11, OECD Development Centre, Paris.

OMAN, C. (1994), *Globalisation and Regionalisation : The Challenge for Developing Countries?*, Development Centre Studies, OECD, Paris.

PRITCHETT, L. (2001), "Where Has All the Education Gone?" *World Bank Economic Review*, Vol. 15, No.. 3, pp. 367–391.

RODRIGUEZ, F. AND D. RODRIK (2000), "Trade Policy and Economic Growth: A Skeptic Guide to the Cross National Evidence", Kennedy School, Harvard University, mimeo.

ROMER, D. (1986), "Increasing Returns and Long–run Growth", *Journal of Political Economy* 94 (5), 1002–1037.

SACHS, J. AND A. WARNER (1995), "Economic Reform and the Process of Global Integration", *Brookings Papers on Economic Activity* 1, pp. 1–95.

SUMMERS, R. AND A. HESTON (1991), "The Penn Mark IV Data Table", *Quarterly Journal of Economics*, 106 (2), 327–368.

UNITED NATIONS EDUCATIONAL, SCIENTIFIC, AND CULTURAL ORGANIZATION (various years), *Statistical Yearbook*, Paris.

WEI S.-J. (2000), *Negative Alchemy? Corruption and Composition of Capital Flows*, Technical Papers No. 165, OECD Development Centre, Paris.

YOUNG, A. (1995), "The Tyranny of Numbers: Confronting the Statistical Realities of the East Asian Growth Experience", *Quarterly Journal of Economics*, 110.

Chapter 4

Convergence Clubs and Underdevelopment Traps

Jean–Claude Berthélemy

Introduction

At the time when the founding theoretical works on endogenous growth were appearing in the late 1980s, a large number of investigations were launched to reassess the question of the convergence of national economies, on the basis of Baumol's work in particular. The 1990s thus saw the appearance of a highly fertile combination of theoretical breakthroughs and fresh analyses of stylised facts on the growth of national economies. The Development Centre's work on growth during this period formed part of this line of research.

The lack of convergence among nations, as a result of which over a billion people are excluded from the globalisation process today, has been thoroughly demonstrated. The majority of the researchers who have examined this issue used Heston and Summers' GDP data, expressed in purchasing power parity, but the demonstration became much more enlightening with the data compiled at the Development Centre by Maddison (1995), which show that over the 1820–1992 period the gap in per capita income between the richest country and the poorest country increased more than tenfold in terms of purchasing power parity.

In order to analyse development and devise development policies, it is essential to understand the reasons for this lack of convergence. The notion of conditional convergence put forward by Barro (1991) provides part of an answer, but this concept assumes that initial conditions have no impact on an economy's long–term growth path. An alternative explanation is that more than one equilibrium state exists and that developing countries do not converge towards the level of the developed countries because they are "trapped" in a low equilibrium.

Introducing the multiple equilibria hypothesis into the analysis of convergence thus allows researchers to return, armed with new analytical tools, to the issue of underdevelopment traps, which was introduced into development theory as early as the 1950s. The aim is not simply to help explain why some countries are excluded from economic progress and globalisation, but also to identify the underlying barriers so as to inform development policy makers about the areas to which they should direct their efforts as a matter of priority. This approach leads to emphasis on the questions of educational development, financial development and infrastructure. It also enables us to discuss some aspects of the role of the institutional framework in development.

Multiple Equilibria in Development Theory

The idea that certain countries can find themselves locked into an unfavourable equilibrium state dates back to the beginnings of development theory, notably in the seminal work of Rosenstein–Rodan. As from the late 1950s, Solow's growth model led the majority of economists to adopt instead the idea that nations should converge towards a single equilibrium state. Even in the work based on Solow's model, however, it was possible to envisage the appearance of multiple equilibria, in connection with the minimum income levels required in order for individuals to save, or with a relationship between population growth and incomes, implying that a high rate of population growth undermines the economic growth of poor countries.

It is only recently, however, with the development of endogenous growth theory, that the hypothesis of multiple growth equilibria has been thoroughly investigated and checked against observational data. Various approaches along these lines were developed at the Development Centre in the 1990s, and subsequently led to empirical testing that helped identify the factors which can stimulate (in a high equilibrium) or hold back (in a low equilibrium) the growth of developing countries.

The question arose first, naturally enough, with respect to human capital, or more precisely with respect to investment in education. The theoretical work of Azariadis and Drazen (1990) clearly showed that a low level of educational development could lock an economy into a situation of underdevelopment. The paucity of human resources available initially reduces considerably the effectiveness of and the return on the education system, and consequently blocks the process of human capital accumulation that the economy needs in order to develop, since the private return on human capital falls so low that parents no longer invest in the education of their children. In these analyses, human capital is thus seen to have a property similar to that attributed to the research and development sector in standard endogenous growth models, namely a dynamic externality. When the stock of knowledge available within the population is insufficient, the gains from this externality cannot appear, and as a result growth will be blocked unless the state implements a strongly proactive education policy.

A similar idea was developed in the Development Centre's work on the role of the financial system. As capital is particularly scarce in developing countries, the opportunity cost of misusing this resource is extremely high, which is sufficient reason for paying special attention to this sector. Berthélemy and Varoudakis (1996a, 1996b) suggest that the initially weak state of the financial system and the low income level of the population may persist as a result of a cumulative process: low incomes imply that the amount of savings to be intermediated is small, which leads to high costs and weak competition in the financial sector; the result is a sluggish and inefficient capital accumulation process — owing to both the insufficient size of the financial sector and imperfect competition — that holds back growth and helps to keep the economy in a low–equilibrium state.

In the last analysis, the argument put forward here, like the theory of development advanced in the 1950s by Rosenstein–Rodan, is based on a pecuniary externality: the productive efficiency of the financial sector is positively correlated with the country's income level.

The existence of such multiple equilibria can lead to the appearance of convergence clubs, i.e. of separate groups of countries, each of which converges towards a different equilibrium state. These equilibria will be steady states, so that a given country will not be able — barring a strong initial push — to move from one convergence club to another over time. One of the contributions made by the Development Centre has been to propose empirical tests for the presence of multiple equilibria, based on the method for detecting convergence clubs put forward by Durlauf and Johnson (1992).

Convergence Clubs: Empirical Results from Cross–country Comparative Data

The proposed tests are in fact rather simple: they are structural stability tests of the parameters of a conditional convergence equation, conducted after the countries under consideration have been regrouped according to their levels of initial educational or financial development. The boundaries of the convergence clubs, as well as the extent to which the human capital effect overlaps with the financial development effect, are then determined through a maximum likelihood procedure.

These tests represent significant progress over other work on convergence clubs because they enable us not only to detect such clubs but also to isolate the economic factors that determine their emergence, whereas the usual tests simply define convergence clubs by ranking countries according to per capita income, and thus have little explanatory power. They also represent progress with respect to the work of the early 1990s, which demonstrated that certain groups of countries — particularly the sub–Saharan African countries — recorded lower growth rates than the others, all other things being equal, but which offered no economic explanation for such divergence.

When applied to cross–country comparative data similar to those used by Barro (1991), these tests showed a twofold division of countries, according to both their initial levels of educational development and their initial levels of financial development. More precisely, the results obtained made it possible to identify four convergence clubs, as shown in Figure 1.

Figure 1. **Results of Convergence Club Tests on a Sample of 95 Countries**

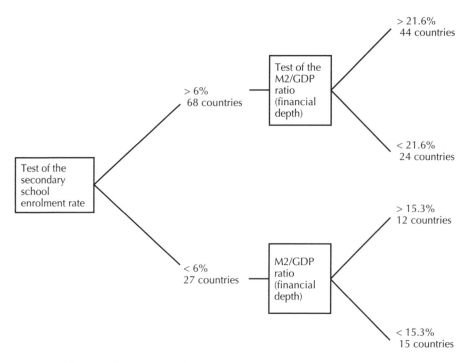

Source: Berthélemy and Varoudakis (1996b).

These two arguments — that the initial level of educational development and the initial depth of the financial system both determine the equilibrium towards which economies might converge — are thus complementary. This provides a key to understanding the paradoxical situation in some Latin American countries which went through a period of considerable economic prosperity (notably because they had relatively well-trained labour forces, due in part to immigration), but which never caught up with the developed countries, partly because they went through episodes of financial repression and hyperinflation which undermined their capacity for development. These countries are still at intermediate levels of development, however, well above the great majority of African countries, which have neither human capital nor a real financial sector.

Additional tests concerning financial development have shown, moreover, that financial depth itself follows a non-linear growth path (Berthélemy and Varoudakis, 1996*b*). When financial depth is low initially, it tends to grow slowly and to be relatively insensitive to changes in interest rate policy and inflation. The opposite properties are observed when the financial sector has considerable depth initially, and in this case the growth of financial depth reacts positively to the amount of human capital available in the economy. What is more, the threshold detected in these tests, which separates countries with low financial depth from those with high financial depth (an M2/GDP ratio of approximately 19 per cent), is of the same order of magnitude as that observed in the procedure used to identify convergence clubs from the growth equation.

Implications for Growth Analysis

The convergence clubs which have been identified offer a natural interpretation for the fact that, whereas a positive correlation between education and growth, and between financial system depth and growth, is often observed on the basis of static cross-country comparative data, these observations are often called into question when growth equations are estimated using panel data. Panel data estimations involve combining the temporal and spatial dimensions of the data in the observations used. They generally lead to the introduction of fixed effects for each country, that is, to allowing different regression constants for different countries. The fixed effects thus capture the impact of differences in growth trajectory from one country to the next — differences connected with the fact that the countries belong to one or another convergence club — whereas in growth equations based on simple cross-country comparisons the impact of such differences is not distinguished from the linear effect of human capital and financial development on growth. In other words, where convergence clubs exist, estimating a linear equation that links educational development or financial development to growth can lead to a seriously erroneous specification, because this approach mistakenly considers that these variables have a continuous influence on growth, whereas in fact their influence may be discontinuous, at least in part. This bias, which leads to overestimation of the growth impact of the underlying explanatory variables, is substantially reduced in a panel data estimation with fixed effects. This argument is illustrated in Figure 2 below.

In the presence of convergence clubs, analysis of growth factors can thus be strongly biased if countries belonging to different clubs are treated in the same way. This argues in favour of carrying out a growth study for each country, or studies of homogeneous groups of countries.

Figure 2. **The Impact of Financial Development on Growth in the Presence of Convergence Clubs**

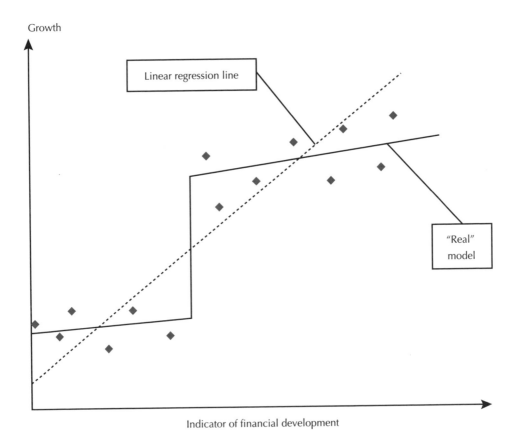

Source: Berthélemy and Varoudakis (1996*b*).

A corollary to the above is that, when one tries to reproduce convergence club tests on panel data instead of cross–country comparative data, in a fixed–effect model, the results are not very significant. The estimation procedure amounts to estimating growth equations for each of the (relatively horizontal) portions of the "stairstep" curve in Figure 2. The reason is that very few countries change their growth regimes over time, which is natural in the presence of stable high and low equilibria.

It is thus more difficult, but also more to the point, to identify growth factors by using only the temporal dimension of the data, instead of cross–country comparative data. However, this requires long–term historical series.

Country–by–country growth analysis using time series also has the virtue of allowing more precise examination of the growth process, by linking it to changes in the historical, political and institutional context of the countries considered. With this in mind, the Development Centre produced a series of monographs on growth in various developing countries, published in a series of volumes on long–term growth. Two of these volumes, on Argentina (Véganzonès and Winograd, 1997) and Brazil (Abreu and Verner, 1997), provide a long–term historical perspective and help us to understand how these economies, which were relatively advanced before the Second World War, started to fall behind from the 1950s. The historical analysis makes it possible to show how much of this was due to the policies implemented, not only to interventionist policies affecting the monetary and financial sector but also, for example, to protectionist industrial and trade policies. Conversely, a study of Chinese Taipei (Dessus *et al.*, 1995) shows how, beginning in 1950, this economy managed to develop through balanced, gradual progress in the training of the labour force and in the allocation of resources, particularly financial resources. The beginnings of a similar pattern were noted in Tunisia (Morrisson and Talbi, 1996), at least after its socialist period in the 1960s.

Where sub–Saharan Africa is concerned, it is more difficult to analyse the history of economic growth owing to the poor quality of the available statistical sources and the limited historical depth of the data, since analyses can be carried out only for the post–independence period. As a result, studies of individual countries, such as the Development Centre studies on Senegal (Berthélemy *et al.*, 1997) and Kenya (Azam and Daubrée, 1997), necessarily reach more qualitative conclusions. The implications of the studies nevertheless concur: regulatory and protectionist policies prove to be costly for growth (Senegal), and in some cases the evasion of state control by private actors, when this was tolerated by government, facilitated economic progress.

To offset the lack of data, it is also possible to combine the available information concerning economies at comparable levels of development, which in all likelihood belong to the same convergence club. This was done by the Development Centre in its "Emerging Africa" project (Berthélemy *et al.*, 2001), in which growth factors in Africa were identified by estimating a production function linking the economy's GDP to the amounts of capital and labour available, as well as to various other variables that may influence factor productivity. These estimations show that the growth factors are not substantially different from those observed elsewhere: capital accumulation, education, the sectoral breakdown of economic activity between high- and low-productivity sectors and the diversification of activity are all found to have a significant impact on growth. This estimation also enabled us to evaluate which factors played a decisive role in the rapid growth episodes observed since 1960 in Africa. In the 1960s and 1970s, these episodes showed the usual characteristics of extensive growth, mainly due to capital accumulation, similarly to what was observed in South–east Asia. In contrast to what happened in Asia, however, this extensive growth occurred in a context of very low productivity. In virtually every case — Botswana was the only exception — it came to an end fairly quickly because it was not sustainable. More recently, however, growth processes have appeared in Africa that are based much more on productivity gains, driven not only by efficiency gains due to structural adjustment but also by proactive educational policies and diversification policies. The characteristic example which shows that development policies can be successfully conducted in Africa is provided by Mauritius. The success recorded in Mauritius was primarily based on the country's educational policy, as a result of which it now has a level of human capital comparable to that of some OECD countries, and on the establishment of an export processing zone, which as from the 1980s stimulated the endogenous diversification of the economy. In sum, growth in Africa is indeed influenced by the usual macroeconomic factors, but it also depends to a large extent on institutional reforms and the microeconomic environment. This result is in line with many other recent studies on Africa (Collier and Gunning, 1999).

Another approach that yields relevant empirical analyses of growth is to study regional growth processes within an economy having a federal structure, where one can be reasonably certain that the observational data are homogeneous. At the Development Centre, this approach has been applied to China's provinces (Démurger, 2000) and to India's states (Nagaraj et al., 1998). In the case of China, the results obtained show that the positive effects of openness are due much more to foreign direct investment than to foreign trade. They also reveal neighbourhood effects, which suggest the possibility that economic progress can be disseminated outwards from the regions which are furthest along in modernisation and the reform process.

Implications for Development Policy

Research on convergence clubs has shown that the impact of economic policies on growth can vary considerably depending on the initial equilibrium state of the economy. For example, observation of those convergence clubs which have been identified shows that an economy lacking a developed financial sector will find it difficult to derive benefit from a policy of trade openness. This is readily explained by the fact that in order to reap the benefits of economic openness, the economy must have a well–developed ability to reallocate factors between sectors so as to exploit its comparative advantages and adapt to changing conditions on the international market. Similarly, lack of human capital seems to be a handicap with regard to benefiting from openness, since an economy that is short of skills cannot make use of the innovations offered by trade contacts with the outside world.

This last observation suggests that, in a low–equilibrium situation, certain traditional "recipes" of structural adjustment programmes may well fail to yield the expected results. This is true not only for trade openness but also for financial liberalisation policies: the results of the studies discussed above clearly show that financial liberalisation, which seeks to restore normal market conditions in the financial sector by replacing low administered interest rates with rates more attractive to saving, has no effect on either overall economic growth or financial sector growth when the financial sector is too weak initially. In the case of Senegal, for example, it was clearly apparent that the financial sector, which initially was very weak, could not be strengthened by mere government fiat, owing to the lack of savings and of know–how concerning resource allocation; under these circumstances, an attempt in the 1990s to revive activity in this sector through a policy of financial liberalisation had no more chance of producing the desired outcome than did an earlier government attempt, in the 1970s, to intervene in the sector by creating banks and public enterprises (Berthélemy, 1997).

In the presence of multiple equilibria, it is thus difficult to devise policies that allow a country to escape from a low–equilibrium state. However, the experience of economies such as that of Chinese Taipei and other economies of emerging Asia suggests that such a change of equilibrium is possible.

To bring such a change about, it is necessary to undertake structural transformation, which is the only means of modifying the terms of the problem in such a way as to strengthen the economy in a sustainable way: trying to change the immediate determinants of growth is futile as long as the economy is drawn towards a low–equilibrium state, which will bring these factors back to their initial equilibrium levels. For example, the research conducted as part of the Development Centre's "emerging Africa" project clearly showed that only deep structural changes — such as those that allow the economy to diversify endogenously, as was observed in Mauritius — could raise African countries' escape out of a slow–growth trajectory (Berthélemy et al., 2001). Such structural transformation cannot be limited to setting up incentive structures, such as the export processing zone in Mauritius, but must also include the establishment of an institutional framework that encourages private initiative. Moreover, in the presence of multiple equilibria, if institutional change gives an initial impetus to growth and actually brings the economy into a different growth path, this may produce far–reaching qualitative effects. Once again, the financial system and educational development provide interesting examples.

The financial systems of poor countries are small and vulnerable not only because of the lack of savings, but also because potential savers cannot trust existing financial institutions to protect and remunerate their savings properly, just as these institutions cannot trust potential borrowers. This state of affairs results not only from the absence of efficient financial intermediaries but also from the quality of the legal system. In African countries, where judicial systems function poorly and where the very definition of property rights is uncertain, there is little chance that a modern financial sector will develop. Conversely, improvements to the legal and institutional framework could enhance the possibilities for development of the financial sector and consequently of the entire economy.

African education systems function poorly owing to the shortage of trained teachers, so that even primary schooling is far from ensured. The paucity of qualified teaching personnel results in part, however, from the fact that a high proportion of the available human capital is wasted in rent–seeking activities. This hypothesis is consistent with the observation that the least open economies, which offer the greatest number of opportunities to capture rent situations, are those where human capital has the least impact on growth, as was shown in a Development Centre research project (Berthélemy et al., 1997; Berthélemy et al., 2000) which is summarised in Pissarides (2000). In support of this argument, it may also be noted that in sub–Saharan Africa in the early 1990s, 37 per cent of the non–agricultural labour force was employed in the civil service, as against 33 per cent in North Africa and the Middle East, 15 per cent in East Asia, 19 per cent in Latin America and 20 per cent in the OECD countries, which does suggest that more human capital is wasted in the form of rent–seeking activities in Africa.

This argument also helps to explain the difficulties involved in demonstrating, for large samples of heterogeneous countries, that the accumulation or the level of human capital has a significant impact on growth. Moreover, in research limited to Africa as part of the "Emerging Africa" project, the educational level reached by countries was indeed found to be linked to their level of development, which is not surprising if one accepts the proposition that the amount of human capital wasted in rent–seeking activities is comparable from one African country to another.

In a context where the bulk of educational investment is made by the state, particularly where primary education is concerned, and where a large proportion of the skilled population is employed in the public sector, in sometimes unproductive tasks, a strong initial boost to this sector by the state can have a permanent rather than transitory effect on the economy's potential for development. This boost would involve both reduction of the waste of human capital in rent–seeking activities and massive investment in education to enable all children to obtain schooling. Such a policy would obviously have a budgetary cost and would show results only in the long term, but it is essential in order to stimulate growth and reduce poverty.

Reform of the institutional framework may also take other forms. In a study conducted for the Development Centre, Brunetti (1998) used cross–country data to show that political instability has a negative effect on growth. Azam *et al.* (1996) present a similar analysis using African data. Here again, it is probable that a cumulative process will be at work between political instability and growth, since poor economic performance can undermine political stability, particularly in a context of fragile political institutions. In that case, this cumulative process may itself be the cause of an unfavourable equilibrium in which political instability and slow growth are mutually reinforcing (Berthélemy and Varoudakis, 1996c). Under these circumstances, governments' attitude towards political and social instability is decisive. Berthélemy *et al.* (2002) show that in African countries the attitude generally observed is a harder line and restriction of democracy freedoms, which can only increase political instability. From this standpoint, efforts to improve political governance are a vital component of the initiatives that need to be implemented to avoid the vicious circle of political crises and economic decline.

Many economic, political and institutional mechanisms thus lead to cumulative processes that can jeopardise whatever progress poor countries manage to obtain. This is particularly true of Africa. For this reason, it is essential for policy makers to have adequate monitoring instruments in order to identify the factors that may undermine the economic situation, so as to be able to forestall them before it is too late. That being the case, the analysis cannot be confined to the macroeconomic situation but must also address questions of governance, which in Africa largely determine whether a vicious or virtuous circle emerges. It is for this reason that the Development Centre and the African Development Bank (ADB) have begun to publish an annual report entitled *The African Economic Outlook,* the first edition of which appeared in February 2002.

Another purpose of this annual report is to allow comparison of the performances of the various African countries. If one accepts the theory of convergence clubs, it is, from an operational standpoint, of little use to compare Africa with the rest of the world, whereas comparing the African countries with one another is essential in order to detect potential for emergence.

In the era of the New Partnership for Africa's Development (NEPAD) project, moreover, the policy value of having such a comparative tool for the African countries needs no further demonstration. A strategic aspect of the NEPAD project will be the implementation in the near future of a peer review process, which is necessary to obtain endogenous improvement of the policies followed by African governments. The peer review process will begin by tackling the thorny problem of governance, but should also address all aspects of economic policy and the fight against poverty. In the coming years, the process should profit from the *African Economic Outlook* report, together with the information sources established by other African institutions, such as the assessment of governance planned by the Economic Commission for Africa. The experience of the OECD shows that one of the keys to success in the peer review process is to have reliable, independent and transparent information and analyses, without which no discussion is possible. Thus, by accumulating a wealth of experience in comparing the economic performances of African countries, an experience which ensures the scientific credibility of such comparisons, the *African Economic Outlook* will allow the OECD, through its partnership with the ABD, to make an operational contribution to the NEPAD process.

Conclusion

Fifteen years after the first studies on endogenous growth theory, this work has proved to have only a moderate influence on development economics. This period has left a legacy, however, in that it strongly encouraged empirical analyses of growth. The Development Centre's contribution was made primarily in this field. As a result, we know much more about the growth process of the developing economies, which according to this body of research is not linear, owing to the presence of multiple equilibria, and which involves interaction among the various aspects of development policy, such as those relating to institutional development, education, the construction of financial and physical infrastructure, and economic openness.

These studies also shed new light on the performance of the standard structural adjustment policies implemented in the 1980s and 1990s in many developing countries. In some countries, e.g. in South–east Asia, these policies have been crowned with success. In the poorest countries, however, it is not clear that re–establishing the normal operating rules of market economies will be enough. It is also necessary to ensure that the economy does not remain trapped in its initial low–equilibrium state. This requires deeper structural transformation, which implies in particular that the country must develop the infrastructure — physical, financial, institutional, legal and human — needed for a market economy to run properly. It also requires that the donor community implement so–called second–generation reform policies, which address the political and institutional factors that can, by turns, lead to a spiral of economic and political crises. To this end, substantial initial investment is needed — not only financial investment, but also and above all investment in building institutional capacity.

This conclusion is in keeping with the recent debates over aid efficiency and selectivity (World Bank, 1998). If the economy remains locked into a low equilibrium, an increase in the amount of aid it receives will not stimulate economic growth. That being the case, it is preferable not to waste financial resources in investment projects there, as long as the conditions required for escaping from the underdevelopment trap have not been met. The observations of Africa carried out at the Development Centre suggest, however, that one type of investment — and one that requires considerable budgetary resources — should be made very early on: investment in education. The aid selectivity approach advocated by the World Bank should thus not be applied to nations only, but also to the sectors in which aid is used. This approach should also recognise that aid targeted to the strategic sector of primary education is desirable in all poor countries where implementation of this policy is feasible.

Bibliography

ABREU, M. AND D. VERNER (1997), *Long–Term Brazilian Economic Growth: 1930–94*, Development Centre Studies, "Long–term Growth" series, OECD, Paris.

AFRICAN DEVELOPMENT BANK AND OECD DEVELOPMENT CENTRE (2002), *African Economic Outlook*, OECD, Paris.

AZAM, J.–P, J.–C. BERTHÉLEMY AND S. CALIPEL (1996), "Risque politique et croissance en Afrique", *Revue Economique*, Vol. 47, No. 3, May, pp. 819–829.

AZAM, J.–P. AND C. DAUBRÉE (1997), *Bypassing the State: Economic Growth in Kenya, 1964–90*, Development Centre Studies, "Long–term Growth" series, OECD, Paris.

AZARIADIS C. AND A. DRAZEN (1990), "Threshold Externalities in Economic Development", *Quarterly Journal of Economics*, 105, pp. 501–526.

BARRO, R.J. (1991), "Economic Growth in a Cross Section of Countries", *Quarterly Journal of Economics*, 106 (2), pp. 407–443.

BERTHÉLEMY, J.–C. (1997), "From Financial Repression to Liberalization – The Senegalese Experience", *in* K.L. GUPTA (ed.).

BERTHÉLEMY, J.–C. , S. DESSUS AND A. VAROUDAKIS (1997), *Capital humain, ouverture extérieure et croissance : estimation sur données de panel d'un modèle à coefficients variables*, Documents techniques No. 121, OECD Development Centre, Paris.

BERTHÉLEMY, J.–C. , C. KAUFFMANN, L. RENARD AND L. WEGNER (2002), "Political Instability, Political Regimes and Economic Performance in African Countries", Oxford Conference on Understanding Poverty and Growth in Sub–Saharan Africa, March, www.economics.ox.ac.uk.

BERTHÉLEMY, J.–C. , C. PISSARIDES AND A. VAROUDAKIS (2000), "Human Capital and Growth: The Cost of Rent Seeking Activities", *in* M. OOSTERBAAN, T. DE RUYTER VAN STEVENINCK AND N. VAN DER WINDT (eds).

BERTHÉLEMY, J.–C., A. SECK AND A. VOURCH (1997), *Growth in Senegal: A Lost Opportunity?*, Development Centre Studies, "Long–term Growth" series, OECD, Paris.

BERTHÉLEMY, J.–C. AND L. SÖDERLING, WITH J.M. SALMON AND H.–B. SOLIGNAC LECOMTE (2001), *Emerging Africa*, Development Centre Studies, OECD, Paris.

BERTHÉLEMY, J.–C. AND A. VAROUDAKIS (1997), "Développement financier, épargne et convergence : une approche de données de panel", in R. HAUSMANN AND H. REISEN (eds.).

BERTHÉLEMY, J.–C. AND A. VAROUDAKIS (1996a), "Economic Growth, Convergence Clubs, and the Role of Financial Development", *Oxford Economic Papers,* 48, pp. 300–328.

BERTHÉLEMY, J.–C. AND A. VAROUDAKIS (1996b), *Politiques de développement financier et croissance,* OECD Development Centre Studies, "Long–term Growth" series, OECD, Paris.

BERTHÉLEMY, J.–C. AND A. VAROUDAKIS (1996c), "Policies for Economic Take–off", Policy Brief No. 12, OECD Development Centre, Paris.

BRUNETTI, A. (1998), *Politique et croissance économique : comparaison de données internationales,* Development Centre Studies, OECD, Paris.

COLLIER, P. AND J.W. GUNNING (1999), "Explaining African Economic Performance", *Journal of Economic Literature,* 37, pp. 64–111.

DÉMURGER, S. (2000), *Ouverture et croissance économique en Chine,* Development Centre Studies, "Long–term Growth" series, OECD, Paris.

DESSUS, S., J.D SHEA AND M.S. SHI (1995), *Le Taipei chinois : les origines du « miracle » économique,* Development Centre Studies, "Long–term Growth" series, OECD, Paris.

DURLAUF, S.N. AND P.A. JOHNSON (1992), "Local versus Global Convergence Across National Economies", Discussion Paper 131, LES Financial Market Group.

GUPTA, K.L. (1997), *Experiences with Financial Liberalization,* Kluwer Academic Publisher.

HAUSMANN, R. AND H. REISEN (eds.) (1997), *Promouvoir l'épargne en Amérique latine,* Development Centre Seminars, OECD, Paris.

MADDISON, A. (1995), *Monitoring the World Economy: 1820–1992,* Development Centre Studies, OECD, Paris.

MITRA, A., A. VAROUDAKIS AND M.A.VÉGANZONÈS (1998), *State Infrastructure and Productive Performance in Indian Manufacturing,* Technical Papers No. 139, OECD Development Centre, Paris.

MORRISSON, C. AND B. TALBI (1996), *La croissance de l'économie tunisienne en longue période,* Development Centre Studies, "Long–term Growth" series, OECD, Paris.

NAGARAJ, R., A. VAROUDAKIS AND M.–A. VÉGANZONÈS (1998), *Long-run Growth Trends and Convergence Across Indian States,* Technical Papers No. 131, OECD Development Centre, Paris.

OOSTERBAAN,M., T. DE RUYTER VAN STEVENINCK AND N. VAN DER WINDT (eds.) (2000),*The Determinants of Economic Growth,* Kluwer Academic Publisher.

PISSARIDES, C. (2000), *Human Capital and Growth: A Synthesis,* Technical Papers No. 168, OECD Development Centre, Paris.

Véganzonès, M.A. and C. Winograd (1997), *Argentina in the 20th Century: An Account of Long-Awaited Growth*, Development Centre Studies, "Long-term Growth" series, OECD, Paris.

World Bank (1998), *Assessing Aid — What Works, What Doesn't, and Why*, Washington, D.C.

Chapter 5

Sustainable Development

David O'Connor

Post–war Development Experience and the First Stirrings of Environmental Awareness

When the Development Centre was founded in 1962, the concept of "sustainable development" was not yet born. For the first generation of the Centre's life economic growth, unconstrained by environmental concerns, was the preoccupation not only of developing countries but of the development research community. The 1960s and 1970s were an era of rapid industrialisation in the OECD countries as well as in several developing ones. Even as Japan and Western Europe rushed to reconstruct and narrow the income gap with the United States (e.g. from the early 1960s to the early 1970s, Portugal's real per capita GDP went from one–fifth to one–third of that in the United States), the former Soviet bloc countries were pouring resources into forced industrialisation in the hope of maintaining military parity with the West. Developing country ambitions to industrialise and reduce their dependency on primary commodity production for export were supported to varying degrees, by either East or West, depending on a particular country's perceived importance as ally in the Cold War.

Even in the industrialised countries of the West and Japan, awareness of the environmental consequences of unbridled industrial expansion was still not widespread. Also, there was little sense of the scope for governments to remedy pollution problems through forceful regulation. Beginning with the 1952 London smog that killed some 4 000 people[1], and the Clean Air Act that was passed by the UK government four years later, industrialised countries began to address the most egregious pollution problems (Long, 2000). Also in the late 1950s, a report commissioned by the government of Japan determined that "Minamata disease" was most probably caused by industrial discharges of mercury into coastal waters.

77

Throughout the 1960s, concern grew in industrialised countries about the health consequences of exposure to a variety of chemicals, from pesticides like DDT to polychlorinated biphenyls (PCBs). In 1968, the first warning flag was raised by Swedish scientists about the problem of acid rain — the atmospheric transport and deposition of sulphur compounds — in Europe's lakes and forests. By the late 1960s, the growing evidence of — and public concern about — environmental hazards of life in an urban, industrial society was causing OECD Member governments to raise environmental issues for discussion in this forum.

Based on a Swedish proposal, the United Nations agreed to convene the first international conference on the environment, which was held in Stockholm in June 1972. In 1969, an important preparatory meeting, held in Switzerland, sought to bridge the North–South divide on whether environmental protection should concern only rich countries that had already achieved industrialisation. The Stockholm Conference on the Human Environment, in its concluding Declaration of Principles, constituted the first body of "soft law" in international environmental affairs; the conference also popularised the notion of "development without destruction", the forerunner to "sustainable development". The creation of the United Nations Environment Programme (UNEP) in 1972 was a direct outcome of Stockholm, which was to be the first in a series of global summits on environment and development, with the next and best–known held a decade ago in Rio de Janeiro and the most recent — the World Summit on Sustainable Development (WSSD) — held in Johannesburg, South Africa, in August–September 2002.

The OECD Development Centre played a modest role in recording if not shaping the early debate on environment and development. In 1973 it published an extensive annotated bibliography on *Environmental Aspects of Economic Growth in Less Developed Countries* (Block, 1973). In the work reviewed there was a strong focus on looming resource scarcities, notably of non–renewables like oil and other minerals. Recall that the first oil price shock occurred just one year later, and the influential, neo–Malthusian report of the Club of Rome, *Limits to Growth*, had been published just one year earlier. This was only the most celebrated of a number of articles and books appearing around this time that argued the inevitability if not the desirability of a zero–growth economy (see also Boulding, 1966; Daly, 1973). The impact of the Club of Rome report owed much to its purportedly scientific method and its use of sophisticated computer models. The basic result was simple and stark: that economic growth would be brought to an abrupt halt in a not–too–distant future by either the exhaustion of non–renewable natural resources, high levels of pollution, or excessive population growth with resultant food scarcities à la Malthus. The study concludes that overshoot and collapse can be avoided only by an immediate limit on population and pollution, as well as a cessation of economic growth.

It is no mystery why this literature did not receive an enthusiastic reception in the development community. The broader economics profession roundly challenged the methodology employed, arguing that little regard was taken of how relative price changes in the face of growing scarcity would force behavioural change and technological innovation. What the mainstream critique did not adequately address is how to ensure that the appropriate incentives are in place to induce technological innovation, especially given the market failures in R&D that more recent economic literature has identified. Also, the preconditions for effective innovation — in terms of human capital and strong educational and research institutions — were not fully appreciated at the time[2]. To the extent that the Club of Rome claims were considered credible, the Southern ("developmental") response was to call on Northern countries to rein in their own profligate consumption so as not to exhaust the earth's natural bounty before the developing country masses have even begun to share in it. While scientific inquiry never solely reflects broader societal trends, there can be little doubt that the "simple living" message of the "limits to growth" school resonated with the countercultural *zeitgeist* of that period.

Growth and the Environment

While the rich countries may be able to debate the possibility of "zero growth" and less conspicuous consumption, poor countries strive to become rich and a growing number — including rather large ones like China and India — are succeeding to varying degrees in reducing poverty and expanding the ranks of the moderately well–off middle classes. Naturally, with higher incomes come consumption patterns more closely resembling those of the OECD countries. The question then is whether, with rising incomes, pollution levels are also bound to increase and, if so, at what point do increasingly prosperous citizens come to demand a cleaner environment?

Fortunately, we already have a sample of countries that achieved rapid industrialisation and high per capita incomes whose evolving environmental problems, public perceptions, policies, and outcomes we can observe. The first–generation East Asian export successes — Hong Kong (China), Korea, and Chinese Taipei — were countries that were poor in land and natural resources and that based their development on relatively abundant labour fed by intensive agriculture (or, in the case of Hong Kong, food imports). The limited absorptive capacity of their environments created strong pollution pressures with adverse effects on health and the quality of life. During the first few decades of rapid industrial growth, Korea and Chinese Taipei remained under authoritarian rule and public protest over worsening pollution was severely restricted. Yet, over time, with rapidly rising real incomes and eventual democratisation, their governments responded to popular demands by allocating more resources to environmental protection. The Development Centre charts the dynamic interplay among economic growth, political liberalisation, and environmental policy in East Asia in its study on *Managing the Environment with Rapid Industrialisation* (O'Connor, 1994).

While effective environmental management is not an oft–remarked feature of East Asia's development story, the comparison of the more advanced to the less advanced countries of the region (*idem.*) suggests that rising prosperity was itself an important part of the story of environmental improvement, though by no means an automatic one. Also noteworthy is the timing of growth, with the newly industrialising countries of Asia able to take advantage of pollution control and less–polluting production technologies developed in response to earlier environmental regulation in OECD countries. There are three broad factors that contribute to aggregate pollution loads: the total level of economic activity (L), its composition (C), and the technologies used in any set of activities (T). Over the course of development, as economic expansion tends to increase pollution loads, sectoral transformation can have either a reinforcing or an offsetting effect — reinforcing if there is a shift of resources into pollution–intensive industries, offsetting if the reverse is true. The technology effect should be positive if — as suggested above — developing countries capture the benefits of borrowed technologies from OECD countries, less positive or negative if there is a transfer of second–hand, polluting technologies from OECD countries to developing countries. How the interaction of LCT plays out in practice is affected by policies, not just environmental ones but economic ones. For instance, a competitive trade and investment policy regime may provide stronger incentives to adopt modern technology (that is usually less polluting) than a protectionist regime. Work of Wheeler and associates at the World Bank has generally borne this out (cf. Wheeler *et al.*, 1993). In a similar vein, the Development Centre argues that "policy matters" to environmental outcomes, so that countries at comparable levels of per capita incomes can have widely varying environmental quality, depending on a combination of economic and environmental policies. In a paper prepared for the 3rd Annual World Bank Conference on Environmentally Sustainable Development, O'Connor (1996) presents a heuristic model in which, for any given pollutant, there may be multiple pollution trajectories as per capita incomes rise, depending on whether *a)* economic policies favour the adoption of efficient, less–polluting technologies and *b)* environmental policies are effectively enforced. The model is then used to compare the developmental and environmental trajectories of East Asia and Eastern Europe. Prior to the 1990s, the latter's emphasis on heavy industry coupled with generous energy subsidies pointed down a highly polluting growth path; at comparable per capita income levels, then, Eastern European economies have tended to be much more energy– (and a *fortiori* pollution–) intensive than East Asian ones.

80

The Polluter Pays Principle

The 1970s saw the passage of major environmental legislation and numerous regulations in developed countries. These regulations were sufficiently stringent, and new, that polluters were concerned that the costs of compliance could undermine their international competitiveness — this in the context of expanding world trade and intensifying global competition, especially among the OECD countries. The pressures to transfer the costs of pollution on to the general taxpayer or someone other than the polluter were sufficiently strong and widespread that the OECD promulgated, in 1972, a set of "Guiding Principles Concerning International Economic Aspects of Environmental Policy". Articulated therein was what has come to be known as the *Polluter Pays Principle*. Contrary to a common misconception, this principle was not intended as an alternative to the Coase theorem stating the indifference on efficiency grounds (in a model of zero transaction costs) between a rule of "polluter pays" and one of "victim compensates". It was rather an attempt to render domestic environmental regulation consistent with a liberal international trade regime. The text reads in part: "Uniform application of this principle, through the adoption of a common basis for Member countries' environmental policies, would encourage the rational use and the better allocation of scarce environmental resources and prevent the appearance of distortions in international trade and investment". The *polluter pays principle* has evolved into something like a general rule for internalising pollution externalities. It was first widely discussed on a global scale at the Rio Earth Summit in June 1992. The principle was endorsed by all attending national representatives and thus became a truly global principle. Note, however, that it is not an efficiency principle à *la* Coase, since it remains agnostic about the particular instrument chosen to make polluters pay. Much work in environmental economics, not least at the OECD, has been preoccupied with choice of efficient instrument.

On the Road to and from Rio

Addressing National Environmental Policy Challenges

The major impetus to the convening of the Rio Summit was provided by the so–called "Brundtland report", *Our Common Future*, published by the World Commission on Environment and Development in 1987. Its main contribution, apart from popularising the concept of sustainable development (defined therein as "development that meets the needs of the present without compromising the ability of future generations to meet their own needs"), was to situate environmental policy within a broader context of governments' economic, social and political concerns. Another important milestone was the OECD Ministerial conference convened in Bergen, Norway, in preparation for the Rio Summit.

There were three distinctive features of this meeting (Long, 2000): it was the first of its kind to involve non–governmental organisations (NGOs) and other stakeholders from the preparatory phase onward; it highlighted the importance of government accountability, and the need for sound information on environmental trends to track progress towards sustainability; it enshrined the *Precautionary Principle*, which has taken its place alongside the *Polluter Pays Principle* as a pillar of international environmental policy. As the name suggests, the *precautionary principle* admonishes decision makers to err on the side of caution in cases of incomplete information about the environmental consequences of current decisions, where those consequences could be irreversible, and where the costs of irreversible damage would be exceedingly high. The concept of sustainable development has itself been formulated in terms of not foreclosing options open to future generations, which comes close to the *precautionary principle*, while extending it beyond strictly environmental outcomes to a broader notion of intergenerational justice. As Dasgupta (1995) points out, however, not only is this broader notion operationally meaningless to policy makers, it is conceptually flawed in failing to value options.

The Development Centre made a significant contribution to the preparations for Rio by organising a conference of international experts on *Environmental Management in Developing Countries* in October 1990 (proceedings in Eröcal, 1991). That conference covered a wide range of issues, from economic incentives for wildlife conservation in Africa to public–sector environmental management, to the role of NGOs and environmental education, and country experiences from Indonesia to Rwanda and Poland to Brazil. Two central themes that emerged from the discussions were the ineffective enforcement of existing environmental regulations in many developing countries, for the interconnected reasons of limited resources, weak institutional capacity and lukewarm political commitment, and the potential role of improved economic incentive structures in encouraging better environmental performance in both the public and private sectors, by both enterprises and individuals.

Building on the analyses presented at the 1990 conference, the Development Centre published in 1992 a Policy Brief on *Environmental Management in Developing Countries* (O'Connor and Turnham, 1992) that anticipated a strong *post*-Rio developing country interest in environmental governance. The Brief argues, *inter alia*, for reform of environmentally damaging subsidies, greater experimentation with economic instruments, a more rational use of limited government capabilities by targeting enforcement at the largest polluters and enlisting civil society in monitoring and enforcement efforts, and a stronger emphasis on forward–looking, preventive measures like improved land use and transport planning.

In the aftermath of Rio, the interest on the part of developing countries in identifying potential uses of economic instruments of environmental policy blossomed and the Development Centre followed up its earlier contribution with analytical guidance to work on designing economic instruments in several developing countries, including India, Mexico, Thailand and Viet Nam. O'Connor (1998) explores the complexities involved in the transition from theory to the design and practical implementation of economic instruments in developing countries, including the vested interests opposed to policy reform, the fiscal issues involved (e.g. use of revenues generated by a pollution tax), and the need for design simplicity and phased implementation to permit learning by doing. Also, drawing upon an earlier Centre study (O'Connor, 1994) that reviews the Japanese experience with public pressure, moral suasion and voluntary pollution control agreements, the author points to the opportunity presented by political liberalisation in many developing countries for wider involvement of civil society in environmental management, e.g. through public information disclosure programmes. The 1994 Centre study may have been one source of inspiration for a major World Bank research programme on what it dubbed "informal regulation" of polluters (Pargal and Wheeler, 1995; Dasgupta and Wheeler, 1996). *Inter alia*, that work applies econometric analysis to data on provincial–level enforcement of environmental standards in China, relating enforcement intensity to characteristics of the provincial population like population density, per capita income, and educational attainment, as well as to frequency of citizens' nuisance complaints. It concludes that differences in enforcement intensity follow prior expectations, with wealthier, better educated populations living in crowded areas demanding/getting stricter enforcement.

In many situations, policy makers are confronted with the need to make trade–offs between environmental and economic objectives or, put differently, to weigh environmental costs against benefits. For this, valuation of environmental resources and/or pollution externalities is essential. Over the years, environmental policy in OECD countries has moved towards greater sensitivity to a cost–benefit calculus, though rarely is this the sole basis for decision making. For the most part, too many uncertainties remain in valuation methods to provide anything more than broad order–of–magnitude estimates of the net social returns to a particular course of action.

The OECD made early contributions to the environmental valuation literature (cf. OECD, 1981), and in the mid–1990s it produced two major methodological studies (OECD, 1994; OECD, 1995). While the first is a rather technical valuation manual, the latter is a "practical guide" for developing country policy makers on *The Economic Appraisal of Environmental Projects and Policies.* The Environment Directorate commissioned the work and the Development Centre participated actively in the peer review process. More recently, the Centre has published a number of studies making use of environmental cost–benefit analysis to assess the net impacts of climate policy in developing countries, once changes in local pollution levels are evaluated (see discussion below).

Addressing Global Environmental Challenges in a Developing Country Context

Even before the Rio Summit, one global environmental problem had emerged in the late 1980s as a test case for international environmental co–operation, viz., depletion of stratospheric ozone. By the mid–1980s, the scientific evidence had become overwhelming that man–made chemicals — mostly in the chlorofluorocarbon and halon families — were reacting in the atmosphere to create a hole in the earth's protective ozone layer, letting through high levels of ultraviolet (UV–B) radiation and posing a variety of health and ecological risks. The international community responded by ratifying, first, the Vienna Convention and, then, the Montreal Protocol, the latter binding signatory nations to a timetable for phasing out domestic use of listed substances. Developing countries enjoyed a 10–year grace period after which they too had to phase out use, with the benefit of technical and financial assistance from the developed countries. The OECD Development Centre provided one of the first analyses of how developing countries were coping with the challenge of phasing out "ozone–depleting substances" (ODS) (O'Connor, 1991).

As a result of that research, the Development Centre was invited to participate in the deliberations of the Economic Options Panel of the Montreal Protocol, providing periodic assessments of the economic aspects of compliance with commitments, especially in developing countries. Also, the researcher involved was invited to participate in meetings of the technical committees formed to assess the feasibility and costs of different options for ODS phase–out and to address regional UNEP workshops for policy makers in Africa, Asia and Latin America.

The Montreal Protocol attracted considerable interest from policy makers and their advisors keen on finding lessons for other international environmental agreements still to be negotiated, in particular the UN Framework Convention on Climate Change (UNFCCC) and the Kyoto Protocol. Noteworthy features of the Montreal Protocol were: *i)* the wide participation in the phase–out effort of both developed and developing countries; *ii)* the extent of willingness of the former to finance the incremental costs of ODS phase out in the latter; *iii)* provision for the use of trade sanctions to discourage free riding. The negotiation of a greenhouse gas control regime has proven far more challenging. Important differences exist between the climate change and ozone problems: in the latter case, *i)* the scientific evidence linking cause to effect is hardly in dispute; *ii)* the scope of the measures required to address the problem has been limited — essentially, persuading a dozen or so chemical companies to stop making the chemicals; *iii)* the total costs of containing the problem are thought to be much smaller for ozone than for climate change (though *ex ante* estimates of ODS phase–out costs were often grossly inflated). Addressing climate change requires a thorough revamp of one of the basic components of a modern economy, viz., its energy system. Thus, in the end, this problem has required much new thinking.

The OECD and its Development Centre have contributed substantially to international research on climate policy, with the latter bringing a strong focus on developing country concerns. The OECD's GREEN computable general equilibrium, or CGE, model (see Burniaux *et al.*, 1992) was one of the earliest and most widely used global models for assessing the economic impacts of climate policies. From the mid–1990s, the GREEN model was maintained by the Development Centre and van der Mensbrugghe (1998) modified it to incorporate the Kyoto targets and permit trading, finding as expected that the non–OECD countries as a group would — if permitted to participate in global permit trading — become sizeable sellers to the OECD countries. Moreover, inclusion of non–OECD countries (allocating them permits in accordance with projected growth of their emissions to 2010) would halve costs of Kyoto compliance from 0.2 to 0.1 per cent of world product.

More recent Development Centre work on climate policy has focused principally on the interface with local environmental problems and their management. Using a common methodological framework, country studies of how climate policy can alter local environmental quality have been completed for Chile (Dessus and O'Connor, 1999) and India (Bussolo and O'Connor, 2001) and one for China is near completion. The studies suggest that, for developing countries that have taken few prior measures to control local air pollution, constraints on fossil fuel consumption designed to slow greenhouse gas emissions could yield significant local air quality improvements, especially in cases where the major fuel used in power generation is dirty coal, as in China and India. Naturally there are costs associated with such constraints, and governments need to weigh these in their decision making. Still, for modest future reductions (up to 15 per cent) of carbon dioxide (CO_2) emissions from a growth baseline, the ancillary benefits in premature deaths averted and reduced health costs can offset most if not all those costs, yielding few or even no "regrets".

The Development Centre's work on ancillary benefits of climate policy has dovetailed with related work in the Environment Directorate having a Member country focus. One result has been collaboration on a major international workshop on "Ancillary Benefits and Costs of Greenhouse Gas Mitigation", held at Resources for the Future in Washington, D.C., in March 2000 (see OECD, 2000, for proceedings). The Centre's work was presented in comparative light (O'Connor, 2000a) and it has subsequently benefited from an intensive exchange with other researchers in the field who were present at the workshop. A key contribution of the papers presented has been to inform environmental policy makers of the full range of possible impacts of specific measures, whether they be directed in the first instance at greenhouse gases or at local pollutants. This should, in principle, lead to better policy design.

On the Road to Globalisation

The effects of Rio were perhaps nowhere felt more strongly than in the international donor community, with concerted efforts at "greening" development assistance. The World Bank's environmental expertise expanded exponentially post–Rio. The international financial institutions and regional development banks put in place stricter environmental safeguards in response to strong criticisms from international NGOs and community groups in client developing countries. The United Nations Development Programme (UNDP) launched a major global initiative called *Capacity 21*, to help developing countries build the institutional and technical capacity to implement their various undertakings outlined in the *Agenda 21* declaration signed by 172 countries at Rio. Among those undertakings were participation in two major global environmental conventions, the Framework Convention on Climate Change and the Convention on Biological Diversity.

The 1990s were not simply the *post*–Rio decade. They were also a decade of sustained and rapid expansion in the world's largest economy, and of closer integration of the developing world into the global economy through accelerating trade and capital flows. The conjuncture of these two developments gave rise to a large body of research into the question of what globalisation means for the environment. The basic hypothesis around which much of the debate centres is that economic liberalisation leads to a "race to the bottom" in environmental standards as countries compete to attract foreign investment and to gain a trading advantage by holding down regulatory costs. Numerous objections have been made to this hypothesis, starting with the empirical observation that the overwhelmingly large share of foreign investment continues to take place among OECD countries with more or less similar (and relatively strict) environmental standards. Oman (2000) summarises the evidence, finding little support for the view that competition for foreign investment causes deterioration in environmental standards. That having been said, numerical models of trade liberalisation (including ones developed at the OECD Development Centre; see Beghin *et al.*, 1996, for a detailed technical description) do point to a sizeable scale effect of trade liberalisation in resource extraction sectors in those countries, like Indonesia, where these sectors possess a clear comparative advantage (Lee and Roland Holst, 1993). The authors point out, however, that better resource pricing to reflect the full social costs of extraction would mute this scale effect. As alluded to above, various studies (including several authored by Wheeler's team at the World Bank) find that more open economies perform better than more closed ones in terms of the adoption of "cleaner" production technologies — not because of explicit concern for the environment but simply because the pressures of competition force investment in newer (usually imported) technologies that also happen to be more efficient in transforming inputs into outputs, using less energy and generating less waste in the process (Hettige *et al.*, 1996).

The OECD has played an active part in stimulating international debate on globalisation and the environment, sponsoring an international conference on the subject in 1997 (see OECD, 1997, for proceedings). Contributions at the conference, in which the Development Centre participated, address the "race to the bottom" hypothesis, examine the relationship between the international trade regime, in particular the WTO, and environmental issues, and document the environmental performance of foreign investors as compared with national firms. The Development Centre's early work on mining and the environment (Warhurst, 1994) was among the first systematic explorations of how multinationals behave in a potentially environmentally damaging industry, and how their performance compares with that of nationally–owned (often state) enterprises in developing countries. Without suggesting that multinational firms always adhere to the same standards in developing countries as in their OECD operations, the study suggests that these firms often possess technologies and management know–how for addressing environmental problems that have been refined over years of having to comply with strict OECD standards. Where the learning associated with introducing these techniques has yielded process cost savings, it would not be rational for these companies to revert to inferior techniques simply because of relatively lax local environmental standards in their host country. Another consideration is the increasingly active monitoring of multinationals' environmental performance, irrespective of location, by international NGOs. Moreover, there is growing evidence of the sensitivity of stock prices to "bad environmental news" from listed companies, although the effect may be short–lived unless the news is expected materially to impact the bottom line — e.g. in the form of major site clean–up costs (O'Connor 2000*b*).

Johannesburg and Beyond

A decade has passed since Rio and, while not by any means a "lost decade" for the environment, the 1990s closed with the shine off the dynamic economies of Asia and with the familiar problems of macroeconomic management once again to the fore. The new millennium has begun with an equity market slump and a US–led recession that are proving stubbornly persistent. In 2001, a controversial new book (Lomborg, 2001) appeared, *The Skeptical Environmentalist*, written by a Danish statistician and former Greenpeace activist, challenging the bleak environmental prognoses of the Washington–based

Worldwatch Institute and, by extension, many environmental activists, including in the academic community. Few of the arguments in the book are new; the author points out correctly that quite a few environmental indicators have shown improvement, not deterioration, over the past decades. The principal shortcoming of the book is that it takes worldwide averages for many indicators, which often mask opposing trends in environmental quality in the developed and the developing world. Indeed, since the quality of the data for the OECD countries is generally much better than for the rest of the world, the author tends to rely more on the very data that show the most noticeable improvements. While it would be inaccurate to say that environmental indicators have not improved at all in the developing world, in many specific instances — e.g. air quality in megacities of Asia and Latin America — there has been marked deterioration. Thus, as with so much else written in the environmental field, this latest tome provides a very imperfect picture of what is happening in those regions of the globe — the developing world — where most of the world's people live.

The global recession, combined with a conservative tilt in the political leadership of several important OECD countries makes 2002 an inauspicious year for a World Summit on Sustainable Development. On the other hand, the location of the summit — Johannesburg, South Africa — provides an opportunity to broaden the focus definitively from environmental sustainability to include social sustainability. For this is a country whose enormous post–apartheid energy is being sapped by the scourge of rampant HIV infection among the prime working age population, leaving millions of orphans in its wake. While poverty is not alone the proximate cause of the epidemic, it is a major reason for people's vulnerability to opportunistic infections, for the unaffordability of AIDS drugs, as well as for the incapacity of health care systems in much of the continent to provide reliable access to medicines and medical care for AIDS sufferers. In addition to HIV, the Report of the WHO Commission on Macroeconomics and Health stresses the debilitating economic effects of such endemic tropical diseases as malaria. Gallup and Sachs (2001) find, for example, that controlling for other variables, countries with intensive malaria have per capita incomes only one–third as high as those without malaria, and they grew (1965–90) by 1.3 per cent less per person per year than the latter countries.

While the focus of much of the literature on sustainable development has been on intergenerational equity, Johannesburg provides the occasion to refocus on the question of intragenerational equity. The recent OECD horizontal project on *Sustainable Development* has given renewed emphasis to this question. Put simply, in an interconnected global economy, can development be sustained indefinitely in some countries if others are permanently left behind? In strictly economic terms, there may be nothing to prevent this outcome, but political and social considerations may make it increasingly untenable. Opinion polls in the United Kingdom, for example, find that more than two–thirds of those surveyed view poverty reduction in developing countries as an important moral issue. While this may not be entirely representative of other OECD countries, public opinion surveys in several OECD countries suggest that civil society's support for humanitarian and development assistance has not waned even if in some instances government budgets for this purpose have shrunk (Mc Donnell, 2001). The crucial test is whether OECD citizens feel strongly enough about poverty reduction to reverse this decline in ODA amounts and even augment significantly the flow of real resources to the developing world. In the context of the March 2002 Monterrey UN Summit on Financing for Development, both the EU and the United States took small but significant steps towards reversing the 1990s decline. This may or may not owe something to events of September 11. In any event, there is some cause for optimism that OECD policy makers are becoming ever more cognizant of the urgency of finding ways to spread the benefits of globalisation as widely as possible, including to the poor and powerless millions living in the developing world.

Notes

1.   The London smog was the result of pollution from multiple sources: not just factories and power plants but also domestic fuel burning and motor vehicles. In effect, London's air pollution problems of the 1950s resemble those of many developing country mega–cities today.

2.   I thank David Turnham for these points.

Bibliography

BEGHIN, J., S. DESSUS, D. ROLAND–HOLST AND D. VAN DER MENSBRUGGHE (1996), *General Equilibrium Modelling of Trade and the Environment*, Technical Papers No. 116, OECD Development Centre, Paris.

BLOCK, D. (1973), *Environmental Aspects of Economic Growth in Less Developed Countries: An Annotated Bibliography*, OECD Development Centre, Paris.

BOULDING, K.E. (1966), "The Economics of the Coming Spaceship Earth", *in* H. JARRETT (ed.), pp. 3–14.

BURNIAUX, J.–M., J.P. MARTIN, G. NICOLETTI AND J. OLIVEIRA–MARTINS (1992), "GREEN: A multi-sector, multi-region dynamic general equilibrium model for quantifying the costs of curbing CO_2 emissions: a technical manual", *Economics Department Working Papers*, No. 116, OECD, Paris.

BUSSOLO, M. AND D. O'CONNOR (2001), *Clearing the Air in India: The Economics of Climate Policy with Ancillary Benefits,* Technical Papers No. 182, OECD Development Centre, Paris.

DALY, H.E. (ed.) (1973), *Toward a Steady State Economy*, W.H. Freeman & Co., San Francisco.

DASGUPTA, P. (1995), "Optimal Development and NNP", *in* I. GOLDIN AND L.A.WINTER (eds.), *op.cit.*, chapter 5.

DASGUPTA, S. AND D. WHEELER (1996), "Citizen Complaints as Environmental Indicators: Evidence from China", Policy Research Working Paper, The World Bank, November; available at: http://www.worldbank.org/nipr/work_paper/compwp/index.htm.

DESSUS, S. AND D. O'CONNOR (1999), *Climate Policy without Tears: CGE–Based Ancillary Benefits Estimates for Chile*, Technical Papers No. 156, OECD Development Centre, Paris.

ERÖCAL, D. (ed.) (1991), *Environmental Management in Developing Countries*, Development Centre Seminars, OECD, Paris.

GALLUP, J.L. AND J.D. SACHS (2001), "The Economic Burden of Malaria", CMH Working Paper Series, WG1 – 10, Commission on Macroeconomics and Health, February.

GOLDIN, I. AND L.A. WINTERS (eds.) (1995), *The Economics of Sustainable Development*, Cambridge University Press for the OECD Development Centre and CEPR, Cambridge, UK.

GROSSMAN, G. AND A. KRUEGER (1994), "Economic Growth and the Environment", WP4634, NBER Working Paper Series, Cambridge, MA, February.

HETTIGE, H., M. HUQ, S. PARGAL AND D. WHEELER (1996), "Determinants of Pollution Abatement in Developing Countries: Evidence From South And Southeast Asia", *World Development*, December, 24(12), 1891–1904.

HETTIGE, H., M. MANI AND D. WHEELER (1997), "Industrial Pollution in Economic Development: Kuznets Revisited", Development Research Group, World Bank, December, processed.

ISLAM, N., J. VINCENT AND T. PANAYOTOU (1999), "Unveiling the Income–Environment Relationship: An Exploration into the Determinants of Environmental Quality", HIID Development Discussion Paper No. 701, Harvard Institute for International Development, Cambridge MA, May.

JARRETT, H. (ed.), *Environmental Quality in a Growing Economy*, Johns Hopkins University Press, Baltimore.

KOLSTAD, C.D. (2000), *Environmental Economics*, Oxford University Press, Oxford.

LEE, H. AND D. ROLAND HOLST (1993), *International Trade and the Transfer of Environmental Costs and Benefits*, Technical Papers No. 91, OECD Development Centre, Paris.

LOMBORG, B. (2001), *The Skeptical Environmentalist: Measuring the Real State of the World*, Cambridge University Press, Cambridge, UK.

LONG, B.L. (2000), *International Environmental Issues and the OECD 1950–2000*, OECD, Paris.

MC DONNELL, I. (2001), "Current Trends in Public Opinion about International Development Co–operation in OECD Countries", presented at the Informal Experts' Meeting on *International Development Co–operation in OECD Countries: Public Debate, Public Support and Public Opinion*, 25–26 October, Dublin.

O'CONNOR, D. (2000a), "Ancillary Benefits Estimation in Developing Countries: A Comparative Assessment", in OECD (2000), *op.cit.*, 377–396.

O'CONNOR, D. (2000b), *Global Capital Flows and the Environment in the 21st Century*, Technical Papers No. 161, OECD Development Centre, Paris.

O'CONNOR, D. (1998), "Applying Economic Instruments in Developing Countries: From Theory to Implementation", *Environment and Development Economics*, 4, 91–110.

O'CONNOR, D. (1996), *Grow Now/Clean Later, or the Pursuit of Sustainable Development?*, Technical Papers No. 111, OECD Development Centre, Paris.

O'Connor, D. (1994), *Managing the Environment with Rapid Industrialisation: Lessons from the East Asian Experience*, Development Centre Studies, OECD, Paris.

O'Connor, D. (1991), *Strategies, Policies and Practices for the Reduction of CFC Usage in the Electronics Industries of Developing Asia*, Research Document, OECD Development Centre, Paris, June.

O'Connor, D. and D. Turnham (1992), *Managing the Environment in Developing Countries*, Policy Brief No. 2, OECD Development Centre, Paris.

OECD (2000), *Ancillary Benefits and Costs of Greenhouse Gas Mitigation*. Proceedings of an IPCC Co–Sponsored Workshop, held on 27–29 March 2000, in Washington, D.C., Paris.

OECD (1997), *Globalisation and Environment: Preliminary Perspectives*, OECD Proceedings, Paris.

OECD (1995), *The Economic Appraisal of Environmental Projects and Policies: A Practical Guide*, Paris.

OECD (1994), *Project and Policy Appraisal: Integrating Economics and Environment*, OECD Documents, Paris.

OECD (1981), *The Costs and Benefits of Sulphur Oxide Control: A Methodological Study*, Paris.

Oman, C. (2000), *Policy Competition for Foreign Direct Investment: A Study of Competition among Governments to Attract FDI*, Development Centre Studies, OECD, Paris.

Pargal, S. and D. Wheeler (1995), "Informal Regulation of Industrial Pollution in Developing Countries: Evidence from Indonesia", Policy Research Working Paper No. 1416, World Bank, Washington, D.C., February; available at: http://www.worldbank.org/nipr/work_paper/1416/index.htm.

Selden, T.M. and D. Song (1994), "Is There An Environmental Kuznets Curve for Air Pollution?", *Journal of Environmental Economics and Management*, 27, 147–162.

Shafik, N., and S. Bandyopadhyay (1992), "Economic Growth and Environmental Quality: Time–Series and Cross–Country Evidence", *Background Paper for the World Development Report 1992*, Policy Research Working Paper WPS 904, World Bank, June.

Stern, D.I., T. Auld, M.S. Common and K.K. Sanyal (1998), "Is There An Environmental Kuznets Curve for Sulfur?" paper presented at the World Congress on Environmental Economics, Venice, June, processed.

Stern, D.I., M.S. Common and E.B. Barbier (1996), "Economic Growth and Environmental Degradation: The Environmental Kuznets Curve and Sustainable Development", *World Development*, 24(7), 1151–1160.

Van der Mensbrugghe, D. (1998), "A (Preliminary) Analysis of the Kyoto Protocol: Using the OECD GREEN Model", in *Economic Modelling of Climate Change: OECD Workshop Report*, proceedings of a workshop held at OECD Headquarters, 17–18 September 1998, Paris.

VINCENT, J. (1997), "Testing for Environmental Kuznets Curves within a Developing Country", *Environment and Development Economics*, 2(4), 417–431.

WARHURST, A. (1994), *Environmental Degradation from Mining and Mineral Processing in Developing Countries: Corporate Responses and National Policies*, Development Centre Documents, OECD, Paris.

WHEELER, D., M. HUQ AND P. MARTIN (1993), "Process Change, Economic Policy and Industrial Pollution: Cross–Country Evidence from the Wood Pulp and Steel Industries", World Bank, Washington, D.C., processed.

Chapter 6

Globalisation and Poverty

Maurizio Bussolo and Christian Morrisson

Introduction

To the uninformed, poverty is an evil immune to economic policy, and to trade policy in particular. Over the last half century (1950–2000), the number of "poor" people grew steadily — by 50 per cent in all — while the number of "very poor" (living on less than $1 per day) remained stable, despite the fact that during the same period, two completely contradictory trade policies were implemented in turn. In the 1950s, 1960s and 1970s, many developing countries pursued import–substitution strategies relegating exports to a secondary role, while only a few Southeast Asian countries successfully pursued an opposite policy of export–led growth. After the "lost decade" of the 1980s — lost owing to the adjustment programmes made necessary by the macroeconomic imbalances generated in the 1970s — the 1990s brought the Uruguay Round and a conversion to trade liberalisation, which indeed had already been initiated in many structural adjustment programmes during the 1980s.

Thus, it is easy today to criticise the choice of globalisation on the grounds that the number of "poor" is still increasing, just as, 30 years ago, protectionist or inward–looking development policies could be criticised because this number was rising then as well.

This scepticism should be tempered, however, by a few solid facts. First, the world's population has risen by 140 per cent, and the percentages of "poor" and "very poor" have dropped considerably, from 72 per cent to 51 per cent for the former, and from 55 per cent to 24 per cent for the latter. A much smaller proportion of the world population is living in poverty today than it was in 1950. Second, one should look at the countries in which poverty has decreased the most. In the 1960s and 1970s, these were the Southeast Asian countries, rather than China under the Maoist regime or the Latin American countries which had opted for import–substitution policies.

95

As the work of the Development Centre has shown, however, opening up to trade does not always reduce poverty: in African countries where mining exports have come to account for a high percentage of GDP, poverty has not declined. Whereas the manufactured exports of the Southeast Asian countries, for example, do reduce poverty, those stemming from mining or large–scale farming do not have this effect. Each export–led growth strategy may, depending on its specific features and the sectors involved, have either positive or negative effects.

The value of in–depth analyses resides precisely in the fact that they take this complexity into account. Since its foundation, the Centre has participated in the debates on the relationships between trade and development and on the impact of trade policy. In this chapter, we will be concerned only with its contributions concerning the relationships between trade policy and the integration of goods markets by international trade on the one hand, and inequality and poverty on the other. It is well known that poverty results from a great number of factors, and no attempt will be made here to explain its overall evolution. We are concerned only with the incidence of trade relations on poverty. Our scope is also limited by a restrictive conception of poverty in which the poverty line is defined in terms of income or consumption. Organisations such as UNDP, however, have for several years been using a multi–dimensional conception of poverty, including aspects such as health, education and access to drinking water. The UNDP incorporates such variables into its indicators of both human development and poverty.

After a brief review of the complex relationships between globalisation and poverty, this chapter presents the Development Centre's contributions to the policy debate in the first period (1950–80): did import–substitution policies and export–led growth policies benefit the poor? It then turns to the second period (1980–2000), when structural adjustment policies and the Uruguay Round induced countries to open up their economies to trade: what has been the impact of this globalisation process on equality and poverty?

The Complex Relationships between Globalisation and Poverty

It should be specified at the outset that we are concerned here with only one aspect of globalisation. This term usually refers to all economic relationships between countries, whether these involve goods, capital, people or technology. Here we consider only the integration of goods markets through international trade, while bearing in mind that trade in goods may have a different impact on poverty than do labour force migration or capital transfers.

Two additional difficulties make the assessment of the link between globalisation and poverty particularly tricky. The first is that international trade is a prime example of a subject in which it is essential to take account of general equilibrium, in which everything affects everything else. For example, should one model the effects of a change in trade protection as if that change is occurring in isolation in a country that faces given world prices? Or should one consider simultaneous changes in various countries, as well as modifications in other policies that offset tariff revenue losses? Should trade–induced variations in factor returns be examined separately from movements in the prices of consumption goods, or should one consider their joint impact on the poor? Partial and general equilibrium approaches can produce opposing predictions about poverty and contradictory policy advice.

The second difficulty, which is connected to the first, has to do with the empirical verification of theoretical predictions. Many different factors influence change in trade volumes and international prices, as well as variations in poverty levels. Controlling all of these variables in such a way as to identify a clear relationship between trade and poverty has proved very difficult. Researchers may come to opposite conclusions depending on which counterfactual scenario they compare to actual observations. If we disregard specific country cases, East Asia and Latin America display two contrasting situations, in which increasing trade flows are accompanied respectively by declining and growing poverty levels. Clearly, in such cases, the counterfactual should include not only lower trade flows but also other variables (growth rates, technology, the stability of macroeconomic balances and levels of development) which may in turn interact with trade flows.

Figure 1 represents in schematic form the direct and indirect linkages between globalisation and poverty, providing a simple illustration of a large and diverse literature.

Figure 1. **A Schematic Representation of Globalisation and Poverty Linkages**

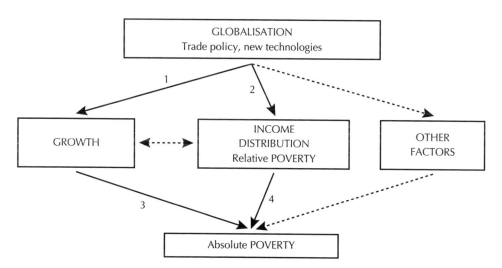

The expansion of international trade, i.e. globalisation, potentially affects poverty through its effects on both growth and income distribution. Trade expansion or contraction is the ultimate objective of trade policy. A country may choose to raise barriers against imports or to impose restrictions on both imports and exports, or, conversely, it may encourage any of these flows. Various instruments that discriminate between domestic and foreign products or markets are available, such as tariffs, taxes, subsidies and quantitative restrictions.

Although "other factors", the most important of which is technological progress, may have contributed, trade policy reforms have played a major role in the post–war growth of trade volumes. However, the effects of these increased trade flows on GDP growth and income distribution still give rise to heated debate. Given that economic growth and income distribution are the main determinants of poverty levels, a description of how increased trade affects these two variables is essential.

Trade Openness and Growth
(arrow 1 in Figure 1)

Economic theory allows for a negative as well as a positive relationship between trade restrictions and growth, and thus is not particularly helpful. Hoping for firmer guidance, researchers have looked to real–world data, and their numerous empirical studies seem to have found some form of positive relationship between openness and growth[1].

Trade Liberalisation and Income Distribution
(arrow 2 in Figure 1)

One of the few firm facts that economists have to offer is that trade liberalisation has strong redistributive effects. One need only observe that, in almost all cases, the question of whether trade reforms will be fully implemented or reversed is determined by governments' ability to cope with the repercussions of reform on real income distribution or by the inability of the potential or actual losers to join forces and block the reforms.

In the simplest international trade model of comparative advantage, a standard prediction is that increased trade causes resource reallocation and production specialisation in the sectors that make intensive use of the country's most abundant factor. When dealing with developing countries, which presumably are endowed with a relative abundance of low–skilled labour (the endowment of the poor), the model concludes that increased trade should shift output towards goods that are intensive in low–skilled labour, increasing demand for unskilled workers and raising their wages relative to the remuneration of other factors.

Does this happen in reality? If not, why not? The broad picture, for two regions that have embarked on extensive trade liberalisation policies, is that income distribution — or, more specifically, wage inequality between skilled and unskilled labour — improved in East Asia but not in Latin America[2]. Various explanations have been put forward to resolve this apparent empirical conundrum. First of all, it may be that the only alteration needed in the above model to account for the observed outcomes is to consider an additional, sector–specific factor of production, such as natural resources in the mining sector. Other aspects may also have played some role: different trade policy instruments (export incentives in East Asia, tariff reductions in Latin America); different external global environments (the East Asian countries opened their economies in the 1960s and 1970s, before the entry of the large low–income exporters — Bangladesh, China, India, Indonesia and Pakistan — that hampered the liberalisation efforts of Latin America in the 1980s and 1990s); different institutional arrangements on domestic labour markets.

Growth, Income Distribution and Poverty
(arrows 3 and 4 in Figure 1)

How do globalisation–induced growth and changes in income distribution affect poverty levels? At first sight, it seems that growth and a more equal income distribution undeniably favour poverty reduction. When one considers the dynamic development process in its entirety, however, one may find that growth generates inequalities; thus, even when growth originating from trade opening is accompanied by a more balanced income distribution, the net result on poverty is uncertain.

In order to understand the relationships between globalisation, income distribution and poverty, consideration of four important factors is needed. First, a clearer understanding of the connection between the functional and personal income distributions is essential. We need to identify more clearly how and from which type of factor of production the poor derive their incomes. Second, some poor people live completely outside market relationships, and in such cases trade liberalisation cannot have any effect on their incomes. Third, there is a presumption that positive trade liberalisation effects will relieve the poor in the end, but that in the short to medium term the whole adjustment process may be more harmful than helpful. Fourth, countries with high levels of poverty do not usually enjoy large government budgets and normally rely quite heavily on trade taxes. Transforming the fiscal structure of these countries may take some time, and social expenditures are often the first to be squeezed when shrinking revenues from trade taxes have to be balanced.

The Policy Debate in 1950–80: The Period of Controversy

The Trade Policy Debate over Arrows 1 and 2: Is Protectionism a Good Strategy?

From the 1950s to the early 1980s, the Prebisch–Singer "terms–of–trade curse" and the ensuing focus on import–substitution industrialisation were the central and almost undisputed ideas in the debate over development strategies. In this intellectual and political environment, the OECD Development Centre study Industry and Trade in Some Developing Countries (Little et al., 1970) broke new ground by clearly showing the limitations and real pitfalls of these ideas. This work was particularly useful because many Latin American, North African and sub–Saharan African countries had opted for an import–substitution policy, imposing many quotas or very high tariff rates.

Using in–depth case studies, the authors showed that an industrialisation policy oriented towards serving a highly protected domestic market worked to the detriment of agriculture, owing to a fall in the terms of trade between the agricultural and non–agricultural sectors. The resulting drop in the ratio of average agricultural income to average non–agricultural income hurt the poor, most of whom live in rural areas. The import–substitution policy also raised the share of profits — another factor of inequality. In the secondary sector, this policy gave priority to the most recent capital–intensive technologies at the expense of traditional labour–intensive techniques, which are favourable to employment and hence to the poor. As a result, the market for production factors showed strong demand for capital, but weak demand for labour. Few jobs were created and urban unemployment rose, since the growing income gap between rural and urban areas provided an increasingly strong incentive for migration. The increased income inequality also affected the goods market, because it changed the structure of demand for goods: to meet the shift in demand, more automobiles and other consumer durables were produced, and fewer goods for current consumption such as textiles, clothing and shoes. Both the decision to favour capital–intensive techniques and this shift in demand and output increased foreign exchange requirements, but foreign exchange could not be obtained because the export sectors had been neglected, which led to under–utilisation of production capacity in many cases.

In a recent economic history of Latin America, Thorp (2001) provides a clear description of how prescient the study by Little et al. had been. She argues that "inequality was knit deeply into the fabric of the model and was part of its effectiveness in generating growth", and that although the failure of this new industrialisation model to raise the purchasing power of the population and create a wider domestic market was temporarily concealed by the abundance of foreign loans in the 1970s, it became immediately apparent when international conditions changed. For Latin America, the debt crisis of 1982 marks the bitter realisation of the need for deeper institutional and economic policy reforms — ten years after Little *et al.* (1970) had published their book suggesting some of these very reforms.

Some years later, when structural adjustment loans and conditionality had been implemented in many countries, the Development Centre's research on the consequences of these reform programmes for poverty was crystallised in a series of studies with the eloquent title of "Adjustment and Equity". Adjustment is achieved in the short term through stabilisation, and in the long term through reform. The aim of stabilisation programmes is to bring about a rapid reduction of the external deficit and restore macroeconomic balances by restricting overall demand. Structural adjustment programmes, in contrast, are implemented over a number of years and aim to increase supply through structural reforms, notably trade liberalisation.

An economy can be stabilised in several ways: by devaluing the currency, cutting public spending, restricting the money supply or reducing imports through a sudden rise in customs tariffs (this last measure being in contradiction with trade liberalisation, a key objective of structural adjustment programmes). The impact of these measures can be estimated using a computable general equilibrium (CGE) model that disaggregates all households in a country by socio–economic group. According to the simulations comparing the effects of all these measures in the case of Morocco (Morrisson, 1991), a substantial rise in tariffs (+ 60 per cent) increases both inequality and the percentage of poor. Some other measures have the same negative effect, but this pitfall can be avoided (or its effects strongly attenuated) by devaluing the currency or cutting either public investment spending or civil service wages. Even a monetarist policy has a slightly less negative effect. There is thus a clear contrast between devaluation and protectionism: the former encourages exports and openness (while at the same time reducing inequality), while the latter increases both inequality and poverty. This relationship between protectionism and inequality had already been demonstrated by Bourguignon and Morrisson (1989) for a sample of 20 countries. It was observed that the more protectionist the policy, the more inegalitarian is the country. The result is an increase in poverty: the share of the poorest 60 per cent, which amounts to approximately 22 per cent of the total income of households, falls by five percentage points.

What about Export–led Growth? Is It Working? Does It Benefit the Poor?

The emergence of the Southeast Asian tigers and their seemingly strong performance in terms of growth and poverty brought another key policy debate to the attention of economists. In the 1970s, the performance of these countries was spoken of as a "miracle", and some analysts came prematurely to the conclusion that any trade liberalisation policy reduces poverty. The Development

Centre took part in this debate and showed that the true situation is more complex, by analysing the effects of this policy on income distribution and poverty in a series of case studies, collected in Bourguignon and Morrisson's *External Trade and Income Distribution* (1989).

This study shows that export orientation favours the poor only in those cases where exports originate mainly in labour–intensive manufacturing and agriculture, and where the latter is not dominated by large–scale landowners (Malawi, Costa Rica, Malaysia). In those countries where natural resource sectors are the major export sources (Peru and Morocco), relative poverty worsens under an export–led strategy.

More precisely, in Costa Rica a 10 per cent rise in total exports stemming from an increase in coffee exports raises employment and incomes by 4 per cent, whereas if the rise is due to textile exports, the increase amounts to 6 per cent for employment and 5.5 per cent for incomes. In Morocco, if the rise is due to textiles, clothing and leather products, the effect on employment is + 1 per cent and that on incomes +0.7 per cent. In Peru, where coffee is produced by smallholders, a 10 per cent rise in total exports driven by coffee exports increases employment by 3.6 per cent and incomes by 1.4 per cent. As these manufacturing or agricultural exports increase, labour demand from export sectors absorbs the surplus labour supply in both rural and urban areas. As soon as this surplus is exhausted, wages shoot up (e.g. Chinese Taipei as from 1970). This analysis also applies to other export activities that mainly employ low–skilled labour, such as fishing and the tourist industry.

The picture is quite different, however, for activities that regularly employ large amounts of capital or of a specific production factor (e.g. mining) but little labour. If other factor markets are competitive, any rise in the price of the exported good (ore) will be siphoned off by the specific factor, i.e. the owners of the mine. In agriculture, large plantations, which use relatively little labour and a great deal of capital that is not substitutable for labour, can pay their workers very low wages precisely because a labour surplus exists. In both cases, the distribution of export–related incomes is highly inegalitarian, and the above analysis (in which the export sector profits from an abundant labour supply) does not apply. The state can soften this inegalitarian effect by imposing a minimum wage well above the equilibrium rate in these sectors, but the impact of this measure is limited by the small size of the labour force. A more effective measure is for the state to appropriate the mining rent, provided that it redistributes the proceeds primarily to the benefit of poor households, which is often not the case.

These sectoral differences are confirmed by estimations of the impact of a 10 per cent rise in total exports due to increased mining exports. In Morocco, such an increase in phosphate exports raises employment by 0.3 per cent and incomes by 0.8 per cent; in Peru, mining exports increased employment by 0.8 per cent and incomes by 1.4 per cent. Thus, the income effects in Morocco and Peru are comparable to those for textiles and coffee, but there is much less job creation. Exports of mining products create well–paid jobs, but very few of them, so the poor derive no direct advantage from such exports.

This assessment of the benefits of exports for the poor is confirmed by the World Bank's World Development Report (1990) on poverty. This report shows the benefits that trade liberalisation would bring to developing countries, taking textiles and clothing as examples: liberalisation would raise the number of jobs by 20 to 45 per cent, to the benefit of the poor. However, poor countries and net importers of agricultural products would lose from liberalisation, because it would raise world agricultural prices. Moreover, middle–income countries would derive greater benefit from full trade liberalisation than less developed countries such as those of sub–Saharan Africa. The effect would be favourable, however, for the two countries having the greatest number of poor: China and India.

Since the 1980s: A Preference for Globalisation

Liberalisation under the Uruguay Round and Poverty

Although Little *et al.* (1970) had shown that inward–looking import–substitution strategies were likely to fail owing to the narrowness of the domestic market, the surge in loans to rechannel petrodollars beginning in 1973 allowed these countries to revive demand. This growth "on credit" without simultaneous development of exports led to the financial crisis of 1982, however, and the countries that had opted for this strategy were forced to implement adjustment programmes in order to be eligible for further loans. Trade liberalisation was an important condition of these programmes, and was gradually implemented from 1982 to the early 1990s. Meanwhile, the Uruguay Round negotiations, which began in 1986, reached their end in 1994. This agreement marked a turning point in favour of globalisation in developing countries. For the first time, developing countries' interests were fully recognised in the negotiations, which also included efforts to broaden the world trading system to include services and intellectual property rights and to subject agriculture, textiles and clothing to the same set of rules as that governing manufactures. This major step forward was made possible by the political willingness of all participating governments and the continuing efforts of professional economists to convince negotiators and the public at large of the benefits of free trade.

The Development Centre distinguished itself in this role by producing state–of–the–art estimations of the potential effects of the trade agreement. In the words of François *et al.* (1996), "Quantitative studies influenced this [negotiation] process, from the setting of the agenda to the ratification process. For example, … work at the OECD Development Centre signalled the potentially adverse impact of agricultural liberalisation on net food importers and helped lead to the Agreement on Agriculture being supplemented at the conclusion of the Uruguay Round with a 'Decision on Measures Concerning the Possible Negative Effects of the Reform Program on Least–Developed and Net Food–Importing Countries'."

The Development Centre work referred to comprises a number of contributions. The first to appear was the most ambitious in scope: Goldin et al. (1993) estimate the effects of agricultural and non–agricultural trade liberalisation for the entire world economy. Beginning with a baseline simulation, the three authors estimate the impact of partial and full trade liberalisation (including the elimination of producer subsidies) on the incomes of the rural and urban populations. The rural/urban disaggregation is very important, as the majority of the poor live in rural areas. The results obtained for full liberalisation in four countries are instructive. In Brazil, for example, the ratio of average rural income to average urban income rises by 16 per cent. In Mexico, the rural sector benefits from a rise in world agricultural prices and a reduction in taxation owing to the elimination of duty on non–agricultural imports. In China, all of the gains from full liberalisation accrue to the rural sector, whereas the urban sector sees its welfare decrease. This rise in rural incomes relative to urban incomes greatly slows off–farm migration and consequently reduces income inequality in urban areas, since the pressure on the labour market eases. This gain for the rural population is the direct result of increases in agricultural producer prices. It should be noted that the rural poor benefit much more from complete liberalisation than from partial liberalisation.

In India, full liberalisation raises both rural and urban incomes, but the increase is greater for rural incomes. The agricultural prices that rise the most are those for sugar and livestock products, which account for only a low share of rural consumers' expenditures. The rural population is subject to double taxation in this rather closed economy, owing to the maintenance of agricultural producer prices at a low level and strong protection of the urban sector. As poverty in India is concentrated in the rural environment, it is clear that full liberalisation would reduce both inequality and poverty.

Goldin and van der Mensbrugghe sum up this research project in their policy brief "Trade Liberalisation: What's at Stake?" (1993), in which they conclude that liberalisation would be favourable to all the poor, in developed and developing countries alike. They point out, however, that small farmers in developing countries will benefit only if the rise in world prices is wholly passed on to producers and if crop yields increase (owing to improvements in production techniques, storage conditions and distribution). In addition, there is a genuine risk that the poorest countries, such as those in sub–Saharan Africa, will benefit the least from liberalisation or will even lose out, and that it will be necessary to compensate them for their losses. Thus, this research project leads to a qualified conclusion: liberalisation can reduce poverty only if several conditions are met.

More Recent Contributions on Trade Policy and Globalisation

In the new context resulting from the Uruguay Round, many globalisation–related topics have been addressed in discussions and studies, in which the Development Centre has participated (see Chapter 9). Only the analyses concerned with poverty will be considered here.

Regional Integration versus or together with Multilateral Liberalisation

Following on the work published in 1993, Collado *et al.* (1995) studied the effects of liberalisation on employment in Latin America. They used a global model, but gave special emphasis to the effects in the region concerned. This model also differed from the preceding one in breaking down labour into four categories.

The model shows the favourable effects of liberalisation on production and employment in Latin America — job creation reduces unemployment, thus reducing poverty — but it also reveals a negative aspect of liberalisation: the portion of the working population that benefits the most from liberalisation consists of the most highly skilled workers, and income distribution within the working population becomes more unequal. This happens because, in contrast to the Southeast Asian countries, the Latin American countries have fallen behind in terms of secondary education, which is under–funded; as a result, skilled labour is relatively scarce, and when liberalisation strengthens the demand for such labour, wages rise.

Lee and Roland–Holst (1994) focus on another region: the Pacific Basin. Their CGE model encompasses ten countries on the Pacific Ocean (United States, Japan, China, Korea, Chinese Taipei, Singapore, Malaysia, Thailand, Indonesia and the Philippines). Their simulations examine the effects of *1)* the elimination of tariff barriers, *2)* the elimination of tariff and non–tariff barriers and *3)* the extension of the liberalisation process to the rest of the world. The positive effects on employment increase from one simulation to the next. Most important, the less developed and more labour–intensive the economy, the stronger these effects are (and virtually no effect was found for the United States and Japan).

Increases of over 5 per cent in total employment, as in Malaysia, Thailand, Indonesia and the Philippines, undoubtedly work to the benefit of the under–employed and unemployed poor in these countries. In contrast, Japan would create 3 million jobs abroad through its increased demand for labour–intensive goods, but would derive no benefit for itself. The results for Singapore and Chinese Taipei in terms of domestic job creation are little better.

These studies of the impact of a somewhat speculative regional liberalisation process were followed by a real–world case with the liberalisation of trade among the Maghreb countries, the Middle East and the European Union (agreements have already been signed with some countries, while others are still at the negotiating stage). The Development Centre took part in the discussions on the consequences of this liberalisation. The volume edited by Dessus et al. (2001) contains a dozen contributions on this topic, two of which (on Tunisia and Morocco) are concerned with the impact of liberalisation on the poor and on differences in average income between the rural and urban populations. The chapter on Tunisia builds on a Development Centre technical paper by Chemingui and Dessus (1999), the value of which lies in its fairly high level of disaggregation (five types of labour distinguished by type of qualification; two representative Tunisian households, one urban and the other rural; 57 sectors of activity, of which half are in agriculture), which makes it possible to estimate the impact of liberalisation on inequality and poverty. The baseline simulation starts with the existing environment and the measures to which Tunisia has already committed, estimating the variables over the period 1992–2010. Next, various scenarios are simulated. The first assumes a decline in tariffs on agricultural and agri–food imports from the European Union, which fall to zero in 2010. Scenario 2 considers a gradual reduction of agricultural subsidies, which are also eliminated by 2010. Scenario 3 assumes that the European Union gradually eliminates tariffs on agricultural imports from Tunisia (to zero in 2010). When the three scenarios are combined, there is admittedly an overall gain (GDP increases by 1.2 per cent in 2010), but the average income of rural dwellers falls slightly, while that of the urban population rises by 2.4 per cent. Thus, inequality increases, but there is probably no increase in poverty owing to a favourable impact on the urban poor. It may be concluded that no liberalisation is possible unless the European Union opens up its markets to Tunisian agricultural products and unless essential redistributive measures (transfers by the state to rural populations) are taken to ensure that the end result is positive for rural households as well.

The chapter by Löfgren et al. in Dessus et al. (2001) offers a comparable analysis of Morocco. Here again, the general equilibrium model focuses on agriculture (38 activities out of 45) and uses fairly detailed breakdowns (skilled/unskilled labour, poor/non–poor rural households, poor/non–poor urban households) to estimate the impact of liberalisation on inequality and poverty. The first scenario assumes reduced protection on agricultural products, which has a negative effect on agriculture and on other rural activities (owing to the slower growth of agricultural incomes). If this measure is combined with the elimination of non–tariff barriers (scenario 2), household incomes grow at a higher rate, except for those of the rural poor. The authors then combine liberalisation with redistributive measures (scenario 3): a uniform tariff rate is adopted (10 per cent) and the state subsidises farmers or finances training for unskilled rural labour (the growth rate of the skilled rural workforce doubles). The incomes of the rural poor (and non–poor) show much higher growth in this case than in the baseline simulation. As 70 per cent of the country's poor live in rural areas, this combination of measures would certainly reduce poverty in Morocco, whereas poverty would increase with the liberalisation of agricultural imports under scenarios 1 and 2.

Taken in isolation, then, liberalisation has no direct favourable impact on the poor. In both Morocco and Tunisia, the state needs to take redistributive measures to ensure that the rural poor benefit from liberalisation as other groups do.

Will the Next Multilateral Liberalisation Round Focus on Poverty?

The World Bank's World Development Report for 2000, which is devoted to poverty, regards liberalisation of trade in agricultural products as a crucial issue. This report denounces the policy of the developed countries, which are protecting their markets through high tariffs and subsidies. As a result, trade in agricultural products rose by only 1.8 per cent a year from 1985 to 1994, as against 5.8 per cent for manufactured goods. According to the report, exports of agricultural products would allow effective poverty reduction in rural areas, where over two–thirds of the poor are to be found, because such exports would raise employment, including non–agricultural employment, and incomes, thus stimulating the entire rural economy.

The most recent work on liberalisation and poverty (McCulloch *et al.* 2001) makes the same argument, but qualifies it somewhat. The authors point out that the impact of agricultural exports will depend on agrarian structures: for a positive effect to be felt, these structures must encourage intensive use of labour. Since liberalisation would raise agricultural prices, poor rural households could derive a net benefit even if they are not producers, but poor urban households would undoubtedly lose from liberalisation.

The volume edited by Dessus *et al.* (2001) is clearly one of the works on agricultural market liberalisation and poverty reduction that will make a contribution to future negotiations, but this is not the only topic addressed by the Development Centre. O'Connor and Lunati (1999) examine the relationships between workforce qualifications, technology and investment when a country adopts an open trade policy. If openness leads to the adoption of new technologies, demand for skilled labour rises and hence there is increased wage inequality. In addition, openness seems to stimulate investment in physical capital. If there is complementarity between physical capital and new technologies, however, we have three complementary factors: capital, technology and skilled labour. In this case, foreign investment would go not to poor countries, where skilled labour is unavailable, but to middle–income countries. In these countries, openness and foreign investment would increase the growth rate (which reduces poverty) and simultaneously increase wage differentials. In low–income countries, individuals would have even less incentive to acquire skills, because openness is unfavourable to moderately human–capital intensive industries. Consequently, wage and income inequalities in these countries would tend to decline, while poverty could well increase. Empirical tests seem to confirm these complementarities between skills, technology and capital. It is therefore important in middle–income countries to co–ordinate openness with educational investment in order to reduce wage inequality. This is also necessary, despite appearances, in low–income countries: if the state does not train a skilled workforce to meet the requirements of the private sector, even though there is no immediate demand for it, the country will never be able to attract investment in the future. Thus, where technology is concerned, liberalisation may well benefit middle–income countries rather than the countries where the majority of the poor are to be found. These results agree with the conclusions of McCulloch et al. (2001) on the effects of access to technology — conclusions that are pessimistic for poor countries, and optimistic for middle–income countries.

Conclusions

We should begin with a reminder that the favourable impact of trade liberalisation on poverty is no longer in doubt. The World Bank study *Globalization, Growth and Poverty* (2002) provides the proof. It shows that during the 1990s, 24 countries, with a combined population of 3 billion, which doubled their exports/GDP ratios attained a per capita GDP growth rate double that of the developed countries, while other countries have suffered a drop in per capita GDP. Poverty continued to increase in these countries, whereas it declined rapidly in the 24 countries that opted for an open trade policy. The most striking example is that of China, where the number of poor in rural areas is believed to have fallen by over 200 million in 20 years. As the study concludes, "globalization clearly can be a powerful force for poverty reduction".

Bhalla (2002) reaches the same conclusion. Global income inequality, which stood at the same level in 1980 as in 1950, has fallen over the last 20 years. From 1960 to 1980, income per capita in the developed countries grew at a rate nearly twice that of the less developed countries. The period from 1980 to 1999 saw an inverse trend, owing to the strong performance of the Asian countries (while Latin America and sub–Saharan Africa stagnated), and these successes have brought a rapid fall in the percentage of poor in Asia. It was Asia that participated the most in the globalisation process, while Africa watched from the sidelines.

Although this review is positive on the whole, in–depth analyses are still needed to determine which negative impacts are possible and to identify all the conditions required for reconciling openness with the reduction of inequality and poverty. The Development Centre has produced a number of such analyses of the effects of liberalisation on inequality and poverty, which yielded the following results:

— Although manufactured exports and agricultural exports produced by small farmers do reduce poverty effectively, this is not true of other exports unless the state intervenes (e.g. by redistributing part of the oil rent to the poor).

— Small farmers in developing countries will not benefit from the liberalisation of agricultural trade unless several other conditions are met, such as increased yields or redistributive measures by the state.

— Liberalisation may well be of greater benefit to the "poor" than to the "very poor", because middle–income countries (whose populations include many "poor" people but few "very poor") are better prepared to take advantage of it than are the poorest countries, such as those of sub–Saharan Africa.

— An open, simple trade policy can foster some external discipline, helping to reduce distortions on domestic markets, and narrow the scope for mistaken or unbalanced policies in other areas, as well as rent–seeking and corruption, which normally do not favour the poor (Bonaglia *et al.*, 2001). Rejection of the globalisation process rarely helps the poor. Trade isolationism is usually worse than other, more targeted fiscal measures (e.g. food stamps) to protect special segments of a population or their incomes (a well–known second–best result).

— Embracing globalisation may not bring immediate positive results. It is true that in the long run, more open economies, exposed to more foreign competition and investing abundantly in institution building, will obtain better governance and stronger growth; in the short run, however, domestic policies may be more valuable than pursuing globalisation at all costs. This may be especially important for poorer countries that may face serious trade–offs between complying with international agreements and investing in basic development infrastructures such as education, health and social security.

Notes

1. There is a huge econometrics literature on this topic. A few of the most recent and most cited works are Dollar (1992), Sachs and Warner (1995), Ben–David (1993) and Edwards (1998). For a good survey of previous studies see Edwards (1993).

2. See, for example, Wood (1997).

Bibliography

BEN–DAVID, D. (1993), "Equalizing Exchange: Trade Liberalization and Income Convergence", *Quarterly Journal of Economics, 108(3)*.

BHALLA S.S. (2002), *Imagine There's No Country: Poverty, Inequality, and Growth in the Era of Globalization*, Institute of International Economics, Washington, D.C.

BONAGLIA, F., J. BRAGA DE MACEDO AND M. BUSSOLO (2001), *How Globalisation Improves Governance*, Technical Papers No. 181, OECD Development Centre, Paris.

BOURGUIGNON, F. AND C. MORRISSON (1989), *External Trade and Income Distribution*, Development Centre Studies, OECD, Paris.

BOURGUIGNON, F. AND C. MORRISSON (1990), "Income Distribution, Development and Foreign Trade: A Cross–sectional Analysis", *European Economic Review*, pp. 1113–32.

CHEMINGUI, M. AND S. DESSUS (1999), *La libéralisation de l'agriculture tunisienne et l'Union européenne : une vue prospective*, Document techniques No. 144, OECD Development Centre, Paris.

COLLADO, J., D. ROLAND–HOLST AND D. VAN DER MENSBRUGGHE (1995), "Latin American Employment Prospects in a More Liberal Trading Environment", *in* TURNHAM, D., C. FOY AND G. LARRAÍN (eds.).

DESSUS, S., J. DEVLIN AND R. SAFADI, eds (2001), *Towards Arab and Euro–Med Regional Integration*, Development Centre Seminars, OECD, Paris.

DESSUS, S., K. FUKASAKU AND R. SAFADI (1999), "Multilateral Tariff Liberalisation and the Developing Countries", Policy Brief No. 18, OECD Development Centre, Paris.

DOLLAR, D. (1992), "Outward–oriented Developing Economies Really Do Grow More Rapidly: Evidence from 95 LDCs, 1976–85", Economic Development and Cultural Change, pp. 523–544.

EDWARDS, S. (1993), "Openness, Trade Liberalization, and Growth in Developing Countries", *Journal of Economic Literature*, 31(3), September, pp. 1358–1393.

EDWARDS, S. (1998), "Openness, Productivity and Growth: What Do We Really Know?", *Economic Journal* 108, March, pp. 383–398.

FRANÇOIS, J., B. MCDONALD AND H. NORDSTRÖM (1996), "A User"s Guide to Uruguay Round Assessments", CEPR Discussion Paper no. 1410, Centre for Economic Policy Research, London, http://www.cepr.org/pubs/dps/DP1410.asp.

GOLDIN, I., O. KNUDSEN AND D. VAN DER MENSBRUGGHE (1993), *Trade Liberalisation: Global Economic Implications,* Development Centre Seminars, OECD Paris.

GOLDIN, I. AND D. VAN DER MENSBRUGGHE (1993), "Trade Liberalisation: What's at Stake?", Policy Brief No. 5, OECD Development Centre, Paris.

LAWRENCE, R. (1996), *Single World, Divided Nations?,* published by the OECD Development Centre and the Brookings Institution Press, Paris and Washington, D.C.

LEE, H. AND D. ROLAND–HOLST (1994), *Trade Liberalization and Employment Linkages in the Pacific Basin,* Technical Papers No. 94, OECD Development Centre, Paris.

LITTLE, I., T. SCITOWSKY AND M. SCOTT (1970), *Industry and Trade in Some Developing Countries,* Oxford University Press, Oxford.

LÖFGREN, H., M. EL–SAID AND S. ROBINSON (2001), "Trade Liberalisation and the Poor: A Dynamic Rural–Urban General Equilibrium Model of Morocco", pp. 129-146 *in* DESSUS, S., J. DEVLIN ET R. SAFADI (eds.), *op. cit.*

MADDISON, A. (1995), *Monitoring the World Economy 1820–1992,* Development Centre Studies, OECD, Paris.

MADDISON, A. (2001), *The World Economy: A Millennial Perspective,* Development Centre Studies, OECD, Paris.

MCCULLOCH, N., A. WINTERS AND X. CIRERA (2001), *Trade Liberalization and Poverty: A Handbook,* CEPR, London.

MORRISSON, C. (1991), *Adjustment and Equity in Morocco,* "Adjustment and Equity in Developing Countries" series, Development Centre Studies, OECD, Paris.

O'CONNOR, D. and M. LUNATI (1999), *Economic Opening and the Demand for Skills in Developing Countries,* Technical Papers No. 149, OECD Development Centre, Paris.

SACHS, J. AND A. WARNER (1995), "Economic Reform and the Process of Global Integration", *Brookings Papers on Economic Activity,* 1995:1, pp. 1–118.

THORP, R. (2001), *An Economic History of 20th Century Latin America, Vol. 2: Latin America in the 1930s: The Role of the Periphery in World Crisis,* St Martin's Press.

TURNHAM, D., C. FOY AND G. LARRAÍN (eds.) (1995), *Social Tensions, Job Creation and Economic Policy in Latin America,* Development Centre Seminars, OECD Paris.

WOOD, A. (1997), "Openness and Wage Inequality in Developing Countries: The Latin American Challenge to East Asian Conventional Wisdom", *The World Bank Economic Review,* Vol. 11, No. 1, January.

WORLD BANK (2002), *Globalization, Growth and Poverty,* Washington, D.C.

WORLD BANK (2000), *World Development Report: Attacking Poverty,* Washington, D.C.

WORLD BANK (1990), *World Development Report: Poverty,* Washington, D.C.

Chapter 7

The Changing Role of the Firm in Development

Charles P. Oman[1]

The emergence of corporate capitalism, and the concomitant transition from Adam Smith's "invisible hand" to Alfred Chandler's "visible hand", led by the rise of the giant limited–liability joint stock corporation, occurred rather suddenly in the final decades of the 19th century (Chandler, 1977, 1990). It did so in conjunction with a major wave of globalisation, then underway, which largely collapsed during the War and Depression years of 1914–1945. A new wave of globalisation followed the Second World War, driven, at the microeconomic level, by the spread of taylorist approaches to the organisation of activity in large corporations, both in OECD countries and in the "modern sector" of many developing countries. Marked by high productivity growth, this period saw many developing (and some OECD) countries seek actively to promote "national" firms and industries — and especially national industrialists — in a context of both spectacular growth and rising criticism of multinational corporations (MNCs).

The 1970s were a watershed. Productivity growth stagnated or slowed sharply in all OECD countries and "stagflation" (high or rising inflation and unemployment combined) then emerged in the United States and Europe (where it was called "eurosclerosis"). Market deregulation, notably in financial and other services, and monetary "shock treatment", were the principal US and European policy responses, in the late 1970s and early 1980s. The 1970s also witnessed a strengthening of developing countries' bargaining power *vis–à–vis* OECD–based MNCs, a growing use of "new forms" of international investment in developing countries, and an explosive growth of relocation of manufacturing to some developing countries (largely under the control of OECD–based firms) for markets in OECD countries.

The 1980s and 1990s have not only witnessed the emergence of a new wave of globalisation — the third in the last 100 years — and a resurgence of MNCs' bargaining power *vis–à–vis* developing countries. They have seen a sea change in government policies on MNCs, with many governments in both developing and OECD countries now competing actively to attract investment by such firms. These years have also witnessed fundamental change in the way leading firms organise production, and compete, worldwide. That change, and especially the difficulties of adapting to it, much more than globalisation or imports from developing countries, are in turn largely responsible for the relatively poor performance of OECD labour markets over the last two decades, compared to the 1950s and 1960s. That change also creates major challenges for developing countries.

Setting the Stage: the 1960s and 1970s

Following the Second World War, the proliferation of MNCs (at first mainly United States–based, later also European and Japanese) drove expanding investment and trade flows between OECD and developing countries as well as among OECD countries. Many of these firms looked to developing countries as growing markets for manufactured products.

On the receiving end of these investments, many developing countries had come to see industrialisation as a requisite of development. Market forces had already launched import–substituting industrialisation (ISI) in 1914–1945 in some of the larger and more advanced developing countries, notably Argentina and Brazil, when those countries were largely cut off from the industrialised countries that constituted both their export markets for primary products and their principal sources of manufactured goods. Following the Second World War, many more developing countries, throughout Latin America but also in Asia and subsequently in Africa, turned to ISI as a development strategy and pursued policies to promote it.

Some countries (e.g. India, Korea, Algeria) largely restricted inward investment by MNCs. Other countries, especially in Latin America, sought, on the contrary, both to attract MNCs and to enhance the contribution of their investment to the host economy. These countries widely used regulations or "performance requirements", notably with respect to MNCs' foreign–exchange contribution (or cost) to the local economy, and their contribution to technology transfers and other "linkages" with local industrialists (Blomström, 1989; Kokko, 1994). While an unintended consequence could have been to reduce the net inflow of investment, there is little evidence of such an effect — perhaps because many developing countries that sought to enhance MNCs' contribution to the local economy also offered incentives to attract their investment (Root and Ahmed, 1978). The MNCs nevertheless operated in local manufacturing behind protective import barriers, in relatively closed and often relatively small national markets widely plagued by weak inter–firm price–competition and low levels of productive efficiency and productivity growth. Also significant, though widely ignored, was the considerable overseas borrowing undertaken by MNCs' subsidiaries in Latin America especially during the 1970s — borrowing that appears to have contributed significantly to the build up of debt that eventually led, in 1982, to the emergence of the debt crisis (Guimaraes et al., 1982)[2].

Export–oriented industrialisation was subsequently pursued by a number of developing countries. Beyond their avoidance of ISI's marked policy bias against manufactured exports, the greater success of these strategies would owe much to the rapid growth of moves by OECD–based firms to relocate manufacturing production destined for consumers in OECD countries to low–wage production sites in some developing countries. Faced at home, especially during the 1970s, with growing rigidities in their taylorist systems of production (rigidities that slowed productivity growth and squeezed profits), a growing number of Japanese and US firms, then some European (especially German) firms, moved to relocate relatively labour–intensive products (e.g. clothing) or segments of production (e.g. assembly and testing of semi–conductors) destined for consumers in high–wage markets — mainly the United States, and later in Europe — to low–wage production or assembly sites "offshore" in some developing countries[3]. The manufacturing export success of several of the latter in turn led the OECD, in 1979, to call for "positive structural adjustment" in its Member countries — then suffering from "stagflation" and "eurosclerosis" — in a study that coined the term "NICs" (newly industrialising countries) in reference to South Korea, Chinese Taipei, Hong Kong, Singapore, Brazil and Mexico (OECD, 1979).

A further result of the growing difficulties of ISI, particularly from the late 1960s and early 1970s, was growing (often vociferous) debate on the role or impact of MNCs in the economy hosting their investment (Servan–Schreiber, 1967; Vernon, 1971; Lall and Streeten, 1977). That debate gave political impulse, at the international level, to the creation in 1975 of the United Nations Centre on Transnational Corporations and to the adoption in 1976 of the OECD Guidelines for Multinational Enterprises (amended in 2001). At the national level, those concerns led many developing countries to increase policy restraints on MNCs[4] and to adopt policies favouring investments in which local firms owned a majority of the equity — including joint ventures, international licensing and sub–contracting agreements, and other contractual arrangements between local and foreign firms (Oman, 1984*a*, 1984*b*, 1989).

Subsequent analysis of these phenomena — dubbed "new forms" of international investment (NFI) — showed that they were widely used in the dynamic East Asian NICs and ASEAN countries. In this region, their rapid growth benefited from a strong propensity by Japanese firms operating in industries undergoing restructuring at home to employ NFI to relocate production to developing countries — including for export to the US market (Ozawa, 1984; Kojima and Ozawa, 1985; Lim and Pang, 1991). In Latin America (where accumulated foreign direct investment (FDI) in manufacturing was considerably greater than in Asia), NFI tended more to be oriented to serving the local market (Peres Nuñez, 1990*a*; Fritsch and Franco, 1991).

The 1970s thus also witnessed a relative strengthening of the bargaining power of developing countries *vis-à-vis* foreign investors — as reflected both in the sustained growth of their FDI inflows despite growing restrictions and regulations, and in the even more rapid growth of NFI. Several factors contributed to that strengthening. One was the marked slowdown in productivity growth and income growth in the OECD countries, coupled with the stronger overall growth of income and investment demand in the developing countries, during that decade. Also important were the oil-price shocks and the role played by the OPEC countries as suppliers of vast sums of capital to international financial markets. The latter was in turn central to a third, and probably the single most important, factor: the low — sometimes negative — real interest rates in international financial markets during much of the 1970s.

Many developing-country governments promoted NFI over traditional (wholly or majority foreign-owned) FDI because — rightly or wrongly — they saw NFI as means of strengthening the local business class, and of enhancing host-country control over production and accumulation. Some also viewed NFI as means to circumvent or reduce the perceived and often feared oligopolistic powers of MNCs, which they saw as embodied in FDI. Moreover, for many, the abundance and low cost of finance in international financial markets meant not only that international borrowing was a politically expedient move on the domestic front. It was also cheaper and easier to obtain foreign loans for major investment projects, and to rely more on NFI to obtain non-financial investment resources (notably technology) from abroad, than to negotiate with MNCs over the terms of new inflows of traditional FDI (Oman, 1986).

Yet a growing number of OECD-based MNCs were discovering they could use NFI to shift much of the normal commercial risk (in addition to the political risk) associated with investment projects in developing countries to their host-country business associates, or to local and/or international lending agencies. They could often maintain their profits through a high degree of effective control over such investment projects, notably via their control over the supply of technological or other key intangible assets to the projects. Just as the separation of ownership from control in large corporations at home had long made it possible for managers effectively to control corporate resources without owning them, in other words, so were OECD-based corporate managers increasingly finding it possible, via NFI, effectively to control investment projects in developing countries with little or no ownership of equity in those projects. In doing so, many were also able to shift significant business risks to local firms and/or to suppliers of finance, and thus actually to increase their financial leverage over the non-financial assets they supplied to developing countries via NFI.

A Swing of the Pendulum: the 1980s and 1990s

The situation changed markedly in the 1980s, and with it the focus of policy debates. Contributing to this change in the early 1980s were the dramatic increase in real interest rates (induced by the US Federal Reserve's use of monetary "shock treatment" to break the back of inflation of the dollar) and, from 1982, the onset of the debt crisis, the virtual disappearance of voluntary bank lending to developing countries, and relatively sustained economic growth in the OECD countries (which combined with slowed growth in many developing countries to reduce or reverse the growth–rate differential that had favoured the latter during the 1970s). Also important was the decline in commodity prices, including the 1986 drop in oil prices. Among the consequences were the undermining of the international debt–financed approach to industrialisation and of the important vestiges of ISI that remained in the developing world, and the strengthening of the relative bargaining power of MNCs *vis–à–vis* host countries. For many developing countries, the depth and severity of the debt problem became such that they felt they could no longer afford the "luxury" of trying to promote the development of locally owned firms through NFI. What they needed above all was investment. Many saw the financial component of the traditional FDI "package" as particularly important.

This new perception of the advantages of FDI was reinforced in many developing countries, from the 1980s, by a perception that the previously feared oligopolistic bargaining and rent–extracting powers of MNCs rather paled in comparison with the quasi–monopolistic bargaining and foreign–exchange–extracting powers of the international financial community. Experience with NFI also showed that while NFI could contribute to industrial development, they were no panacea: host countries often assumed major financial risks, but continued to depend heavily on MNCs for access to technology and to world export markets.

Sustained growth of the OECD economies, and the generally pro–cyclical behaviour of FDI flows (Turner, 1991), help explain both the phenomenal growth of global FDI flows that has emerged since 1985 and the OECD countries' major share of global inflows, as well as Asia's greater share (for the first time) of the flows going to developing countries (Fritsch and Franco, 1991; Peres Nuñez, 1990a, Lim and Pang, 1991). In parallel, the rapid growth of export–oriented manufacturing FDI and NFI in developing countries to serve consumers in OECD countries, noted earlier, persuaded some observers that a "new international division of labour" was emerging. They believed an ever growing share of global manufacturing would relocate, largely under the control of OECD–based MNCs, to low–wage production sites in developing countries (Fröbel *et al.*, 1980).

117

From the early 1980s, profound balance–of–payments problems induced a rapidly growing number of developing countries to pursue industrialisation strategies based on that view. They were generally encouraged to do so by the multilateral development lending agencies as well. The 1980s thus witnessed a proliferation of moves to eliminate anti–export policy biases, set up export–processing zones, etc., in developing countries seeking to attract export–oriented manufacturing FDI. At the same time, popular concerns began to grow in OECD countries that "globalisation" was siphoning off jobs to low–wage production sites in the developing world.

However, as this policy re–orientation was gaining momentum in the developing world, the dynamics of competition changed in the OECD countries. Several factors converged to give impulse to this change. Particularly important were *a)* the rapid development and diffusion, from the late–1970s, of the new microelectronics–based information and communications technologies, *b)* the coming–of–age of a highly flexible post–taylorist system of industrial organisation (variously called "lean" production or "flexible specialisation"[5]) whose markedly superior capacity to take profitable advantage of the new technologies, compared to that of taylorist organisations, began to drive global competition, and *c)* the US and European policy responses to stagflation (Oman, 1994, 1996*a*, 2000*b*). Combined, they gave strong impulse to the new wave of globalisation.

Equally visible, from the mid–1980s, was the emergence of a new wave of *regionalisation,* both de facto (e.g. in the Pacific region) and de jure (e.g. Europe's Single Market programme — which can be understood as continental Europe's response to US and British deregulation — followed by NAFTA, Mercosur, AFTA, etc.). Driving the renewed trend towards regional integration, at the microeconomic level, were two partially contradictory sets of pressures. On one hand, significant increases in the size of firms' fixed costs (e.g. expenditures on R&D, on global advertising, on global marketing) as a share of firms' total operating costs, and the riskiness of R&D expenditures, pushed firms to seek to spread those costs over larger markets. Yet, on the other hand, the considerably greater importance for flexible "lean" producers, than for taylorist firms, of physical proximity, both with suppliers (as in the case of "just in time" systems) and with customers ("think global, act local"), meant that firms tended to develop production networks, internationally as well as inside countries, much more within each of the major regions — Asia, the Americas, greater Europe (including central and eastern Europe, perhaps also North Africa) — than between those regions. Reinforcing the trend towards regionalisation were also the size and volatility of exchange–rate fluctuations among the major currencies, which induced many globally competitive firms to seek more closely to match financial outlays and revenues in each of the major currency areas.

As firms have developed international sourcing networks for parts, intermediate goods and services, many have thus tended — more than is commonly perceived — to develop those networks within each of the major regions, i.e., to develop them intra–regionally rather than inter–regionally. While it makes empirical sense to speak today of a globalisation of inter–firm competition, and of many of the things corporations do (such as creating and managing information systems, managing financial flows, etc.), when it comes to the internationalisation of physical production per se, it is more accurate to speak of a trend towards regionalisation (Wells, 1992). Since the mid–1980s, this trend has also been an important factor, at the microeconomic level, in driving the emergence of new or strengthened regional integration agreements among governments.

The new regionalisation led in turn to considerable debate over the relationship between globalisation and regionalisation, and its policy implications for developing as well as for OECD countries (Peres Nuñez, 1990b; Lawrence, 1991; Drobnick, 1992; Fishlow and Haggard, 1992; Fritsch, 1992; Fukasaku, 1992; Gee, 1992; Han, 1992; Lincoln, 1992; Page, 1992; Stopford, 1992; Mytelka, 1994). Analysis focused on the microeconomic forces that drive globalisation, notably the competitive strength of flexible post–taylorist firms, and the crisis of taylorist firms. This drew attention to the potential value of regionalisation as a policy means, both *a)* to help weaken the resistance to needed change by powerfully entrenched interest groups within nations, and *b)* to enhance policy stability and credibility needed, among other reasons, to help attract productive long–term corporate investment. It also pointed up the importance for governments to pursue policies that ensure globalisation and regionalisation tend to be mutually reinforcing, and that strengthen rather than weaken social cohesion along with economic efficiency.

The capacity of developing countries to build modern industry and compete in world markets was shown by Lall (1990) to depend in part on their ability to apply new technologies. This research established a framework to assess relative country performances — in terms of promoting technology–oriented industrial development — by policy choices affecting trade, competition and intellectual property rights, capital and labour markets, science and technology programmes and, most importantly, human capital development. It also showed how successful technological and industrial development strategies in developing nations can have direct consequences for industrial restructuring in OECD countries, reinforcing other OECD work calling for positive structural adjustment in OECD Member countries.

Separate studies focused on the challenge of new technologies for newly industrialising economies (Ernst and O'Connor, 1989), on the significance of new technologies for enterprise development in Africa (Tiffin et al., 1992), on their impact in mining and food industries in developing countries (Bomsel et al., 1990; Rama, 1992), on the diffusion of advanced telecommunications in developing countries (Antonelli, 1991), and on the role of competition and innovation in developing industrial competitiveness in developing countries (Mytelka, 1999). This research pointed up important windows of opportunity for all categories of developing countries, including in sub–Saharan Africa, as well as the importance of addressing the question of what sort of intellectual property regime they should adopt and enforce. It also drew attention to a) the importance of a country's overall macroeconomic environment for successful technology diffusion in the country, and the destructive inflationary effects of foreign debt and trade deficits that discourage long–term investment by domestic as well as foreign firms in productivity–enhancing new technologies; b) the different challenges faced by countries that have large domestic markets and those that do not, including that of fomenting more trade among developing countries (e.g. through deeper regional integration) and of responding to trade protection by OECD countries; c) the need for domestic firms as well as governments to find the right balance between building long–term relationships with particular technology suppliers and avoiding the vulnerability that comes with over–reliance on a single or few key sources of technology; and d) the appropriate role for governments in helping small and medium–size firms to realise economies of scale and scope, for example in R&D, basic support services, marketing and distribution. Even in countries with a high concentration of industrial activity in a few very large firms, for example, clusters of dynamic and flexible smaller firms are generally crucial for the large firms to have access to a versatile domestic supplier network which they need for building, and sustaining, competitiveness in global markets.

Effects of Globalisation

Much attention has also focused in recent years on two inter–related debates. One is over the extent to which the relocation of manufacturing to developing countries contributes significantly to labour–market problems in OECD countries (especially high unemployment in Europe, and stagnant wages, growing numbers of working poor and rising inequality in the United States). This is an issue to which the OECD has given much attention (OECD, 1994, 1995). The other debate concerns the extent and effects of policy–based competition among governments to attract FDI.

Research on the first issue found that the relocation of production for OECD consumers to developing countries cannot explain much of the shift away from unskilled jobs in the demand for labour in OECD countries — a shift that is largely responsible for the relatively poor performance of OECD labour markets over the last two decades (compared to the postwar period), and is in turn blamed by many on "globalisation". The reason it cannot is that OECD countries' trade with developing countries has had little impact on OECD labour–market performances compared to the effects of change in technology and in the dominant business model (i.e. the shift from taylorist to more flexible post–taylorist organisations by the leading competitors) in the OECD countries themselves (Lawrence, 1996; see however Wood, 1995). Contrary to the "new international division of labour" thesis, to which many anti–globalisation activists seem to subscribe, moreover, the relocation "offshore" of production for high–wage markets by OECD–based firms — relocation which accelerated through the 1970s and into the early 1980s as many firms in OECD countries sought international taylorist solutions to growing rigidities in their taylorist production organisations at home — has in fact decelerated since the late 1980s, with the formidable rise in competitive strength of "lean" organisations. Many large taylorist "dinosaurs" (firms, and other large bureaucracies, which still account for significant shares of output and employment) in OECD countries have nevertheless faced major difficulties to become effective, dynamic, lean organisations, owing notably to resistance to change (often starting with top management) in the firms themselves. Much more than trade with developing countries, those difficulties and resistance to change within taylorist firms go far to explain OECD countries' relatively poor labour–market performance over the last two decades (Oman, 1999, 2000*b*).

Analysis of competition among governments to attract FDI has in turn spotlighted the importance of sub–national governments (especially state or provincial governments in federal countries, also local and municipal governments) as active competitors for FDI, internationally as well as domestically, and confirmed that the competition has grown markedly since the mid–1980s in OECD and developing countries alike (Oman, 2000a). Little evidence has been found of actual (downward) movement in governments' de facto or de jure standards of protection either of the environment or of workers' rights to organise and bargain collectively, as a result of the competition. The downward pressure exerted on those standards by the competition, and policy makers' fear of losing investment to competing jurisdictions, may still, of course, prevent them from rising to socially or economically optimal levels.

Significant evidence has been found, on the other hand, of bidding wars among governments using discretionary fiscal and financial incentives to try to attract major FDI projects. The direct and especially the indirect costs of governments' use of such discretionary incentives — costs that are difficult to measure, but are potentially large especially because an incentive system's lack of transparency and public accountability can spread through government like an infectious disease, and counteract the development of a modern state and competitive markets — point to significant potential benefits of effective FDI policy co–ordination among governments to avoid such bidding wars. That such competition effectively occurs among governments largely within regions, and that enhanced regional integration can serve in its own right as an effective means to attract FDI, point to significant potential benefits of enhanced FDI policy co–ordination especially among governments within a region (Oman, 2001*b*).

Emerging Challenges

The shift in bargaining power from governments to MNCs since the 1980s, reflected in and reinforced by the growth in competition to attract FDI during the 1990s, and the attention drawn by the 1997–1998 Asian financial crisis to "crony capitalism", have in turn awakened interest in corporate governance in developing countries (OECD, 1999, 2001; Oman, 2001a). Fanning this interest has also been the significant increase in domestic corporations' demand for extra–firm sources of finance in developing countries. Firms in those countries have seen their need for extra–firm sources of finance (as distinct from reinvested earnings) grow substantially, owing to the increased investments they must make in tangible and intangible assets to be able to compete in the context of accelerated change that characterises globalisation today. This increase in firms' demand for extra–firm finance has occurred, moreover, precisely at a time when the national development banks and other traditional — largely state–directed — sources of investment finance in developing countries are no longer able to supply that finance. The significant moves to deregulate markets and liberalise trade and investment policy regimes in developing countries have increased those demands as well, by increasing the competitive pressures on local firms.

Sound corporate governance not only helps to increase the flow and lower the cost of the financial capital that firms in developing countries need to finance their investments in real assets (tangible and intangible). It can significantly enhance corporate performance in the real economy, and thus help increase long–term productivity growth in developing countries. An important reason is the potential for improved corporate governance to constrain the actions of distributional cartels, reflected in ubiquitous self–dealing and rent–seeking behaviour by corporate insiders in a context of clientelistic relationship–based systems of local governance. In the absence of adequate corporate governance, those actions can create significant rigidities and lead both to major wastages of real investment resources and to excessive volatility. By helping to constrain self–dealing and rent–seeking behaviour, and to transform predominantly relationship–based into more rules–based systems of governance, improved corporate governance has a vital role to play in many developing countries today.

Close attention must also be given to sector–specific regulatory reform (see also Chapter 8) and to competition policy (Oman, 1996*b*). The importance of the latter, and the need to avoid regulatory capture by powerful corporate insiders, mean that sound corporate governance also requires sound political governance, and vice–versa (Oman, 2001a). The role of the firm as the locus of productivity growth in society, and the importance of healthy inter–firm price competition in driving that growth, mean that, more than ever, the firm is at the heart of development.

Notes

1.   Hans Christiansen, of the OECD's Directorate for Financial, Fiscal, and Enterprise Affairs, along with the Development Centre's Koji Miyamoto and the authors of the other chapters in this volume provided valuable comments on a draft of this chapter (the usual caveat applies).

2.   MNCs' use of connected lending to circumvent host–country restrictions on profit remittances is reportedly a "hot" policy issue in some developing countries today, notably in Africa.

3.   The spread and rapid development of taylorist approaches to the organisation of mass production in the OECD countries drove the phenomenal growth of productivity in those countries during the 1950s and 1960s, but contributed simultaneously to a building up of bureaucratic rigidities in production whose accumulation over time finally led, in the 1970s, to a dramatic slowdown of productivity growth. Stagnant productivity growth and excessive rigidities led in turn to the emergence of stagflation in North America and Europe in the latter half of the 1970s. Starting already in the late 1960s, and accelerating through the 1970s, many OECD–based firms pursued what can be understood as a taylorist response to the building crisis in taylorist production: they internationalised the logic of taylorist production by relocating labour–intensive parts of production destined for OECD consumers "offshore", in low–wage developing countries. Other OECD–based firms, however, responded to those rigidities by developing more flexible, post–taylorist, "lean" approaches to the organisation of production at home (Piore and Sabel, 1984; Best, 1990; Oman, 1994, 1996a; see also footnote 5).

4.   These commonly included the demarcation of sectors or specific industries where FDI was forbidden or restricted, limitations on MNCs' remittances abroad of profits and royalties, restrictions of foreign takeovers of local firms, local–integration and/or export–performance requirements on MNCs' subsidiaries, the establishment of government boards for screening and registering FDI, and restrictions of foreign equity ownership to minority shares (including the Andean Pact's 1968 "Decision 24" to limit foreign ownership on investments in all member countries to minority equity positions). See for example Oman, 1993.

5. Even before the end of the 1970s, not all OECD–based firms that sought to overcome the growing rigidities of taylorism turned to low–wage production sites "offshore" in developing countries. Some succeeded, over time, in developing significantly more flexible forms of organising production at home. They achieved higher productivity levels and greater responsiveness to market demands notably by: *a)* integrating "thinking" and "doing" in production (thereby also eliminating many layers of middle management that are dysfunctional to information flow); *b)* organising workers into small teams and emphasising teamwork in order to avoid the compartmentalisation of workers and loss of potential synergies and group learning that can result from excessive specialisation (as often occurs in taylorist organisations); and *c)* emphasising continuous innovation in the organisation of production, as well as in products and product features. See for example Piore and Sabel, 1984; Best, 1990; Womack, *et al.*, 1990; and Alcorta, 1998.

Bibliography

ALCORTA, L. (1998), *Flexible Automation in Developing Countries: The Impact on Scale and Scope and the Implications for Location of Production*, Routledge in assoc. with UNU Press, London and New York.

ANTONELLI, C. (1991), *The Diffusion of Advanced Telecommunications in Developing Countries*, Development Centre Studies, OECD, Paris.

BEST, M. (1990), *The New Competition: Institutions of Industrial Restructuring*, Harvard University Press, Cambridge.

BLOMSTRÖM, M. (1989), *Foreign Investment and Spillovers*, Routledge, London and New York.

BOMSEL, O., WITH I. MARQUÈS, D. NDIAYE AND P. DE SA (1990), *Mining and Metallurgy Investment in the Third World*, OECD Development Centre, Paris.

BRADFORD, C. (1993), *Mobilising International Investment for Latin America*, Development Centre Seminars, OECD and the Inter–American Development Bank, Paris.

CHANDLER, A. (1990), *Scale and Scope: The Dynamics of Industrial Capitalism*, Harvard University Press, Cambridge, Mass. and London.

CHANDLER, A. (1977), *The Visible Hand: The Management Revolution in American Business*, Harvard University Press, Cambridge, Mass., and London.

DROBNICK, R. (1992), *Economic Integration in the Pacific*, Technical Papers No. 65, OECD Development Centre, Paris.

ERNST, D. AND D. O'CONNOR (1989), *Technology and Global Competition: The Challenge for Newly Industrialising Economies*, OECD Development Centre, Paris.

FISHLOW, A. AND S. HAGGARD (1992), *The United States and the Regionalisation of the World Economy*, Development Centre Document, OECD Development Centre, Paris.

FRITSCH, W. (1992), *Latin America in a Changing Global Environment*, Technical Papers No. 66, OECD Development Centre, Paris.

FRITSCH, W. AND G. FRANCO (1991), *Foreign Direct Investment in Brazil*, Development Centre Studies, OECD, Paris.

FRÖBEL, F., J. HEINRICHES AND O. KREYE (1980), *The New International Division of Labour,* Cambridge University Press, Cambridge.

FUKASAKU, K. (1992), *Economic Regionalisation and Intra–Industry Trade: Pacific–Asian Perspectives,* Technical Papers No. 53, OECD Development Centre, Paris.

GEE, S. (1992), *Taiwanese Corporations in Globalisation and Regionalisation,* Technical Papers No. 61, OECD Development Centre, Paris.

GUIMARAES, E., P. MALAN AND J. TAVARES (1982), *The New Forms of Investment in Brazil,* OECD Development Centre, Paris.

HAN, S.T. (1992), *European Integration: The Impact on Asian Newly Industrialising Economies,* Development Centre Document, OECD Development Centre, Paris.

KOJIMA, K. AND T. OZAWA (1985), *Japan's General Trading Companies: Merchants of Economic Development,* Development Centre Studies, OECD, Paris.

KOKKO, A. (1994), "Technology, Market Characteristics, and Spillovers"? in *Journal of Development Economics,* 43.

LALL, S. (1990), *Building Industrial Competitiveness in Developing Countries,* OECD Development Centre, Paris.

LALL, S. AND P. STREETEN (1977), *Foreign Investment, Transnationals and Developing Countries,* MacMillan, London.

LAWRENCE, R. (1996), *Single World, Divided Nations? International Trade and OECD Labor Markets,* OECD Development Centre and Brookings Press, Paris and Washington, D.C.

LAWRENCE, R. (1991), *Scenarios for the World Trading System and Their Implication for Developing Countries,* Technical Papers No. 47, OECD Development Centre, Paris.

LIM, L. AND E.F. PANG (1991), *Foreign Direct Investment and Industrialisation in Malaysia, Singapore, Taiwan and Thailand,* Development Centre Studies, OECD, Paris.

LINCOLN, E. (1992), *Japan's Rapidly Emerging Strategy Towards Asia,* Technical Papers No. 58, OECD Development Centre, Paris.

MYTELKA, L. (1999), *Competition, Innovation and Competitiveness in Developing Countries,* Development Centre Studies, OECD, Paris.

MYTELKA, L. (ed.) (1994), *South–South Co–operation in a Global Perspective,* Development Centre Document, OECD Development Centre, Paris.

OECD (forthcoming), *Foreign Direct Investment for Development: Maximising Benefits, Minimising Costs,* OECD, Paris.

OECD Global Forum on International Investment (2002), *New Horizons for Foreign Direct Investment,* OECD, Paris

OECD (2001), *Corporate Governance in Asia: A Comparative Perspective,* OECD, Paris.

OECD (1999), *OECD Principles of Corporate Governance,* OECD, Paris.

OECD (1996), *Competition Policy: 1994 Workshop with the Dynamic Non–Member Economies,* OECD, Paris

OECD (1995), *Linkages: OECD and Major Developing Countries,* OECD, Paris.

OECD (1994), *The OECD Jobs Study,* OECD, Paris.

OECD (1979), *The Impact of the Newly Industrialising Countries on Production and Trade in Manufactures,* OECD, Paris.

OECD (1976, revised 2001), "Guidelines for Multinational Enterprises", OECD, Paris.

OMAN, C. (2001a), *Corporate Governance and National Development,* Technical Papers No. 180, OECD Development Centre, Paris.

OMAN, C. (2001b), "The Perils of Competition for Foreign Direct Investment", *in Foreign Direct Investment Versus Other Flows to Latin America,* Development Centre Seminars, OECD, Paris.

OMAN, C. (2000a), *Policy Competition for Foreign Direct Investment: A Study of Competition among Governments to Attract FDI,* Development Centre Studies, OECD Paris.

OMAN, C. (2000b), "The Business Model of the New Economy" in Economic Reform Today, No. 1, Center for International Private Enterprise, Washington, D.C.

OMAN, C. (1999), "Globalisation, Regionalisation and Inequality", *in* A. HURRELL AND N. WOODS (eds.) *Inequality, Globalization, and World Politics,* Oxford University Press, Oxford and New York.

OMAN, C. (1996a), *The Policy Challenges of Globalisation and Regionalisation,* Policy Brief No. 11, OECD Development Centre, Paris.

OMAN, C. (1996b), "The Contribution of Competition Policy in Economic Development" *in* OECD (1996).

OMAN, C. (1994), *Globalisation and Regionalisation: The Challenge for Developing Countries,* Development Centre Studies, OECD, Paris.

OMAN, C. (1993), "Trends in Global FDI and Latin America", *in* C. BRADFORD (ed.).

OMAN, C., D. BROOKS AND C. FOY (eds.) (1997), *Investing in Asia,* Development Centre Seminars, OECD, Paris.

OMAN, C. (1986), "New Forms of Investment in Developing Countries", *in* T. MORAN *et al., Investing in Development: New Roles for Private Capital?,* Overseas Development Council, Washington, D.C.

OMAN, C. (1984a), *New Forms of International Investment in Developing Countries,* Development Centre Studies, OECD, Paris.

OMAN, C. (ed.) (1984b), *New Forms of International Investment in Developing Countries: The National Perspective,* Development Centre Seminars, OECD, Paris.

OMAN, C. (with the collaboration of François Chesnais, Joseph Pelzman and Ruth Rama) (1989), *New Forms of Investment in Developing Country Industries: Mining, Petrochemicals, Automobiles, Textiles, Food,* Development Centre Studies, OECD, Paris.

OZAWA, T. (1984), "Japan's Revealed Preference for the New Forms of Investment" *in* C. Oman (ed.) (1984*b*).

PAGE, S. (1992), *Some Implications of Europe 1992 for Developing Countries,* Technical Papers No. 60, OECD Development Centre, Paris.

PERES NUÑEZ, W. (1990*a*), *Foreign Direct Investment and Industrial Development in Mexico,* Development Centre Studies, OECD, Paris.

PERES NUÑEZ, W. (1990*b*), *From Globalization to Regionalization: The Mexican Case,* Technical Papers No. 24, OECD Development Centre, Paris.

PIORE, M.J. AND C.F. SABEL (1984), *The Second Industrial Divide: Possibilities for Prosperity,* Basic Books, New York.

RAMA, R. (1992), *Investing in Food,* Development Centre Studies, OECD, Paris.

ROOT, F. AND A. AHMED (1978), "The Influence of Policy Instruments in Manufacturing Direct Investment in Developing Countries" *in Journal of International Business Studies,* Vol. 9, Winter.

SERVAN–SCHREIBER, J.J. (1967), *Le défi américain,* Denoël, Paris.

STOPFORD, J. (1992), *Offensive and Defensive Responses by European Multinationals to a World of Trade Blocs,* Technical Papers No. 64, OECD Development Centre, Paris, May.

TIFFIN, S. AND F. OSOTIMEHIN, WITH R. SAUNDERS (1992), *New Technologies and Enterprise Development in Africa,* Development Centre Studies, OECD, Paris

TURNER, P. (1991), "Capital Flows in the 1980s", BIS Economic Papers No. 30, Bank for International Settlements, Basel, April.

VEIGA, P. DA MOTTA (1997), *L'industrie brésilienne dans la transition: Vers un nouveau modèle productif?,* Development Centre Document, OECD Development Centre, Paris.

VERNON, R. (1971), *Sovereignty at Bay: the Multinational Spread of U.S. Enterprises,* Basic Books, New York.

WELLS, L. (1992), *Conflict or Indifference: U.S. Multinationals in a World of Regional Trading Blocs,* Technical Papers No. 57, OECD Development Centre, Paris.

WOMACK, J., D.T. JONES AND D. ROOS (1990), *The Machine that Changed the World,* Rawson MacMillan, New York, 1990.

WOOD, A. (1995), *North–South Trade, Employment and Inequality,* Clarendon Press, Oxford.

Chapter 8

State–owned Enterprises in Development: Privatisation and Beyond

Andrea Goldstein[1]

State Ownership in Economic Development Policies

State ownership has characterised most market and, a *fortiori*, planning economies in the 20th century (Toninelli, 2000). Financial, strategic, political, and technological reasons have been advanced to justify either the nationalisation of existing private–sector firms or the ex *novo* creation of state–owned enterprises (SOEs) (Hanson, 1966). For a long time the links between state ownership and development appeared self–evident, as many governments in late industrialising and developing countries argued that only the public sector could overcome critical "bottlenecks" in terms of physical, financial, and human capital investments required by industrialisation. Different forms were adopted to organise the SOE sector, with OECD influences often proving important. The Italian model of state–owned holdings, very successful in the country's catch–up after the Second World War (Barca and Trento, 1997), proved particularly influential, for instance in Egypt (Waterbury,1992). Elsewhere, the desire of foreign donors and lenders to bypass the public administration, regarded as inefficient, led to the concentration of scarce human resources in a limited number of relatively autonomous SOEs. The establishment of some Brazilian SOEs was indeed suggested in the 1950s by the Joint Brazil–United States Economic Development Commission (Sikkink, 1991).

State ownership of utilities, for its part, has been justified on the grounds of technological conditions leading to natural monopolies, external economies, and diverging social and private discount rates. A further motive has been the desire to keep domestic control on monopoly rents produced exploiting non–renewable natural resources. On weaker economic grounds, SOEs have been established to build a coalition in support of new regimes and for different distributional aims — to make essential goods and services available, to create new jobs, to reduce

131

geographical concentration of economic power. They were also meant to ensure national independence in strategic industries, in particular in countries run by military regimes; avoid the danger of unpopular minorities' eventual control of the economy — such as the Lebanese in West Africa and the Chinese in Southeast Asia; and support the interests of ruling minorities in other countries — such as the Afrikaaner "white poors" and Afrikaans capital in South Africa under apartheid. A further explanation for the diffusion of state ownership in semi–peripheral countries, especially in Latin America, was advanced by the dependency literature. While accepting the primacy of private ownership, "bureaucratic–authoritarian regimes" considered that the role of the state had to go beyond that of a subsidiary character to that of supplying the complementary inputs to the process of private capital accumulation (Evans, 1978).

SOEs lack a clear–cut objective of profit maximisation, do not face the risk of bankruptcy, and the market for corporate control, because of the state's tight grip through majority stakes, cannot act as an adequate device for disciplining managers. In theory, this concentration of ownership in the hands of a single majority investor could have served to circumvent the collective action problem that impedes small, dispersed shareholders in listed companies from wielding efficient monitoring on corporate managers. This relative advantage of public ownership, however, has often been offset by agency problems stemming from the multiplicity of ties linking the government and ministries with specific competences, parliament, political parties, and the management of SOEs, all have different goals, and are possibly at cross–purposes. Moreover, SOEs' managers are often appointed for political reasons, rather than for their corporate skills. In the 1970s and 1980s, various studies attempted to compare public– and private–enterprise performance. On aggregate, in both OECD and non–OECD countries they found SOEs to be *ceteris paribus* less efficient than the private sector (Shirley and Walsh, 2001). The findings in this literature, while suggestive of the greater productive efficiency and profitability of private ownership, are not compelling. Most analyses focused almost exclusively on cross–sections of US companies operating in heavily regulated industries and, at any rate, "cost comparisons are rarely straightforward in the absence of a controlled experiment, and no such experiments exist for public enterprise" (Domberger and Piggott, 1994, p. 40).

More nuanced conclusions, indeed, emerge when examining the contribution of SOEs to the learning process of development countries' firms in catching up with the world technological frontier. This literature relies heavily on country–specific case studies and is rich in contextual detail, although aggregation and generalisation are inherently much more difficult. A nationalistic and highly–educated elite of bureaucrats, who made subsidisation contingent on the achievement of monitorable performance standards, devised a variety of subsidies in Asian countries such as Korea and Chinese Taipei (Amsden, 1989). One sector where this strategy created the economies of scale necessary to compete internationally was petrochemicals. In Korea, by buying equity stakes from foreign investors that had initially provided the technological know–how, SOEs set up large integrated complexes under single management (Chesnais and Kim, 1999). Although state ownership was not as widespread as in Latin America, one of the architects of that country's outstanding development trajectory, SaKong (1993, pp. 79–83), considered the high linkage that the public enterprise sector created to the rest of the economy and its substantial contribution to the nation's overall fixed capital formation as proof if its strategic importance for the economy as a whole.

Similarly, "it is doubtful that Brazil could have recorded such important economic successes in the 1965–80 period without the results achieved by the public sector enterprises" (Trebat, 1983, p. 9). Project execution capabilities were particularly important in Brazil's SOEs and public managers that mastered them often moved on to very successful careers in government or in the domestic private sector (Schneider, 1991). What little innovation activity took place in Brazil, expressed as research and development outlays, was also mostly undertaken by SOEs such as CVRD, Embraer, and Petrobras (Dahlman and Frischtak, 1993). Acknowledging these features does not mask the serious problems that plagued Brazilian SOEs — *in primis* the inability to generate the cash flows needed to keep investing in fixed assets and human capital. As the large SOE sector became associated with inflation, fiscal imbalances and slow economic growth, policy makers embarked in the second half of the 1990s on the then world's largest privatisation programme (Goldstein, 1999).

The Dynamics of Privatisation

Since the rise of oil prices in the 1970s, the whole post–war model of economic development has been heavily criticised, and SOEs have not been exempted from this swing in the ideological pendulum from the structuralist to the neo–liberal end. Summarising a major research programme on industrialisation in seven large developing countries, Little *et al.* (1970) noted that "investment decisions can be efficiently made only in the light of a detailed knowledge of the circumstances of each case, and central planners have not had access to the information which is really required. Nor have they had large enough or sufficiently expert staffs to process the information available" (p. 5). Very often SOEs had become crucial elements for playing patronage politics through jobs and the servicing of constituencies and the appropriateness of public management of productive units was put in doubt. For instance, in a thorough examination of conflicts in post–independence Chad, Azam and Morrisson (1999) conclude that allocating a disproportionate share of public resources to the southern regions to the detriment of the peoples of the Sahel and Tibesti was one the main causes.

SOEs were also found to have negative income distribution effects, to worsen budget and trade balances, and to divert resources from more essential social goals, such as education and health expenditures.

Over the past two decades, the initially timid progress recorded in some pioneering countries (United Kingdom, Chile, New Zealand) were matched and sometimes even surpassed by new countries joining the privatisation bandwagon, first in the developing world (Argentina, Mexico, Malaysia), then in Europe (France, Italy), and finally in transition economies[2]. Depending on the political, economic, and technological context, privatisations have been partial or full and different strategies have been used, including block sales, voucher plans, and initial public offers on the stock market (e.g. Bouin and Michalet,1991).

Yet, while a central issue in the debate for almost two decades, privatisation has been a rather restricted phenomenon from a quantitative point of view (Shirley, 1998). Selling SOEs is part of the political game: it requires the creation of supportive coalitions and it impacts on the distribution of power resources. Strong vested interests, such as organised labour, the military, parts of the urban bourgeoisie, and most economic groups, mount in defence of nationalisation. Moreover, privatisation is a typical example of a collective action situation: benefits are uncertain and far from immediate, actors more likely to appropriate them are widely dispersed, and beneficiaries of the status quo may then find it easier to organise an opposition than future beneficiaries to create a support group. Finally, in developing countries where capital markets are thin and scarcely organised, and where it is thus difficult to realise popular capitalism through public placing of SOEs, the potential of privatisation for coalition–building is rather remote.

In this respect it is very telling to observe that even in the two OECD democracies that "pioneered" privatisation, implementing this policy was not an explicit objective in the policy makers' electoral manifestos. British Conservatives were "unfavourably disposed towards the nationalised industries" but "the party placed little emphasis on the denationalisation and liberalisation proposals in the [1979] manifesto" (Galal et al., 1994, p. 43). In 1984, the New Zealand's "Labour Party stated unequivocally that it had 'no plans to sell off any publicly–owned concerns'" (Williams, 1990, p. 140). The case of Chile's radical conservative experiment is obviously different because the "seven modernisations", including SOE reform, were implemented by an authoritarian government that did not face the threat of losing power through elections. Even there "it was not clear at the time [of the *coup*] what type of change (restoration? revolution?) would be possible" (Foxley, 1983, p. 92). The priority assigned to privatisation (and to using for this purpose the resources that, even when politicians do not have to be elected, still have to be spent for implementing policies) resulted from the political leeway gained by the so–called "Chicago Boys", a group of economists expressing strong free market views (see Valdés, 1995 and the review by Barber ,1995).

In practice, the intrinsic allure of free market economics has proved less important a factor for the success of privatisations than more conjunctural conditions (Armijo, 1998). First, the nature and the seriousness of crisis deeply influence both the perceived need of radical changes and the central themes of the political debate. The tighter the fiscal constraint, and the greater the contribution of SOEs to the deficit, the quicker the recourse to divestiture to solve problems. The need for the financial support from international organisations and donors does indeed play a strong role in convincing governments to adopt privatisation, as shown for instance by Campbell White and Bhatia (1998) in the case of Africa. An important issue is therefore the choice of firms to be sold and the method of sale. Understanding the economic goals to be met through divestiture, in particular the choice between an immediate reduction of macroeconomic imbalances and the medium–term achievement of efficiency improvements by liberalisation and more effective regulation, is crucial. The least productive enterprises are harder to dispose of, which might make it necessary to concede easy terms well beyond a low price, when not eliminating them altogether. At the same time, countries in dire economic straits need quick "leading cases" to build their reputation *vis–à–vis* foreign investors. The choice has thus often been to start from the best managed and more profitable SOEs, such as telecommunications, at the risk of making learning mistakes in those very cases where state assets should be more coveted by international investors. Moreover, such industries present technological and tariff complexities, requiring sophisticated tools for asset valuation and regulation that developing countries seldom possess.

Timing and organisational structure also matter. New political incumbents have higher chances of implementing reforms, thanks not only to the "post–election honeymoon", but also because, according to the electoral cycle theory, there are fewer incentives to deter adopting risky and painful actions. Likewise, although the relationship between regimes and economic policies is indeterminate, being able to use emergency powers opens smoother roads on the reforms' path. "Insulated change teams" (Nelson, 1992) or "technopols" (Williamson, 1994 and Domínguez, 1997) are important, especially where governments came to power with the backing of the lower class and need to prove themselves credible in the face of international investors' fears.

Thirdly, given the short–term adjustment costs of economic reforms, it is necessary to introduce compensatory mechanisms. While scholarly attention has been focused on specific, targeted measures to face the reduction of fiscal subsidies to the poor, large business groups that dominate the industrial sector in most developing countries are hit by falling trade barriers, positive real interest rates, and more careful awarding of public credit. In order to win their support, some countervailing measures may be needed, such as setting low (relative to book value) prices (Schamis, 1999). More generally, privatisation can be used as a strategy to realign the institutional framework so as to privilege the aims of some goals over the competing aspirations of others (Feigenbaum and Henig,1994).

The Outcome of Privatisation

Studies of privatisation in developing economies reveal significant increases in profitability, operating efficiency, capital spending, output, and employment, which are usually greater in countries with higher *per capita* income (Boubakri and Cosset, 1998). In less developed regions, the statistical significance of profitability improvements is generally lower. A sample of 16 privatised firms in Africa suggests that efficiency, as well as output measured by real sales, decreased slightly but not significantly, while capital expenditures rose significantly in the post–privatisation period (Boubakri and Cosset, 2002). In general these results mirror those for OECD countries that also report very positive results in firms' performance (e.g. Meggison and Netter, 2001).

The evidence on the better productivity and profitability performance of privately–owned firms is generally compelling in competitive industries. Counterfactual analyses comparing the performance of private firms with their hypothetical performance had they remained public, or "natural experiments" in which a market is liberalised and some firms are privatised while other (similar) firms are not, also tend to confirm the conclusion that it is the combination of privatisation and product market competition that is associated with the best outcomes (Galal et al., 1994). It must be borne in mind, however, that factors such as the type of corporate control (insider, such as former public managers and/or employees, or outsider), the nature of monitoring mechanisms, and the structure of managers' incentives impinge on post–privatisation performance (Gönenç et al., 2001). In the case of transition economies, in particular, empirical tests of the relationship between enterprise performance and ownership generally refute the hypothesis that privatisation *per se* is associated with improved performance (Estrin and Rosevaer, 1999). Economic performance gains come only from "deep" privatisation, that is when change–of–title reforms occur once key institutional and agency–related reforms have exceeded certain threshold levels (Zinnes et al., 2001). The belief that mass privatisation, by providing powerful incentives for efficient restructuring, would release entrepreneurial endeavours has also proved naive. The chances of fostering entrepreneurship appear greater in a gradualist environment permitting negotiated solutions to restructuring as opposed to market–driven reforms (Spicer et al., 2000).

If privatisation is a technical, albeit qualified, success why then does it remain widely and increasingly unpopular? Recent polls in countries such as Brazil and South Africa show that most people perceive divestiture policies to be fundamentally unfair, both in conception and execution[3]. Although the findings in this area are affected by data limitations, Birsdall and Nellis (2002) conclude that, at least in the short run and especially in transition economies, most divestiture programmes have worsened assets and income distribution. This conclusion appears to be rather robust in the case of banks, oil companies, and other natural resource producers. In electricity and telecommunications, on the other hand, the poor have tended to benefit from much greater access. The case of Bolivia, for instance, suggests that capitalisation and regulation, and the liberalisation of the utilities sector more generally, succeeded both in attracting foreign investment and increasing access to basic services in urban areas (Barja and Urquiola, 2001). In terms of connection, service expansion in the urban areas — although not in rural ones — did not bypass the poor.

The Requirements of Regulatory Capitalism

Utilities regulation

In the hitherto natural monopolies that constituted the core of public enterprises (telecoms, energy, water and transport), fast technological advances have substantially weakened the argument that public ownership of integrated monopolies is necessary to ensure investment growth, service quality and price declines in real terms. The substitution of private for public ownership, however, has been accompanied by the emergence of new regulatory challenges as policy makers try to prevent the new private owners from simply pocketing monopoly rents. The nature of the inputs used by the utilities (assets' specificity) and of the services supplied (non tradability), means that for privatisation to be accompanied by regulatory reform the (prior or simultaneous) development of safeguarding institutions is crucial (Spiller, 1993)[4]. Where local capital markets remain too small to absorb large scale privatisation, attracting foreign investors is a priority and this precondition is especially relevant. An additional argument for making policy and institutional reforms before involving the private sector is that, rather than speeding up policy reforms, individual transactions may actually delay them by relaxing the resource constraints and creating a false sense of achievement. Further, individual transactions could complicate reform later if, for example, the government decides to increase competition but finds it too costly because it has to renegotiate existing contracts with independent power producers. In sum, "utility regulation has two goals: to encourage investment and to support efficiency in production and use" (Levy and Spiller,1994, p. 216).

Safeguarding institutions must signal policy makers' commitment not to engage in opportunistic behaviour and reassuring potential and actual investors against the risk of administrative expropriation of their assets. This reduces the regulatory risk and premia on financial markets. Two features are important, *regulatory governance* and *regulatory incentives*. The former refers to "all the mechanisms that a society uses to restrain government discretionary moves and to solve conflicts between firms and regulators" (Abdala, 2000), while the latter encompasses specific norms on issues such as market structure, tariffs, access[5], unbundling, interconnection and universal service obligations.

No quick institutional, one–size–fits–all fixes are available. In each country, the evolution, and indeed the performance, of these two sets of variables depend on the *institutional endowment*, itself composed of many different dimensions, including the interactions between the executive and the legislative power, the ability of the judicial system to uphold property rights and review administrative agencies, the development of administrative capabilities, the pattern of conflict between contending social groups, and the nature of informal norms that tacitly constrain the actions of individuals or institutions. Political and social institutions not only affect the ability to restrain administrative action, but also have an independent impact on the type of regulation that can be designed, and hence on the appropriate balance between commitment and flexibility. In particular, to complement regulatory procedures in a welfare–enhancing way, three mechanisms restraining arbitrary administrative action must be in place (Levy and Spiller, 1994):

a) substantive restraints on the discretion of the regulator;

b) formal or informal constraints on changing the regulatory system; and

c) institutions that enforce the above formal — substantive or procedural — constraints.

In the electricity industry, in particular, weaknesses in the regulatory framework have sometimes reduced the benefits of privatisation and deregulation. Public authorities must devise sectoral policies that introduce and maintain competition; establish and maintain a sound regulatory framework for the remaining monopolies, public and private; keep transparency in transactions and convince investors that their investments are secure; negotiate, monitor, and enforce contracts with private suppliers of management and financing; ensure that resources from privatisation sales are put to productive uses; and manage the inevitable political and social tensions that arise as enterprise reforms are implemented, especially the critical issues of foreign ownership and labour layoffs (e.g. Pinheiro and Fukasaku, 1999). There is, however, much less agreement on how to approach the next set of challenges (second–generation issues) for countries facing the consolidation of initial reforms. In general, these issues are related to post–privatisation disputes and renegotiations between governments and the private sector and to the mechanisms necessary to promote competition in the reformed industries (Pires and Goldstein, 2001).

Corporate Governance

In view of the goal of creating "people's capitalism", how to provide appropriate mechanisms of corporate governance that protect small shareholders, while allowing management flexibility to pursue long–term corporate goals? Advances in the theory of corporate finance and industrial organisation, as well as the ongoing debate over the "best" capitalist model, have made the analysis of corporate governance — the mechanisms whereby economic systems (in their broadest possible sense) cope with the information and incentive problems inherent in financing investments and facilitate the intertemporal transfer of income claims — a burgeoning theme in comparative institutional economics (Oman, 2001). Key elements of this literature are the sources of financial resources for corporations, the concentration of ownership, the relevance of listing, the role and composition of boards of directors, the rules governing the market for corporate control and the obstacles that they may pose to corporate control activity, the relative importance of the voice and exit mechanisms (boardroom pressures and takeovers, or internal and external control, respectively) in disciplining managers.

Links between privatisation and corporate governance are of two main kinds: selling SOEs exposes them to takeover and bankruptcy threats, thereby easing the corporate governance problems proper of public ownership, and it provides an opportunity to modify the distribution of ownership rights among different classes of investors, by extending public listing among large firms, increasing the number of small shareholders, and reducing ownership concentration.

As mentioned before, if privatisation is associated with the transfer of enterprises charged with symbolic values to domestic conglomerates and/or foreign investors it is difficult to find popular support. No surprise then that creating "people's capitalism" has ranked highly among governments' goals. The total market value of privatised firms grew from less than $50 billion in 1983 to almost $2.5 trillion in 1999 and former SOEs are the most valuable companies in most developing countries (Meggison *et al.*,2000). Listed privatised firms generally have a far larger number of stockholders than do capitalisation–matched private firms in the same country, although their ownership structure is often unstable. This partly reflects the fact that tackling the issues that remain after ownership is transferred from public to private hands and when no (absolute) majority shareowner emerges has seldom been an overriding concern. Potential improvements in technical efficiency following control transfer may be jeopardised if corporate control is not contestable: in this case, and especially if conduct regulation proves insufficient to open up protected markets, managers can exploit rents accruing from market position without having to worry about the threat of takeovers. Privatisation policies should take such elements into account, making it imperative to introduce reforms and redress perceived inefficiencies. Governments have great discretion in pricing the SOEs they sell, especially those being sold via public share offerings, and they use this discretion to pursue political and economic ends. Most experiences, however, suggest the limited power of privatisation in changing the modes of governance which are prevalent in each country's large private companies. Further, those countries which have chosen the mass (voucher) privatisation route have done so largely out of necessity and face ongoing efficiency problems as a result.

OECD countries' experiments and experiences in this area have proved very influential in developing countries through the circulation of skilled personnel — in particular advisors, consultants, and merchant bankers. In Italy, for example, privatisation was accompanied by a legislative effort aimed at providing non–controlling shareholders (i.e. both individual and collective investors) with more adequate safeguards and at introducing the necessary conditions to allow them to monitor managers (Goldstein and Nicoletti, 1996). Successive governments were unsuccessful in broadening the number of large private business groups, whereas enhancing the mobility of control to investors outside of the traditional core of Italy's capitalism was explicitly included among the authorities' strategic goals. On the other hand, experiences such as those of Britain and Chile underscore the fact that mass sell–offs require the development of new institutional investors, such as pension funds, that may later play an active role in corporate governance[6]. Nonetheless, after the steep rise experienced in the immediate aftermath of privatisations, the slow but constant decline in the number of small shareholders in the United Kingdom highlights the difficulties in sustaining people's capitalism in the longer run. Even in a country whose policies in this area are often taken as a benchmark, "control [of privatised companies] is not exerted in the forms of threats of take–over or bankruptcy; nor has it for the most part come from direct investor intervention" (Bishop et al., 1994, p. 11).

The Road Ahead

Looking into the future, if public opinion and policy makers wish, much remains to be sold. Entire countries and regions — indeed not the smallest — have so far remained largely immune from privatisation. China provides the best example in this regard. While the reform period has witnessed a shift from a wholly state–owned industrial sector toward one increasingly dominated by "non–state" enterprises, starting with township and village enterprises (TVEs) and other collectively owned businesses, enterprises either wholly owned or controlled by government entities still account for 30 per cent of industrial output (OECD, 2002). While the government provides the with preferential credits and shelter from competition, it also constrains flexibility and their performance is often lacklustre. SOEs still employ nearly half of the urban workforce in the formal sector and concerns for social stability have so far dictated a gradual approach to SOE restructuring. China's WTO accession is accelerating the pace of the process, but important complementary reforms in the social security system and in training programmes still largely remain on the drawing board (Fan et al. 1997). In comparison, Viet Nam's greater success in reducing the size of the SOE sector in the 1990s was due to the introduction of a safety net composed of severance pay and early retirement schemes (O'Connor, 1996).

Likewise, WTO membership and closer integration with the European Union in the context of the Euro–Mediterranean Partnership are reinforcing pressures on MEDA countries to improve their competitive position (Goldstein, 2002a). Privatisation, regulatory reform and the creation of independent regulatory agencies in telecoms are key elements of this reform package for a number of reasons: the direct effects that divestiture receipts and foreign investment flows may have, the indirect contribution of an efficient service sector to the rest of the economy, and the positive externalities of well functioning institutions on the rest of society. A recent analysis of telecoms in five MEDA countries — Algeria, Egypt, Morocco, Tunisia, and Turkey — that together account for more than two–thirds of the total 2000 GDP of Middle East and North Africa shows that the institutional endowment is proving a stumbling block on the reform path (Goldstein, 2002b). Even more than the quasi stalemate that characterises three of the countries, the difficult transition of Morocco and Turkey on the road from state capitalism to regulatory capitalism highlights the importance of understanding the role of interests, policy learning, institutional isomorphism, and path dependence.

Analytical challenges also remain for improving the dialogue between theorists and empiricists (Shirley and Walsh, 2001). Much of the recent theoretical critiques of privatisation address deviations from optimal firm behaviour. Not surprisingly, given the difficulty in finding such an ideal firm, the flaws and shortcomings of privatisation are magnified in such a framework. Choosing a counterfactual is part of the problem. On the other hand, although in most cases gains can be documented by taking state ownership as such, this may not be ideal since the decision to relinquish control suggests that the utility function of the government has changed. A government that puts higher value on efficiency or sound fiscal policies would operate its SOEs differently as well. Empirical research consists largely of before–and–after comparisons that do not capture any change in government preferences, nor controls for changes in markets. An important exception here is the OECD regulatory reform project, the methodology of which could be replicated for analysing emerging, transition, and developing economies.

In sum, if the pressures of globalisation make it imperative to redefine the function of the state, understanding the development role of different forms of ownership requires focusing on hard analysis and resisting the temptation of ideology. Although privatisation's promise has been frequently oversold (Bouin, 1992), not least by international organisations[7], its ills have also been greatly exaggerated[8]. The future challenges for the regulatory state therefore remain substantial to ensure maximisation of welfare benefits. When ownership transfer has been accompanied by market liberalisation and proper implementation, in OECD and non–OECD countries alike, consumers and end users have benefited in terms of choice, quality and prices. When talking about regulation, however, the devil is in the details — and the boundary between a good and a bad framework is very thin. If it tilts towards rent–seeking and drags the pursuit of high and sustainable growth, the risk of provoking a backlash against market reforms is indeed great — the current predicaments of Argentina do indeed seem to fit this hypothesis. That countries have historically reacted differently to shocks, and that "retrogression" is one such possibility, does not of course come as a surprise to development scholars and practitioners (Emmerij,1987).

Notes

1. I thank Peter Kingstone and other contributors to this volume for substantive comments on earlier drafts of this paper.

2. Possibly the first large–scale sale of a public enterprise was the Volkswagen issue in the early 1960s. Nonetheless, the dramatic fall of the share price after markets were hit by the Cuban missile crisis had a lasting negative impact on equity ownership culture in Germany.

3. See "Cracks open up beneath Cardoso", *The Economist,* 12 May 2001 and "Haunted by a hat", *ibid.,* 30 June 2001.

4. Firms enjoy an informational advantage over regulators, so the first–best solution to solve this problem would be to introduce competition.

5. The multicarrier system allows consumers equal access to a multiplicity of operators by dialling the same number of digits irrespective of the identity of the phone company. A less transparent way of introducing more competition is to let the incumbent keep the advantage of "owning" the traditional numbering system and impose on new entrants multi–digit selection codes; this system is in use in Italy for instance.

6. In Chile, for example, the takeover of the country's dominant electricity utility, Enersis, one of the largest in emerging markets, was stalled for some months in 1998 as pension funds disputed lucrative additional terms that the management had negotiated for themselves based on important agreements concerning the future strategic direction of Enersis that they never told other shareholders about.

7. The candid admission of two former IMF resident representatives in Eastern Europe is probably valid elsewhere: "A major lesson for economists that have had the experience of living with transition is that attention must be paid to establishing the institutional underpinnings of the market. The task of creating market economies has reminded us that markets are embedded in a set of institutions and behavior patterns that economists have normally taken for granted. [...] Economists in general have paid no more attention to the institutional structure in which markets work than fish pay to the water they swim in" (Allen and Haas, 2001, p. 25).

8. In the *Porto Alegre Call for Mobilisation*, for example, the 2001 World Social Forum said that "privatisation is a mechanism for transferring public wealth and natural resources to the private sector. We oppose all forms of privatisation of natural resources and public services. We call for the protection of access to resources and public goods necessary for a decent life".

Bibliography

ABDALA, M. (2000), "Institutional Roots of Post–Privatization Regulatory Outcomes", *Telecom Development*, Volume 24, Nos. 8/9.

ALLEN, M. AND R. HAAS (2001), "The Transition in Central and Eastern Europe: The Experience of Two Resident Representatives", *IMF Staff Papers*, Vol. 48, Special Issue, Washington, D.C.

AMSDEN, A.H. (1989), "Asia's Next Giant : South Korea and Late Industrialization", Oxford University Press, Oxford.

ARMIJO, L. (1998), "Balance Sheet or Ballot Box? Incentives to Privatize in Emerging Democracies", *in* P. OXHORN AND P. STARR (eds.) *The Problematic Relationship between Economic and Political Liberalisation*, Lynne Rienner, Boulder CO.

AZAM, J.–P. AND C. MORRISSON (1999), *Conflict and Growth in Africa: The Sahel*, Development Centre Studies, OECD, Paris.

BARBER, W.J. (1995), "Chile con Chicago: A Review Essay", *Journal of Economic Literature*, 33, 4.

BARCA, F. AND S. TRENTO (1997), "State Ownership and the Evolution of Italian Corporate Governance", *Industrial and Corporate Change*, 6:3, Sept., pp. 533–60.

BARJA, G. AND M. URQUIOLA (2001), "Capitalization, Regulation and the Poor: Access to Basic Services in Bolivia", World Institute for Development Economics Research (WIDER), *Discussion Paper*, No. 2001/34.

BIRDSALL, N.AND J. NELLIS (2002*), Winners And Losers: Assessing The Distributional Impact of Privatization*, Center for Global Development, Washington, D.C.

BISHOP, M., J. KAY AND C. MAYER (1994), "Introduction: Privatisation in Performance", *in* M. BISHOP, J. KAY AND C. MAYER (eds.) *Privatisation and Economic Performance*, Oxford University Press, Oxford.

BOUBAKRI, N. AND J.–C. COSSET (2002), "Does Privatization Meet the Expectations? Evidence from African Countries", *Journal of African Economies*, vol. 11, AERC supplement 1.

BOUBAKRI, N. AND J.–C. COSSET (1998), "The Financial and Operating Performance of Newly Privatized Firms: Evidence from Developing Countries", *Journal of Finance*, 53: 1081–1110.

Bouin, O. (1992) *Privatisation in Developing Countries: Reflections on a Panacea,* Policy Brief No. 3, OECD Development Centre, Paris.

Bouin, O. and C.–A. Michalet (1991), *Rebalancing the Public and Private Sector: Developing Country Experience,* Development Centre Studies, OECD, Paris.

Campbell White, O. and A. Bhatia (1998), *Privatization in Africa,* World Bank, Washington, D.C.

Carreras, A. and X. Tafunell (1997), "Spain: Big Manufacturing Firms between State and Market, 1917–1990" *in* A.D. Cahndler, F. Amatori, and T. Hikino (eds.), *Big Business and the Wealth of Nations,* Cambridge University Press, New York.

Chesnais, F. and H.–S. Kim (1999), "Petrochemicals in Korea and Brazil, *in* L. Krieger Mytelka (ed.), *Competition, Innovation and Competitiveness in Developing Countries,* Development Centre Studies, OECD, Paris.

Dahlman, C. and C. Frischtak (1993), "National Systems Supporting Technical Advance in Industry: The Brazilian Experience", *in* R. Nelson (ed.), *National Innovation System,* Oxford University Press, New York, NY.

Domberger, S. and J. Piggott (1994), "Privatization Policies and Public Enterprise: A Survey", *in* M. Bishop, J. Kay and C. Mayer (eds.) *Privatization and Economic Performance,* Oxford University Press, Oxford.

Domínguez, J.I. (ed.) (1997), *Technopols: Freeing Politics and Markets in Latin America in the 1990s,* The Pennsylvania State University Press, University Park, PA.

Emmerij, L. (1987), "The Future of Development Research in the OECD Development Centre", *in* L. Emmerij (ed.), *Development Policies and the Crisis of the 1980s,* Development Centre Seminars, OECD, Paris.

Estrin, S. and A. Rosevaer (1999), "Enterprise Performance and Ownership: The Case of Ukraine", *European Economic Review,* Vol. 43: 1125–1136

Evans, P. (1978), *Dependent Development,* Princeton University Press, Princeton, NJ.

Fan, G., M. Lunati, and D. O'Connor (1997), *Labour Market Aspects of State Enterprise Reform in China,* Technical Papers, No. 141, OECD Development Centre, Paris.

Feigenbaum, H.B. and J. Henig (1994), "The Political Underpinnings of Privatization: A Typology", *World Politics,* Vol. 46, No. 2, pp. 185–208.

Foxley, A. (1983), *Latin American Experiments in Neo–conservative Economics,* University of California Press, Berkeley, Calif.

Galal, A., L. Jones, P. Tandon and I. Vogelsang (1994), *Welfare Consequences of Selling Public Enterprises,* Oxford University Press for the World Bank, New York, N.Y.

Goldstein, A. (2002a), "Improving the Basis of Long–Term Growth in the MEDA Region: Privatisation and Regulatory Reform", *mimeo,* OECD Development Centre, Paris.

Goldstein, A. (2002b), "Institutional Endowment and Regulatory Reform in Telecoms: A Five–Country Comparison in the MEDA Region", *mimeo,* OECD Development Centre, Paris.

GOLDSTEIN, A. (1999), "Brazilian Privatisation: The Rocky Path from State Capitalism to Regulatory Capitalism", *Industrial and Corporate Change*, Vol. 8, No. 4.

GOLDSTEIN, A. AND G. NICOLETTI (1996), "Italian Privatisations in International Perspective", *Cuadernos de Economia*, No. 33, pp. 425–51.

GÖNENÇ, R., M. MAHER AND G. NICOLETTI (2001), "The Implementation and the Effects of Regulatory Reform: Past Experience and Current Issues", *OECD Economic Studies*, No. 32, OECD, Paris.

HANSON A.H. (1966), "Government Organisation for Government Enterprise", *in* G. MOODIE (ed.) *Government Organisation and Economic Development. Papers and Proceedings of the Fourth Study Conference on Problems of Economic Development*, OECD Development Centre, Paris.

LEVY, B. AND P. SPILLER (1994), "Regulation, Institutions, and Commitment in Telecommunications", *in Proceedings of the World Bank Conference on Development Economics 1993*, Washington, D.C.

LITTLE, I., T. SCITOVSKY AND M. SCOTT (1970), *Industry and Trade in Some Developing Countries: A Comparative Study*, Oxford University Press for the OECD Development Centre, Oxford.

MEGGISON, W. AND J. NETTER (2001), "From State to Market: A Survey of Empirical Studies on Privatisation", *Journal of Economic Literature*, Vol 39, No. 2.

MEGGISON, W., J. NETTER AND M.K. BOUTCHKOVA (2000), "The Impact of Privatisation on Capital Market Development and Individual Share Ownership", Fondazione Eni Enrico Mattei, *Nota di lavoro*, No. 53.

NELSON, J. (1992) "Poverty and Equity", *in* S. HAGGARD AND R. KAUFMAN (eds.), *The Politics of Economic Adjustment*, Princeton University Press, NJ.

NICOLETTI, G. (2000), "The Implementation and the Effects of Regulatory Reform: Past Experience and Current Issues", *mimeo*, OECD Economics Department, Paris.

O'CONNOR, D. (1996), *Labour Market Aspects of State Enterprise Reform in Viet Nam*, Technical Papers No. 117, OECD Development Centre, Paris.

OECD (2002), *China in the World Economy: The Domestic Policy Challenges*.

OMAN, C. (2001), *Corporate Governance and National Development*, Technical Papers No. 180, OECD Development Centre, Paris.

PINHEIRO, A.C. AND K. FUKASAKU (eds.) (1999), *A privatização no Brasil. O caso dos serviços de utilidade pública*, OECD Development Centre and BNDES, Paris and Rio de Janeiro.

PIRES, J.–C.L. AND A. GOLDSTEIN (2001), "Agências Reguladoras Brasileiras: Avaliação e Desafios", *Revista do BNDES*, Vol. 16: 3–42.

SAKONG, I. (1993), *Korea in the World Economy*, Institute for International Economics.

SCHAMIS, H. (1999), "Distributional Coalitions and the Politics of Economic Reform in Latin America", *World Politics*, Vol. 51: 236–68.

SCHNEIDER, B.R. (1991), *Politics within the State*, University of Pittsburgh Press, Pittsburgh, PA.

SHIRLEY, M. (1998) "Bureaucrats in Business: The Roles of Privatization versus Corporatization in State–Owned Enterprise Reform", *World Development*, Vol. 27, pp. 115–36.

SHIRLEY, M. AND P. WALSH (2001), "Public vs. Private Ownership: The Current State of the Debate", *Working Paper*, No. 2420, World Bank, Washington, D.C.

SIKKINK, K. (1991), *Ideas and Institutions' Developmentalism in Brazil and Argentina*, Cornell University Press, Ithaca.

SPICER, A., G. MCDERMOTT AND B. KOGUT (2000), "Entrepreneurship and Privatisation in Central Europe: The Tenuous Balance Between Destruction and Creation", *Academy of Management Review*, Vol. 25, No. 3.

SPILLER, P. (1993), "Institutions and Regulatory Commitment in Utilities' Privatization", *Industrial and Corporate Change*, Vol. 2, No. 3.

TONINELLI, P.A. (ed.) (2000), *The Rise and Fall of State–Owned Enterprise in the Western World?*, Cambridge University Press, Cambridge.

TREBAT, T. (1983) *Brazil's State–Owned Enterprises*, Cambridge University Press.

VALDÉS, J.G. (1995), *Pinochet's Economists: The Chicago School of Economics in Chile*, Cambridge University Press, Cambridge.

WATERBURY, J. (1992), "The Heart of the Matter? Public Enterprise and the Adjustment Process", *in* S. HAGGARD AND R.R. KAUFMAN (eds.), *The Politics of Economic Adjustment*, Princeton University Press, NJ.

WILLIAMS, M. (1990), "The Political Economy of Privatisation", *in* M. HOLLAND AND J. BOSTON (eds.), *The Fourth Labour Government. Politics and Policy in New Zealand* (2nd ed.), Oxford University Press, Auckland.

WILLIAMSON, J. (1994), "In Search of a Manual for Technopols", *in* WILLIAMSON (ed.), *The Political Economy of Policy Reform*, Institute for International Economics, Washington, D.C.

ZINNES, C., Y. EILAT AND J. SACHS (2001), "The Gains from Privatization in Transition Economies: Is "Change of Ownership" Enough?", *IMF Staff Papers*, Vol. 48, Special Issue, Washington, D.C.

Chapter 9

Trade and Investment Liberalisation

Kiichiro Fukasaku

Introduction

Trade liberalisation has been one of the defining characteristics of, and a prime mover behind, globalisation of the world economy throughout much of the post–war years, and especially since the 1980s. During the latter period, the vast majority of developing countries have embarked on trade policy reform as part and parcel of the outward–oriented development strategies. Such policy initiatives have been in many cases instigated or supported by the Bretton Woods institutions. The case for trade liberalisation based on multilaterally sanctioned rules has been well established, as testified by a rapid expansion of the membership of the GATT (General Agreement on Tariffs and Trade) and its successor, the WTO (World Trade Organisation). The rules–based, global trading system under the auspices of the GATT/WTO serves as the cornerstone for developing countries to implement reform programmes in a gradual manner.

Another defining characteristic of globalisation has been a strong surge in foreign direct investment (FDI) since the mid–1980s. Behind this phenomenon is the fact that a large number of developing countries have altered their attitudes and policies towards FDI significantly, and in some cases dramatically as in the case of China. Indeed, attracting FDI has become one of the top agenda items for liberalising economies. This motive also lies at the heart of many regional trade policy initiatives undertaken during this period to create new free trade agreements (FTAs) or revitalise existing ones. Yet, the case for investment liberalisation still remains politically sensitive for many countries and even contentious for some. This may be due in no small part to political, social and other concerns over foreign ownership of national property. While there are no universal rules governing international private investment, bilateral investment treaties, the OECD Codes of Liberalisation and other plurilateral agreements act as important vehicles for protecting and promoting international private investment.

Major Policy Trends

The inward–oriented, import–substitution strategies of the 1950s and 1960s came under critical scrutiny in the 1980s. For instance, the World Bank's 1981 report on sub–Saharan Africa, often referred to as the "Berg Report" after its principal author, presented a critical assessment of post–independence Africa's attempt at industrialisation through inward–oriented development strategies (World Bank, 1981). This report pointed to the adverse economy–wide effect of the "anti–export" bias caused by heavy taxes on agriculture, high protection on local production, overvalued exchange rates and foreign exchange controls. Subsequently, the need for trade liberalisation and exchange rate policy reforms was repeatedly emphasised as a prerequisite for improving Africa's capacity to trade in the international market. These policy reforms were implemented successively in much of the developing world under the so–called structural adjustment programmes (SAPs). In reviewing the development policy experience at that time, Rodrik (1995) notes:

> By the end of the decade [the 1980s], the anti–export and anti–private enterprise bias of the prevailing policy regimes was largely discredited. Public enterprise, industrial promotion, and trade protection were out; privatisation, industrial de–regulation, and free trade were in (*ibid.* p. 2927).

The call for change in trade policies in developing countries also led to a major review of the global trade rules in the 1980s. Since the early years of the GATT (the 1947 GATT), developing countries had been accorded special rights to nurture infant industries, preferential access to developed–country markets and non–reciprocity in multilateral trade negotiations. Such special rights and privileges legitimised "free–riding" on the part of developing countries and allowed them to opt out of MFN–based liberalisation commitments. However, doubt was increasingly raised over the effectiveness of such an approach to trade and development. One of the major critiques came from within the GATT Secretariat. The Leutwiler report (GATT, 1985), commissioned in November 1983 by the then Director–General, Arthur Dunkel, recommended 15 specific, immediate actions in order to meet the "present crisis in the trading system", one of which addressed the problem of trade and development. This recommendation reads:

> Developing countries receive special treatment in the GATT rules. But such special treatment is of limited value. Far greater emphasis should be placed on permitting and encouraging developing countries to take advantage of their competitive strengths and on integrating them more fully into the trading system, with all the appropriate rights and responsibilities that this entails (*ibid.* 44).

Meanwhile, the apparent success in adjustment and growth in several high–performing Asian economies in the 1970s and 1980s stirred policy debates among academic researchers and policy makers. Considerable research was devoted to seeking the exact policy mix that might have enabled them to achieve superior performances (see, for example, Amsden, 1989; Wade, 1990 and Young, 1992 and 1995). This debate received a further boost following the publication of World Bank report on the "East Asian Miracle" (World Bank, 1993). In retrospect, it is worth repeating that there is *no* single East Asian model for trade and development. Beyond the general tenet of "getting fundamentals right", these economies vary significantly in terms of the actual combination of policies (from hands off to highly interventionist), including attitudes and policies towards FDI. Rethinking the development experiences of newly industrialising economies in East Asia and other regions still continues (Amsden 2001; Stiglitz and Yusuf, 2001).

As noted in the Introduction, the period since the mid–1980s has witnessed trade and investment liberalisation on a significant scale at various levels: multilateral, plurilateral, bilateral and unilateral. First, the Uruguay Round of multilateral trade negotiations was launched in 1986 under the auspices of the GATT. For the first time in history, international direct investment was brought under the purview of the multilateral trading system in the context of TRIMs (Trade–related Investment Measures) under the GATT. Cross–border investment was also incorporated into the GATS (General Agreement on Trade in Services) as one of the four modes of international transactions in services. This round was unprecedented in terms of the scope of negotiations and the number of participating members (Table 1). As a successful conclusion of the Uruguay Round (1986–94), the WTO came into being in January 1995. Three agreements are of particular interest to developing countries:

— to phase out the quotas that have been maintained under the so–called Multi–fibre Arrangement (MFA) and progressively integrate the textile and clothing sector into the WTO (by 2005);

— to introduce market–oriented rules and disciplines into agriculture, based principally on bound tariffs, and to limit the use of export subsidies; and

— to prohibit the use of voluntary export restraints (VERs) and other "grey–area" measures.

Numerous studies based on different scenarios have assessed the potential benefits arising from trade liberalisation under the Uruguay Round. The Development Centre has developed a model of global production and trade, which is known as the Rural/Urban–North/South model or RUNS (Burniaux and van der Mensbrugghe, 1991). The quantitative analysis using the RUNS model clearly demonstrates that there would be substantial gains from removing trade distortions and production subsidies for all commodities. The aggregate amount

Table 1. **Multilateral Trade Negotiations 1947-2004**

Year/Period	Place/Name	Subjects Covered	Participation
1947	Geneva	Tariffs	23
1949	Annecy	Tariffs	13
1951	Torquay	Tariffs	38
1956	Geneva	Tariffs	26
1960-1961	Geneva (Dillon Round)	Tariffs	26
1964-1967	Geneva (Kennedy Round)	Tariffs, anti-dumping measures.	62
1973-1979	Geneva (Tokyo Round)	Tariffs, non-tariff measures, "framework" agreements.	102
1986-1994	Geneva (Uruguay Round)	Tariffs, non-tariff measures, rules, agriculture, services, textiles, intellectual property, dispute settlements, creation of WTO, etc.	123
2002-2004 (planned)	Geneva (Doha Development Agenda)	Tariffs, non-tariff measures, rules, agriculture, services, special & differential treatment, etc.	144

Source: Based on WTO (1998, p.9).

of world income gains from full liberalisation could be $450 billion (in 1992 dollars) or more per annum, while partial reform, as envisaged by the Uruguay Round would add around $213 billion (in 1992 dollars) per annum to world income or about 50 per cent of the income of China (see Goldin and van der Mensbrugghe, 1992 and Goldin et al., 1993).

However, many poor countries came to share the view that they were unable to participate effectively in actual negotiations. Participation in multilateral trade negotiations, such as the Uruguay Round, requires a large amount of public resources to be devoted to international trade diplomacy, which costs them dear. This problem has become acute during the course of implementation of the Uruguay Round Agreements and has led donor countries to pay increased attention to issues relating to trade capacity building in least–developed countries (see the final section).

Second, trade liberalisation has continued and even accelerated at both bilateral and plurilateral levels. The United States took a major turn in external trade policy when it concluded an FTA with Israel in 1985, followed by an FTA with Canada in 1989. The conclusion of the North American Free Trade Agreement (NAFTA) in 1994 might well be construed as a North Atlantic response to the EC–1992 process (1985–1992) and the Maastricht Treaty (in force since November 1993). In Asia, the ASEAN Free Trade Area (AFTA) was launched in 1993. Similarly, four major countries in South America embarked on MERCOSUL in 1995. Many more developing countries followed suit. As of July 2000, WTO (2001*a)* reported that 114 regional trade agreements (RTAs) were in force and notified to the WTO (GATT Article XXIV, Enabling Clause and GATS Article VI). Most WTO members are now partners in at least one RTA, and many have become partners in two or more. With the launching of an FTA between Japan and Singapore signed in January 2002, only China, Chinese Taipei, Hong Kong–China, Macau–China, Korea and Mongolia are not currently partners in an RTA among WTO Members.

It should be noted, however, that RTAs, such as FTAs and customs unions, are distinctly different from other regional integration or co–operation agreements, such as the APEC. While the former accord partners preferential tariff treatment on a reciprocal basis, the latter aims to promote open trade and co–operation among member countries. APEC was launched in 1989 as a brainchild of Bob Hawke, then Australian Prime Minister who coined the term "open regionalism". At the Bogor summit meeting in 1994, the member states of APEC announced their intention to pursue "free trade and investment" in the region by 2010 (for developed members) or 2020 (for the rest), according to this principle, in other words, *concerted* unilateral liberalisation.

Third, in the area of international direct investment and multinational enterprises, the OECD has long provided an international framework for co–operation among Member countries by adhering to the Declaration and Decisions on International Investment and Multinational Enterprises, which was originally adopted in 1976. The most recent review was completed in 2000. At the same time, bilateral investment treaties (BITs) have become increasingly important as an instrument for providing legal security to foreign investors and their investments. During the three decades leading up to 1990, only 500 BITs were signed, whereas by the end of the 1990s this number had almost quadrupled. In 1999 the vast majority was concluded between developing countries (UNCTAD, 2000).

There was an important attempt on the part of OECD Member countries to establish a free–standing international treaty, so–called Multilateral Agreement on Investment (MAI), which was also open to non–member countries. The MAI was intended to provide a broad multilateral framework for international investment with high standards for the liberalisation of investment regimes and investment protection and with effective dispute settlement procedures. Intense negotiations that were launched in May 1995 continued for three years. After a six–month pause, the negotiations ceased in December 1998 (see www.oecd.org/daf/mai for detailed documentation). Despite this setback, the experience of MAI negotiations, along with existing bilateral and regional arrangements, provides an important input to the future work on the relationship between trade and investment under the WTO.

Fourth, developing countries have also unilaterally undertaken trade and investment liberalisation during the last two decades. During the eight years of the Uruguay Round, more than 60 developing countries undertook unilateral measures to lower their barriers to imports (OECD 1997). While a review of individual country cases is beyond the scope of this chapter, Bonaglia et al. (2000) provide a useful overview of trade and other policy reforms in African countries. One of the most successful episodes to date is that of China. The country embarked on the so–called "Reform and Opening–up" in late 1978 and moved to embrace the coastal development strategy in the mid–1980s in order to promote trade and attract FDI. Indeed, China's reform process was closely related to long and often painstaking accession negotiations at the GATT/WTO, which began in 1986 (Fukasaku and Wall, 1994, Fukasaku and Solignac Lecomte, 1998 and Fukasaku et al., 1999).

Openness and Growth

The relationship between openness (to international trade and investment) and growth is a subject of long debate. Two of the Development Centre's publications in the early 1970s made direct and important contributions to this debate. One was Little, Scitovsky and Scott (1970), who presented a detailed analysis of trade and industrial policies adopted by seven newly–industrialising economies in Asia and Latin America (Argentina, Brazil, Mexico, India, Pakistan, the Philippines and Chinese Taipei). Though published more than 30 years ago, this book still provides readers with useful insights regarding the political economy of policy reform. The central policy message of this seminal work is succinctly summarised in the Foreword by André Philip, then President of the OECD Development Centre:

> "[T]hese countries have now reached the stage where policies that are followed to promote import–substitution are proving to be harmful for the economic development of these countries. Industrialisation sheltered by high levels of protection has led to the creation of high–cost enterprises; these enterprises are producing expensive products, many of which are for use by a restricted middle class, and so production is rapidly coming up against the limits of the home market (Ibid., p.xviii)".

This book, however, does not advocate *laissez–faire* policies as alternative strategies for these countries. Instead, it carefully analyses and recommends what governments should do in terms of complementary policies to support trade liberalisation. In particular, it draws attention to the problem of transition from import substitution to export promotion, as these economies face capacity constraints, including the initial difficulties of entering export markets and inadequate infrastructure.

Another important contribution to the early debate on openness and growth was Reuber *et al.* (1973). The authors of this book cast new light on the role of FDI in development by collecting and analysing a large amount of statistical data on the structure and distribution of FDI in developing host economies. Some of the main findings include:

— A strong, positive two–way association between the level of income and the stock of FDI. Similarly, there was a positive association between the level of exports and imports and the stock of FDI, though the relationship with the balance of trade was mixed.

— Foreign–controlled manufacturing firms were estimated to employ about 1.6 million persons directly in developing host economies in 1967. Local employees were mostly paid at or above prevailing wages and salary rates.

— The production costs of foreign affiliates engaged primarily in production for exports were highly competitive with production costs in developed countries. Foreign affiliates played a significant role in the transfer of technology and skills to the host economy and also provided substantial training for local personnel.

The authors conclude that the effects of FDI appear to be complementary to many aspects of local development. Yet they also acknowledge the difficulties in designing host–government policies which increase net benefits per unit of direct investment, without simultaneously reducing the level of FDI flows *to the point where losses due to reductions in the number of units more than offset gains due to higher returns per unit* (*italics* added). The role of FDI in development is indeed an important theme that has continued to attract much attention among policy makers and academic researchers even today (see OECD Development Centre, 2002, for an extended review).

Openness can potentially bring many benefits to liberalising economies. First, imports are an important source of new ideas, new goods and new services that are essential to improve productivity and sustain growth (Romer, 1993 and 1994). Import liberalisation also stimulates domestic competition and can act as a catalyst for greater efficiency and innovation. Second, exports are crucial to financing imports essential for development. In addition to this obvious role, exports of manufactures and non–traditional goods and services provide a useful yardstick against which policy makers can design and implement the most effective policy mix (World Bank, 1993). Third, FDI stimulates inflows of capital, technology and know–how from more advanced countries and enhances competition in domestic markets. Although much of FDI flows into developing countries in the 1960s and 1970s were oriented towards natural resource extraction, FDI flows in manufacturing and service sectors have become increasingly important in recent years. In order to attract the best FDI on a sustained basis, host governments must ensure stable macroeconomic conditions and reduce the degree of product market distortions in their economies (Hiemenz et al. 1991).

The positive relationship between openness and growth appears to be fairly robust (see, among others, Dollar, 1992; Sachs and Warner, 1995; Frankel and Romer, 1999; and Dollar and Kraay, 2001), though it is difficult to establish the causation in a rigorous manner. Three points are worth noting in this respect. First, several conventional measures of "openness" (i.e. trade–GDP ratio, tariff rates, the extent of non–tariff barriers, and the degree of distortions in foreign exchange markets) frequently applied to the cross–country regression analysis has been criticised, because they do not necessarily reflect the impact of trade policy per se. They may well capture the impact of good institutions and government policy in general (Pritchett, 1996 and Rodriguez and Rodrik, 1999). Second, the transmission mechanisms through which freer trade may cause higher growth in liberalising economies are not well specified in these cross–country studies. Some argue that it is import liberalisation, rather than export expansion, that may have a stronger impact on productivity and growth (Clerides et al., 1998, and Lawrence and Weinstein, 2001). Or the causation might run in the opposite direction: higher productivity in manufacturing industries leads to higher exports (Bradford, 1994). Third, empirical analysis needs to take into account more explicitly the trade–FDI–growth dynamic in liberalising economies (Urata, 2001). In this respect, Démurger (2000) makes a useful contribution to the understanding of this dynamic in the Chinese context by investigating the effects of opening up to foreign capital on the country's growth and on the evolution of inter–provincial disparities over the last two decades. It also demonstrates an added value of the country–specific approach to empirical research on openness and growth.

From the policy perspective, more analytical work is required to address the question of transitional measures (including selective intervention and industrial targeting) and capacity constraints facing liberalising economies, as already noted in Little et al. (1970). One important line of work in this context is the role of export–processing zones (EPZs) and other special zones as a transitional policy (see, among others, Basile and Germidis, 1984; Oborne, 1986; Warr, 1990; and Wall, 1993). More recently, Schrank (2001) highlights contrasting experiences in the development of EPZs between the Dominican Republic on the one hand and Korea and Mexico on the other. This study provides an important reminder that the success of EPZs depends not so much on the attitudes and capacities of

156

foreign investors but on those of *local* manufacturers. Furthermore, Subramanian and Roy (2001) attribute the success of EPZs in Mauritius to the quality of domestic institutions in managing rent–seeking and inefficiency involved in selective intervention. These studies point more generally to the question of trade–capacity building in developing countries, and in particular least–developed ones. This is the topic that has gathered increased attention since the late 1990s and will be discussed below in more detail in the context of post–Doha development challenges.

New Regionalism

The phenomenon of a dramatic rise in the number of RTAs in the 1990s is often referred to as "new regionalism" as opposed to "old regionalism" in the 1960s and 1970s (see, for example, World Bank, 2000). A key difference between the two is that many of the RTAs signed in the early years were established among developing countries (mostly in Africa and Latin America) based on an import–substitution development model with high external trade barriers in place. The new wave of RTAs in the 1990s, on the other hand, is generally characterised by outward–oriented policies, as external trade barriers have been declining at the same time. New RTAs, often composed of both developed and developing countries as equal partners, aim at *deeper* integration – freer movements of goods, services, capital and knowledge — through effective market integration that requires more than just eliminating trade barriers at the border. Underlying the popular appeal of new regionalism is a significant shift of development policy thinking regarding the role of FDI for development as a major channel of transferring capital, technology and knowledge to developing countries (OECD Development Centre, 2002).

Since the implementation of the Single Market Programme, the EU has been playing a pivotal role in promoting new regionalism around the globe. Indeed, the EU's own trade regimes *vis–à–vis* developing countries have been undergoing a profound transformation. Behind this change is the tightening of the WTO rules and procedures with respect to waivers, which provides a strong incentive for developed countries to take a dual–track approach to their trade relations with developing countries, with non–reciprocal trade preferences being reserved only for least–developed countries. In the case of the EU, the current all–ACP non–reciprocal trade preferences will be maintained until the end of 2007 and then replaced by a set of reciprocal trade arrangements under the so–called Cotonou Agreement signed in June 2000.

Another important feature of new regionalism is to "put politics first" (Goldstein, 2002). Partners to new RTAs are normally requested to make political commitments to a set of core values, such as respect for human rights, democracy and the rule of law. In the Cotonou Agreement, "good governance" is also considered as one of such fundamental elements for partnership, and serious cases of corruption can lead to the suspension of co–operation. In the case of the Euro–Mediterranean Partnership launched in Barcelona in 1995, "regional security and stability" are an important component of the political commitments between the EU and the Mediterranean countries.

Finally, new regionalism also attempts to link existing RTAs *across* regions, as seen in the talks between the EU and MERCOSUL as well as the planned Free Trade Agreement for the Americas (FTAA) scheduled for 2005. In this context, APEC stands out as a unique case of regional integration and co–operation agreements, based on two pillars. One is to undertake non–discriminatory confidence–building measures, such as enhanced exchange of macroeconomic information, increased transparency of trade policies among member states, trade and investment facilitation, consultation, voluntary codes and networking. The other is to design and implement voluntary but common liberalisation programmes under the principle of "open regionalism". As noted earlier, the Bogor Summit declaration provides an ambitious vision. Among the habitual incentives for trade negotiations between and among countries, the APEC route towards free trade and investment among member economies is indeed a novel approach. However, if traditional political economy is a guide, it would not be realistic to expect concerted unilateral liberalisation to succeed beyond marginal measures, because of the free–riding problem under voluntarism and the non–binding nature of policy commitments (Pelkmans and Fukasaku, 1995).

Following the Barcelona declaration in 1995, the Development Centre sponsored a number of studies on new regionalism in the context of evolving relations between the EU and the Southern Mediterranean countries and conducted policy dialogue meetings in collaboration with regional and international organisations (see among others Fontagné and Péridy, 1997; Dessus and Suwa, 2000; Dessus *et al.*, 2001). Some major policy conclusions emerged:

—   there are short–term risks associated with the Euro–Mediterranean Partnership through a worsening of trade balances and a substantial net loss of tariff revenues. However, market opening to the EU does no more than reveal existing structural weaknesses in the Mediterranean economies characterised by, *inter alia*, fiscal deficits, weak public finances, labour market rigidities and the limited capacity for export promotion and diversification;

—   the pursuit of a regional integration strategy envisaged in the Barcelona declaration thus requires the simultaneous implementation of domestic reforms in order to reap the full benefits of deeper integration between the two shores of the Mediterranean. The financial aid and technical co–operation programmes of the Euro–Mediterranean Partnership can and should help facilitate these reforms;

— liberalisation of agriculture and services is not included in the present provisions of the association agreements under the Euro–Mediterranean Partnership. The opening of these two sectors, however, would greatly increase the potential for trade and FDI flows between the two regions;

— rules of origin, technical barriers to trade and government procurement are identified as major areas of concern from the regional rule–making perspective. Furthermore, two potential shortcomings of the Euro–Mediterranean Partnership include the lack of explicit commitments in customs reform and the problem of hub–spoke effects. To the extent that individual Mediterranean countries implement FTAs with the EU but maintain trade barriers between themselves, the EU as "the hub" will become the centre of attraction for FDI flows in the whole region, with limited gains for the Mediterranean economies as "spokes".

Developing Countries and the Multilateral Trading System

Despite (*and* because of) the proliferation of new RTAs over the past years, it is imperative that the momentum of further trade liberalisation under the rules–based multilateral trading system be sustained. Two important benefits accrue from multilateral trade negotiations under the auspices of the WTO. One is enhanced prospects for political saleability when reform of domestic protection is part of a global effort (e.g. agriculture and services). Another is the additional gain from liberalisation by others. Owing to the size of domestic markets and a narrow range of goods and services produced for exports, most developing countries have a much larger stake in a healthily growing world trade than do industrial countries.

The large reductions in import duties and the establishment of non–discriminatory tariffs as the principal means of trade protection are commonly viewed as one of the most significant success stories of post–war multilateral trade negotiations under the GATT. Prior to the Uruguay Round, the past seven rounds had succeeded in lowering the average (trade–weighted) MFN tariff rates of Canada, the EU, Japan and the United States (the so–called Quad–4 countries) on industrial goods from a high of 40 per cent at the end of the Second World War to around 6 per cent at the end of the Tokyo Round. The Uruguay Round further reduced the average trade–weighted tariff rates to 4 per cent (Safadi and Laird, 1996).

Yet, market access still represents perhaps the single most important trade issue between developed and developing countries. First, developed countries' tariffs continue to show significant peaks on products, such as textiles, clothing and leather products, and the practice of tariff escalation against imports of semi–processed and processed products. Second, the overall mean bound rate remains much higher in other developed countries than in the Quad–4 countries. Third, developing countries' tariffs are often either not bound or bound at relatively higher levels than applied rates. Fourth, many OECD countries make an extensive use of the so–called core non–tariff barriers (including anti–dumping and countervailing actions). Fifth, in the case of agriculture, border measures such as quotas and variable levies have been converted to tariffs following the Uruguay Round Agreement on Agriculture. In most cases, such "tariffication" process has resulted in the establishment of tariff rate quotas, involving very high rates. Last but not least, market access in the service sector (including the movement of temporary workers) has been brought under the purview of multilateral trade negotiations only after the completion of the Uruguay Round (see, for example, OECD, 1999a and WTO, 2001b for further discussion). Therefore, much remains to be done in reducing trade barriers to and improving market access for goods and services from developing countries.

While the early models essentially estimated static efficiency gains from multilateral tariff liberalisation, more recent models have attempted to capture "dynamic gains" from freer trade. Four sources of dynamic gains have been identified and empirically estimated: dynamic accumulation of static gains, imperfect competition and scale economies, endogenous total factor productivity (TFP) and endogenous capital flows (see World Bank, 2002b, for a detailed discussion). Although empirical analysis requires further refinement, dynamic effects through better market access, greater domestic efficiency and higher productivity could be substantial. In the case of full tariff liberalisation on agricultural and manufactured products in both OECD and non–OECD countries, the global welfare gains could reach $1 200 billion (in 1995 prices), which is equivalent to about 3 per cent of world GDP. The dynamic gains from positive trade externalities in terms of higher TFP are manifested as a substantial rise in household disposable income, which is two and half times higher than traditional gains from consumer surplus (Dessus et al., 1999).

The results of this and other economy–wide simulation models offer several policy implications. First, any future tariff liberalisation effort has to pay attention to the heavy reliance of developing countries on trade tax revenues. The simulation results reported by Dessus et al. (1999) highlight the significance of this fiscal effect on a country's net welfare. In order to reap the full benefit of future tariff liberalisation, developing countries must undertake major efforts to improve the government fiscal position, in tandem with trade liberalisation. Second, a recent study by the Australian Department of Foreign Affairs and Trade (1999) suggests that the welfare gains from lowering barriers to trade in services would be as large as those from trade liberalisation in goods. Third, and related to the above, more attention needs to be paid to the complementary relationship between liberalisation of goods and liberalisation of services when considering the relationship between trade externalities and productivity. Developing more efficient, dynamic service sectors is of crucial importance for facilitating trade and investment flows into developing countries (see OECD, 2001*b* for further discussion).

Finally, it is worth repeating that dynamic gains from trade will not accrue automatically. To achieve these gains, developing countries, particularly least–developed ones, must secure macroeconomic stability and continue complementary policy reforms so as to improve the domestic supply response to the emerging market opportunities and challenges that will follow from future trade liberalisation. Admittedly, this is easier to say than to do for any country, but is particularly difficult in slow–growing, low–income countries. For those working in the sectors that are currently receiving heavy government protection, the opening–up of national borders and the ensuing adjustment to foreign competition imply a loss of privileges and economic hardship. Nonetheless, such adjustment is an important source of productivity gains and higher real income in society at large. This is an area where development assistance should play a catalytic role in helping weaker countries to develop competitive capacities and to promote foreign trade.

Development Challenges after Doha

One of the most important results of the Uruguay Round multilateral trade negotiations is the creation of the WTO in 1995. In contrast to the GATT, under the WTO Agreement, both developed and developing Members are required to adhere to nearly the same sets of rules and obligations, though greater flexibility is allowed for the latter. Subsequently, however, many developing countries have found it very difficult to implement some of the Uruguay Round obligations within an agreed timetable. The question of "capacity building" poses a major challenge for developing countries, particularly the least–developed ones.

While the concept of capacity building is very complex, this can be thought of as comprising three dimensions in the trade area: *capacity to negotiate* with their trading partners; *capacity to implement* trade rules and polices; and *capacity to compete* in the international market (Fukasaku, 2000). The crux of the matter is the question of time–consistency in priority setting and budget allocation in both national and international policy making.

On the first point, Blackhurst *et al.* (1999) point to generally poor capacity of African members dealing with WTO issues in Geneva, but, they argue, net increases in government expenditures to build up their delegations are not a prerequisite for increasing their participation in the WTO. What is more important is to have proper knowledge about what is at stake in WTO negotiations and give a priority to trade rather than political diplomacy in budget allocation. On the second point, Finger and Schuler (1999) highlight the high costs of implementing the reform programmes necessary to make domestic regulations conform with

WTO rules. While the actual costs of implementing certain WTO Agreements, such as Customs Valuation, SPS and TRIPS, may differ considerably across countries, their conclusion is that it will cost developing countries dear — in some cases a full year's development budget.

In this context, technical assistance has come to play an important role as an instrument for meeting the special needs of LDCs. The first major effort to this end was undertaken in 1996 when the first WTO Ministerial Conference was held in Singapore. On this occasion, WTO ministers adopted an *Integrated Plan of Action for the Least–Developed Countries* with the aim of improving the overall capacity of these economies to respond to the challenges and opportunities offered by the multilateral trading system. Pursuant to the Plan of Action, it was agreed by the WTO and five other international agencies (IMF, ITC, UNCTAD, UNDP and the World Bank) to establish an *Integrated Framework* for providing trade–related technical assistance to LDCs, including human and institutional capacity–building. The inventory of existing trade–related projects suggests a wide range of activities such as efforts to overcome supply constraints, trade promotion and trade support services, improving product quality standards and technical assistance towards the compliance with WTO Agreements.

The *Integrated Framework* has been applied on a case–by–case basis to meet the development needs identified by individual countries through round–table meetings with donors and international agencies. This approach was endorsed by the High–Level Meeting on *Integrated Initiatives for Least–Developed Countries' Trade Development*, organised by the WTO in October 1997 and extended beyond the six original organisations to involve many other aid agencies, multilateral, regional and national. In a similar vein, the Joint Integrated Technical Assistance Programme (JITAP) was launched in 1998 to address the needs of Africa's least–developed and other poor countries in their relations with multilateral trade negotiations.

Following the recommendations made by an independent mandatory review conducted in 2000, the *Integrated Framework* has been revamped to ensure the mainstreaming of trade in national development strategies and donor priorities and complemented by a global trust fund for IF programmes. A pilot scheme has been formulated to conduct a diagnostic study of trade policy issues and technical assistance needs for individual LDCs. Three pilot case studies (Cambodia, Madagascar and Mauritania) had been completed by November 2001. Meanwhile, the call for mainstreaming trade in national development strategies has been strongly supported by many bilateral donors. The Development Assistance Committee (DAC) of the OECD produced the "Guidelines for Capacity Development for Trade" for its member countries and their partners, with the view to strengthening such efforts on the ground (DAC/OECD, 2001). As a fundamental objective, DAC members attach great importance both to fostering a trade policy process in national development strategy in their partner countries and to promoting competitiveness in the enterprise sector.

In order to contribute to ongoing discussions on trade capacity building at the DAC and elsewhere, a 2002 Development Centre study takes a closer look at the policies and institutions that can help to improve the capacity to trade competitively in Africa's commodity–dependent countries (Bonaglia and Fukasaku, 2002). The following conclusions and policy messages deserve special emphasis:

— a stable macroeconomic environment, competitive real exchange rates and the removal of the anti–export bias inherited from the import–substitution era are key ingredients for successful export promotion and diversification policies in Africa. This is not enough. Complementary measures are needed to encourage long–term investment in non–traditional export sectors;

— high transaction costs facing many African economies continue to be a major obstacle to international business development. Improved supply of trade support services would contribute to reducing such costs. The observed mismatch between government policies and exporters' needs in trade support services, however, points to a more general governance problem. The changes needed in Africa are not just in policy *per se* but also in the national policymaking *process;*

— this calls for establishing a governance mechanism through which the voice of private firms and civil society can be heard and reflected properly in trade policy making process. A key element for improving the public–private partnership is the reform of business advocacy institutions, such as chambers of commerce and industry and business associations, which are important conduits between their members and policy–making bodies. Concerns over their legitimacy and severe resource constraints tend to reduce greatly their capacity to safeguard and promote the interests of their stakeholders;

— the establishment of a real public–private partnership is thus of paramount importance for government support to be effective. Public agencies responsible for promoting trade must be endowed with adequate human and financial resources and operate in the interest of exporting firms, without undue political interference. Furthermore, developments in information and communication technologies make traditional instruments for provision of services obsolete. General business information can be easily obtained through the Internet, while high value–added information can be obtained mostly through specialised service providers or business partners. There is the need for a new approach to providing technical assistance to private firms.

In this respect, the experience of Mauritius provides an interesting example of how an effective institutional framework might be built for trade and investment support. The island's participatory approach is considered essential for the government's ability to elaborate and implement a national export promotion and diversification strategy. More specifically, shared visions, adequate resources, close consultation with the private sector and support for the development of private service providers may explain this success.

Concluding Remarks

Several OECD works have focused on trade and investment relations between OECD and non–OECD countries. Such focus reflects the fact that the fuller integration of developing countries in an open multilateral trading system ranks among the top priorities for OECD countries. The following quotation summarises this point succinctly:

"Openness offers the potential for creation and preservation of value and wealth, and a much more reliable way to develop constructive responses to challenges than bureaucratic centralism. Over fifty years ago, the major economic powers realised that reducing barriers to the international flows of goods and services was vital to economic recovery from the Great Depression and the Second World War, as well as to future growth. This realisation was pursued over succeeding decades in a process of trade liberalisation leading to the establishment of the WTO in 1995 with provisions to support additional liberalisation in the future" (OECD, 2001a, p. 14).

Indeed, the accession of China and Chinese Taipei following the Doha Ministerial Conference has brought the WTO closer to a truly global organisation. Yet, governing the global process of trade and investment liberalisation continues to pose a new challenge for the international community, as demographic, socio–economic and technological conditions in both developed and developing countries are evolving continuously. The successful launch of a new trade round at Doha is a salutary event, but much needs to be done in coming years.

An immediate concern is the inadequate capacity of many poor countries to participate in multilateral trade negotiations actively and to implement global trade rules effectively. At the same time, any move in this direction should be complemented by policies aimed at improving market access for their key export products and helping them to strengthen a domestic supply response to emerging market opportunities. Unless these issues are addressed properly, it might be difficult to sustain the political momentum for keeping them engaged in an open multilateral trading system.

Bibliography

AMSDEN, A.H. (2001), *The Rise of "the Rest": Challenges to the West from Late–Industrialising Economies*, Oxford University, Press New York.

AMSDEN, A.H. (1989), *Asia's Next Giant: South Korea and Late Industrialisation*, Oxford University Press, New York.

AUSTRALIAN DEPARTMENT OF FOREIGN AFFAIRS AND TRADE (1999), *Global Trade Reform: Maintaining Momentum* (available on the web site: www.dfat.gov.au).

BASILE, A. AND D. GERMIDIS (1984), *Investing in Free Export Processing Zones*, Development Centre Studies, OECD, Paris.

BEHRMAN, J. AND T.N. SRINIVASAN (eds.) (1995), *Handbook of Development Economics*, vol. III.

BLACKHURST, R., B. LYAKURWA AND A. OYEJIDE (1999), "Improving African Participation in the WTO", Paper commissioned by the World Bank for a Conference at the WTO on 20–21 September.

BONAGLIA, F. AND K. FUKASAKU (2002), *Trading Competitively: A Study of Trade Capacity Building in Sub–Saharan Africa*, Development Centre Studies, OECD, Paris.

BONAGLIA, F., A. GOLDSTEIN AND C. RICHAUD (2000), "Measuring Reform", *Reform and Growth in Africa*, Development Centre Seminars, OECD, Paris.

BOUIN, O., F. CORICELLI AND F. LEMOINE (eds.) (1998), *Different Paths to a Market Economy: China and European Economies in Transition*, CEPII–CEPR OECD Development Centre.

BRADFORD, C.I. (1994), "From Trade–Driven Growth to Growth–Driven Trade: Reappraising the East Asian Development Experience", Document on Sale, OECD Development Centre, Paris.

BURNIAUX, J.M. AND D. VAN DER MENSBRUGGHE (1991), *Trade Policy in a Global Context. Technical Specification of the Rural/Urban North/South (RUNS) Applied General Equilibrium Model*, Technical Papers No.°48, OECD Development Centre, Paris.

CLERIDES, S., S. LACH AND J. TYBOUT (1998), "Is Learning by Exporting Important? Micro–Dynamic Evidence from Colombia, Mexico and Morocco", *Quarterly Journal of Economics*, Vol. 113, pp. 903–948.

Démurger, S. (2000), *Economic Opening and Growth in China*, Development Centre Studies, OECD, Paris.

Dessus, S., A. Suwa (2000), *Regional Integration and Internal Reforms in the Mediterranean Area*, Development Centre Studies, OECD, Paris.

Dessus, S., J. Devlin and R. Safadi (eds.) (2001), *Towards Arab and Euro–Med Regional Integration*, Development Centre Seminars, OECD, Paris.

Dessus, S., K. Fukasaku and R. Safadi (1999), *Multilateral Tariff Liberalisation and the Developing Countries*, Policy Brief No.18, OECD Development Centre, Paris.

Dessus, S., J–D. Shea and M–S. Shi (1995), *Chinese Taipei: the Origins of the Economic "Miracle"*, Development Centre Studies, OECD, Paris.

DAC/OECD (2001), *Guidelines on Strengthening Trade Capacity for Development*, Development Co–operation Directorate, OECD, Paris.

Dollar, D. (1992), "Outward–oriented Developing Countries Really Do Grow More Rapidly: Evidence from 95 LDCs, 1976–85", *Economic Development and Cultural Change*, Vol. 40, pp. 523–44.

Dollar, D. and A. Kraay (2001), "Trade, Growth and Poverty", *Policy Research Working Paper*, No. 2587, World Bank, Washington, D.C.

Finger, J.M. and P. Schuler (1999), "Implementation of Uruguay Round Commitments: the Development Challenge", Policy Research Working Paper No. 2215, World Bank, Washington, D.C.

Fontagné, L. and N. Péridy (1997), *the EU and the Maghreb*, Development Centre Studies, OECD, Paris.

Frankel, J. and D. Romer (1999), "Does Trade Cause Growth?", *American Economic Review*, Vol. 89, pp. 279–396.

Fukasaku, K. (2000), "Special and Differential Treatment for Developing Countries: Does It Help Those Who Help Themselves?", WIDER Working Paper No.197, the United Nations University, Helsinki, September.

Fukasaku, K. (1995) (ed.), *Regional Integration and Co–operation in Asia*, the Asian Development Bank and the OECD Development Centre, Paris.

Fukasaku, K. and H.–B. Solignac Lecomte (1998), "Economic Transition and Trade Policy Reform: Lessons from China", in O. Bouin, F. Coricelli and F. Lemoine, eds., *Different Paths to a Market Economy: China and European Economies in Transition*, CEPII–CEPR–OECD Development Centre.

Fukasaku, K., Y. Ma and Q. Yang (1999), *China's Unfinished Open–economy Reforms: Liberalisation of Services*, Technical Papers No. 147, OECD Development Centre, Paris.

Fukasaku, K. and D. Wall (1994), *China's Long March to an Open Economy*, Development Centre Studies, OECD, Paris.

GATT (1985), "Trade Policies for a Better Future" (the Leutwiler Report), Geneva.

GOLDIN, I., O. KNUDSEN AND D. VAN DER MENSBRUGGHE (1993), *Trade Liberalisation: Global Economic Implications*, joint OECD Development Centre/World Bank publication, Paris.

GOLDIN, I. AND D. VAN DER MENSBRUGGHE (1992), *Trade Liberalisation: What's at Stake?*, Policy Brief No. 5, OECD Development Centre, Paris.

GOLDSTEIN, A. (2002), *New Regionalism in the Sub–Saharan Africa*, Policy Brief No. 20, OECD Development Centre, Paris.

HIEMENZ, U. *et al.* (1991), *The International Competitiveness of Developing Countries for Risk Capital* (Chapter 8), the Kiel Institute for the World Economy, J.C.B. Moh, Tübingen.

KRUEGER, A.O. (1997), "Trade Policy and Economic Development: How We Learn", *American Economic Review*, Vol.87, pp. 1–22.

KRUEGER, A.O. (1995), "Policy Lessons from Development Experience Since the Second World War", *in* J. BEHRMAN AND T.N. SRINIVASan, eds., *Handbook of Development Economics*, Vol. III (Chapter 40, pp. 2497–2550).

LAWRENCE, R.Z. AND D.E. WEINSTEIN (2001), "Trade and Growth: Import–Led or Export–Led? — Evidence from Japan and Korea", *in* J.E. STIGLITZ AND S. YUSUF, eds. (Chapter 10), pp. 379–408.

LITTLE, I., T. SCITOVSKY AND M. SCOTT (1970), *Industry and Trade in Some Developing Countries*, Oxford University Press, London.

MILNER, C. (eds.) (1990), *Export Promotion Strategies: Theory and Evidence from Developing Countries*, New York University Press, New York.

OBORNE, M.W. (1986), *China's Special Economic Zones*, OECD Development Centre, Paris.

OECD (2002), *The Benefits and Costs of Foreign Direct Investment* (forthcoming), Paris.

OECD (2001a), *The Development Dimensions of Trade*, Paris.

OECD (2001b), *Open Service Markets Matter*, Paris.

OECD (1999a), *Reaping the Full Benefits of Open Markets*, Paris.

OECD (1999b), *Policy Coherence Matters*, Paris.

OECD (1998), *Open Markets Matter*, Paris.

OECD (1997), *The World in 2020: Towards a New Global Age*, Paris.

OECD (1995), *Linkages: OECD and Major Developing Economies*, Paris.

OECD Development Centre (2002), *Foreign Direct Investment and Development: Where Do We Stand?*, mimeo, Paris.

PELKMANS, J. AND K. FUKASAKU (1995), "Evolving Trade Links between Europe and Asia: Towards 'Open Continentalism'?", *in* K. FUKASAKU (ed.)., Paris.

PRITCHETT, L. (1996), "Measuring Outward Orientation in LDC's: Can It Be Done?", *Journal of Development Economics*, Vol. 49, pp. 307–335.

REUBER, G., H. CROOKELL, M. EMERSON AND G. GALLAIS–HAMONNO (1973), *Private Foreign Investment in Development*, Clarendon Press, Oxford.

RODRIK, D. (1999), *The New Global Economy and Developing Countries: Making Openness Work*, Policy Essay No. 24, Overseas Development Council, Washington, D.C.

RODRIK, D. (1995), "Trade and Industrial Policy Reform", *in* J. BEHRMAN AND T.N. SRINIVASAN, eds., *Handbook of Development Economics*, Vol. III (Chapter 45, pp. 2925–2982).

RODRIQUEZ, F. AND D. RODRIK (1999), "Trade Policy and Economic Growth: A Skeptic's Guide to the Cross–National Evidence", *NBER Working Paper*, No. 7081, Cambridge, MA.

ROMER, P.M. (1994), "New Goods, Old Theory and the Welfare Costs of Trade Restrictions", *Journal of Development Economics*, Vol. 43, pp. 5–38.

ROMER, P.M. (1993), "Two Strategies for Economic Development: Using Ideas and Producing Ideas", *Proceedings of the World Bank Annual Conference on Development Economics 1992*, pp. 63–91.

SACHS, J.D. AND A.M. WARNER (1995), "Economic Reform and the Process of Global Integration", *Brookings Papers on Economic Activity*, Vol. 1, pp. 1–118.

SAFADI, R. AND S. LAIRD (1996), "The Uruguay Round and Developing Countries", *World Development*, Vol. 24, pp. 1223–1242.

SAUVÉ, P. (2000), "Developing Countries and the GATS 2000 Round", *Journal of World Trade*, Vol. 34, pp. 85–92.

SCHRANK, A. (2001), "Export Processing Zones: Free Market Islands or Bridges to Structural Transformation?", *Development Policy Review*, Vol. 19, pp. 223–242.

SRINIVASAN, T.N. AND J. BHAGWATI (1999), "Outward–orientation and Development: Are Revisionists Right?", Discussion Paper No. 806, Yale University, CT.

STIGLITZ, J.E. AND S. YUSUF (eds.) (2001), *Rethinking the East Asian Miracle*, Oxford University Press.

SUBRAMANIAN, A. AND D. ROY (2001), "Who Can Explain the Mauritian Miracle: Meade, Roner, Sachs or Rodrik?", *IMF Working Paper*, WP/01/116, Washington, D.C.

UNCTAD (2000), *World Investment Report 2000,* United Nations, New York and Geneva.

URATA, S. (2001), "Emergence of an FDI–Trade Nexus and the Economic Growth in East Asia", *in* J.E. STIGLITZ, AND S. YUSUF, eds. (Chapter 11), pp. 409–59.

WADE, R. (1990), *Governing the Market*, Princeton University Press, Princeton, N.J.

WALL, D. (1993), "China's Economic Reform and Opening–up Process: the Role of the Special Economic Zones", *Development Policy Review*, Vol. 11, pp. 243–60.

WARR, P. (1990), "Export Processing Zones", *in* C. MILNEr (ed.), *Export Promotion Strategies: Theory and Evidence from Developing Countries*, New York University Press, New York.

WORLD BANK (2002a), *Globalization, Growth and Poverty: Building an Inclusive World Economy*, Washington, D.C.

WORLD BANK (2002b), *Global Economic Prospects with the Developing Countries*, Washington, D.C.

WORLD BANK (2000), *Trade Blocs*, Washington, D.C.

WORLD BANK (1993), *The East Asian Miracle: Economic Growth and Public Policy*, Washington, D.C.

WORLD BANK (1981), *Accelerated Development in Sub–Saharan Africa: An Agenda for Action*, Washington, D.C.

WTO (2001a), *Annual Report 2001*, Geneva.

WTO (2001b), *Market Access: Unfinished Business: Post–Uruguay Round Inventory and Issues*, Special Studies 6, Geneva.

WTO (2000), "Integrated Framework for Trade–Related Assistance to Least–Developed Countries", WT/COMTD/LDC/7, 23 February 2000, Geneva.

WTO (1998), *Trading into the Future* (2nd Edition), Geneva.

YOUNG, A. (1995), "The Tyranny of Numbers: Confronting the Statistical Realities of the East Asian Growth Experience", *Quarterly Journal of Economics*, Vol. 110, pp. 641–80.

YOUNG, A. (1992), "A Tale of Two Cities: Factor Accumulation and Technological Change in Hong Kong and Singapore", *National Bureau of Economic Research Macroeconomics Annual 1992*, MIT Press, Cambridge, Mass.

Chapter 10

Governing Financial Globalisation

Helmut Reisen

The 21st century is expected to see a growing share of global output move from the rapidly ageing OECD economies to the younger developing world. This will benefit both regions. With labour forces stagnating or shrinking in the OECD area and with pension assets increasingly decumulated, returns on capital will be depressed. All the world's labour force growth will take place in the developing countries, promising higher returns on capital there. This promise is reinforced by the observation that poor countries have a higher potential to grow than rich countries.

These expectations, though, would not materialise without substantial global capital flows, efficiently allocated to their highest *sustainable* social rate of return. Overcoming world poverty requires private capital to flow from capital–rich ageing countries to those capital–poor countries which host all the current and future world's labour force growth. To this day, the requirement is hardly fulfilled. Ever since commercial banks started to recycle massive OPEC surpluses to a selected group of developing countries in the late 1970s, boom episodes have been followed by financial crises while the geographical distribution of private investment to the developing world has been uneven.

Developing–country governments and central banks have to care about the sustainability of the capital flows which their economies can tap abroad. Global capital markets still suffer from major distortions: herd behaviour, excessive risk taking and occasional detachment from fundamentals. Unlike industrial countries, developing countries need to meet capital reversals with immediate and costly cutbacks in domestic absorption. The expansion of domestic credit connected with unsterilised capital inflows may not be sound enough to stand the rise in domestic interest rates and the fall in domestic asset prices that go with a reversal of these inflows; the resulting breakdown of domestic financial institutions provides incentives for monetary expansion and fiscal deficits incurred by the public bailout of ailing banks. Temporary capital flows may lead to an unsustainable appreciation in the real exchange rate which is in conflict with development strategies based on the expansion of exports and efficient import substitution, which centrally relies on a reliable and competitive exchange rate.

Local and global governance needs to improve in order better to exploit the growth potential of global finance for developing countries. Research at the OECD Development Centre has both defined the potential benefits of strengthened financial globalisation and devised policy orientations towards crisis prevention in developing countries.

Global Pension Flows and Pension Reform

In principle, the case for mutual benefits arising from financial globalisation is nowhere stronger than for funded retirement savings (Reisen, 1994; OECD, 1997). While unfunded (pay–as–you–go) pension schemes are locked into the ageing economy, fully funded pension schemes would not escape demographic pressures if their assets were to remain invested in ageing countries alone. Indeed, when the baby boom generation starts to draw on the funded pension schemes, the impact of that decumulation on local asset prices and thus on pension benefits might be negative. The diversification of OECD pension assets into the non–OECD stock markets provides the prospect of higher expected return for a given level of risk or, put alternatively, lower risk by eliminating non–systemic volatility without sacrificing expected return. It is less the superior growth performance of the non–OECD area than the low correlation of returns generated by the emerging stock markets with those of the OECD stock markets that governs this expectation. The correlation between returns on OECD and emerging stock markets will remain low even when diversification gains are seriously exploited. Differences between the two areas with respect to the exposure to country–specific shocks, the stage of economic and demographic maturity and the (lack of) harmonisation of economic policies suggest that the diversification gains for OECD pension assets will not disappear quickly. The benefits of global portfolio diversification also apply to emerging country pension assets as they could diversify away some of the risks stemming from high exposure to shocks in their own countries by investing a portion of their pension assets in OECD countries (Reisen, 1997).

Several Development Centre studies have contributed importantly to the OECD horizontal activities that resulted in *Maintaining Prosperity in an Ageing Society* (OECD, 1998a) as well as earlier to the *Linkages Study* (OECD, 1997). In the early 1980s, Chile pioneered radical pension reform, moving from a public pay–as–you go to a private funded pension system. While many OECD countries were late to tackle the problems of population ageing, Chile's reform was emulated in much of Latin America. The Development Centre issued the first comprehensive study of pension reform in Latin America (Queisser, 1998). The study showed that the benefits of reform can be important but are easily oversold, giving rise to potential disillusionment. While pension reform was seen to help strengthen a country's financial infrastructure and corporate bond market, noted shortcomings were high administration cost and low effective coverage of the working–age population.

Although it is often assumed that the growth in funded pension assets represents a net increase in savings, such asset growth may simply reflect a shift in the form of saving, with pension funds displacing other savings. Bailliu and Reisen (1997) were the first to produce significant international evidence in support of the premise that the rise of funded pensions does indeed, at least in developing countries, contribute to higher national savings. The biggest impact on savings can be expected from funded pension schemes that are mandatory and that discourage borrowing against accumulated mandatory pension assets.

The recent rise of pension assets in both OECD and non–OECD countries also raised new questions for global finance. A series of papers established the case for the pension–improving benefits of global asset diversification (for a collection of these essays, see Reisen, 2000). They made the case for investing part of the growing OECD pension assets in the developing world, promising a "free lunch" — higher risk–adjusted returns for any portfolio underinvested in developing countries — based on modern portfolio theory. A Development Centre Policy Brief (Fischer and Reisen, 1995) looked into the regulatory needs in developing countries to accommodate pension flows from the ageing economies safely. Another paper, prepared for an experts meeting held by the OECD Committee on Financial Markets (OECD, 1998b) emphasised the demographic impact on stock market valuation. The favourable support on OECD stock market valuations from the strong baby boom cohorts is predicted to be reversed from about 2010, as US funded pensions will cease to be a source of net savings. This is likely to support a shift of OECD–based assets into the emerging stock markets where favourable demographic trends will continue well into the year 2050. A simulation model of global pension fund investment (MacKellar and Reisen, 1998) cautions, however, that capital flows from ageing OECD to younger developing countries can only slightly attenuate, not reverse, the pressure exerted by population ageing and declining labour force on capital returns. The model also sheds a light on the distributive impact of the interaction between financial globalisation and population ageing: global financial integration benefits elderly lifetime savers, but hurts the (poorer) lifetime non–savers in OECD countries, hence increasing the urgency of implementing policies which encourage or force poor households to save.

The sheer size of local pension assets and the uniform investment pattern of Chilean pension funds led Chile's authorities to worry about the impact on the foreign exchange and local bond markets, if the local pension funds were free to invest abroad. At the request of the Ministry of Finance of the Republic of Chile, Reisen and Williamson (1994) prepared a macroeconomic analysis on the desirability of localisation requirements imposed on pension funds in developing countries. The paper argued, by contrast, that such concerns were misplaced.

173

Since the diversification of pension assets fosters stock market integration rather than interest linkages, it does little to limit short–term monetary sovereignty. A related paper (Reisen, 1997) argued that the new pension funds in Latin America (and other emerging markets) stand to benefit from international diversification, just like the funds located in OECD countries. But there will not be a free lunch for a pension fund in a developing country: diversifying into developed markets will reduce risk, at the cost of lower returns. This is a price worth paying for funds whose pension beneficiaries are poor and thus cannot tolerate much risk. *The Economist*, devoting its *Economic Focus Page* to the paper, summarised it aptly: low returns, happy returns. Moreover, restrictions of foreign investment by developing–country pension funds can hardly be justified on grounds of financial–development externalities: the home bias generally observed in pension fund investment should translate into sufficient potential demand for domestic financial assets so as to deepen markets and the institutional infrastructure. A case for initial localisation requirements, however, can be derived from the fiscal costs of moving from unfunded to fully funded pension systems if a rise in domestic interest rates due to fiscal illusion and domestic tax collection costs is important.

The 1980s Debt Crisis

The international debt crisis that erupted in 1982 threatened the world financial system and turned the 1980s into a "lost decade" for Latin America. The curtailment of new bank lending and rising cost of debt service resulted in resource transfers from developing debtor to developed creditor countries. Initially, the debtors' plight was ill–conceived as a dollar problem: countries had to run a sufficient current account surplus to earn their way back to creditworthiness. Yet, despite improved current accounts, debtor countries were unable for most of the 1980s to regain access to world financial markets (Cline, 1995).

A Development Centre study (Reisen and van Trotsenburg, 1988a) helped to shift policy attention from the external dollar problem to the underlying internal budget problem. Not the capacity to raise foreign exchange revenue but the scope for non–inflationary fiscal adjustment was the binding constraint on the way back to international creditworthiness. The foreign debt, mostly owned or guaranteed by the government, had to be financed by the internal transfer of resources from the private to the public sector. As tax base broadening traditionally proves difficult in developing countries, the bulk of debt service was financed through cuts in government investment or higher inflation. Both options strongly reduced the growth potential in much of Latin America.

Related work called attention to the fact that the servicing of foreign debt increasingly led to growing domestic public debt, hence mortgaging future stabilisation policies. That research emphasised currency mismatches in the

174

government budget constraint as debt was mostly denominated in foreign currency while tax receipts were based on local currency. The analysis consequently called for an end to the series of currency depreciation in debtor countries as it was seen to worsen public finances and developed major policy orientations for growth–oriented fiscal adjustement that helped minimise real depreciation of the exchange rate and contain the cost of domestic public debt (Reisen, 1989).

Meanwhile, the debt overhang proposition, most prominently advanced by Sachs (1988) and Krugman (1988), gained international support. It established that the existence of a heavy debt burden would reduce the incentive for debtor countries to adjust (and to grow out of debt). The proposition had given an important rationale for the 1989 switch in international debt management from the Baker to the *Brady Plan*, emphasising debt relief rather than new money for problem debtors. An alternative hypothesis, more in line with the Development Centre study on the debtors' transfer problem, blamed the lack of investment on a scarcity of financial resources as a country's savings are drained off by a net transfer. Hofman and Reisen (1990) provided empirical evidence which rejected the debt overhang hypothesis but was in line with the alternative credit constraint hypothesis. The finding had important implications for policy. Cutting the size of debt as envisaged by the Brady Plan would not by itself be enough to spur investment and growth in debtor countries without new lending as countries needed new funds to take advantage of profitable investment opportunities.

However, the presence of high public debt introduces the possibility of dual equilibria in determining interest and inflation rates: As high interest rates increase government indebtedness, they not only reflect but also determine inflation expectations and sovereign risk (Calvo, 1988). An evaluation of the Brady Plan effects on Mexico (Reisen, 1991) found that while the direct effects of the Brady Plan on the country's external transfer had been weak, it nevertheless improved confidence and thus lowered the cost of Mexico's domestic debt. The plan thus exerted considerable leverage in the form of an automatic improvement in Mexico's public finances that far exceeded its direct effects. Such leverage, Centre analysis cautioned, was only available for countries which ran a primary budget surplus (Berthélemy and Vourc'h, 1991).

Opening the Capital Account

A trend very early identified and covered by OECD Development Centre research has been financial opening of developing countries. The research output has provided influential help to authorities in many developing countries contemplating and implementing *de jure* liberalisation of external capital flows. Leaving the 1980s debt crisis behind, policy makers used the opportunity to tap foreign savings and know–how by dismantling capital controls. Early experiences with financial opening in the Southern Cone of Latin America, however, cautioned that the financial reform process had to be carefully designed. The economic debate sought to explain Latin American reform failure in terms of an incorrect sequencing of the reform programmes. The *sequencing literature* recommended linking the acceptance of capital inflows to the progress in fiscal and monetary stabilisation, domestic financial liberalisation, prudential supervision and trade liberalisation (Edwards, 1990; McKinnon, 1991) .

The traditional sequencing literature tended to regard capital–account liberalisation as an all–or–nothing condition. Fischer and Reisen (1992) were the first to devise guidelines for sequencing the opening of the capital account in developing countries based on macroeconomic and institutional reform. They recommend that capital controls on long–term inward flows and trade–related flows be liberalised immediately, because liberalisation of these flows can be helpful even in the earliest stages of development. They advocate the removal of controls on both long– and short–term outflows only after sound government finances have been established, bad–loan problems have been resolved, and controls on domestic interest rates have been eliminated so that the differential between domestic and world interest rates is brought down to a low level. After the domestic financial system has been liberalised and weaknesses in domestic banks have been resolved, they suggest eliminating the barriers to foreign banks. Finally, they do not recommend liberalising short–term capital inflows until a sufficient level of competition is present in the banking sector and a sound system of banking regulation and supervision is in place. Williamson and Mahar (1998), in a comprehensive survey of financial liberalisation between 1973 and 1996 for 34 countries, have recently surveyed to what extent countries have followed the sequencing of financial opening advocated by Fischer and Reisen.

Some advanced developing countries became subject to pressure in bilateral talks to open up their financial systems. This raised an important policy issue: how open were the capital accounts in such countries? And had there been a trend towards more financial openness, as was often claimed by the governments concerned? How constrained has monetary and exchange rate policy been by the effective degree of opening? These questions could only be answered with sophisticated econometric techniques and the use of time–varying, rather than the usual constant, parameter estimation. Reisen and Yeches (1991) found for the period up to the early 1990s a low degree of capital mobility in some of Asia's newly industrialised countries, and no trend towards more openness. The findings implied that future dismantling of capital controls and of internal financial restrictions was thus likely to impose a considerable loss of monetary autonomy on those countries.

In the aftermath of the Asian crisis, the proponents of open capital markets have been criticised for having offered more "banner–waving" than hard empirical evidence that developing countries can derive from open capital accounts (e.g. by

Rodrik,1998). Reisen and Soto (2001) show, however, that the structure of inflows which the opening process entails will determine its growth impact as equity inflows have been shown to exert a strong independent impact on growth in developing countries during the 1990s. Bonds, by contrast, did not produce any significant impact on growth in the OECD Development Centre research, and foreign bank lending — both short and long term — was found to be negatively associated with tomorrow's per capita income growth in the recipient country, unless local banks were sufficiently capitalised. This finding is consistent with earlier evidence (Polak, 1989) that credit intermediation through the global banking system is often economically inefficient. Arteta *et al.* (2001) show the effects of capital–account liberalisation in developing countries to vary with the quality of the institutional framework, with the degree of macroeconomic balances and with the degree of general openess of the economy. High levels of perceived corruption tilt capital flows towards the short term (Wei, 2000), hence make countries that liberalise vulnerable to costly sudden withdrawals of capital. Countries with significant trade distortions and large black market premia have been shown to grow more slowly if they opened their capital accounts. These observations define the necessary prerequisites for successful opening of the capital account.

Choosing Appropriate Exchange Rate Regimes

Don't Fix, Don't Float (Braga de Macedo *et al.,* 2001) summarises well a message that OECD Development Centre research has consistently produced on the choice of exchange rate regimes in developing countries over the last two decades. Several studies have documented the case for exchange rate management (rather than pure floats or hard pegs) and building (rather than lending abroad) macroeconomic credibility. Further, the limits and scope for monetary integration have been explored for Africa, Asia and Latin America.

"Corner" solutions to the choice of the exchange rate regime — pure floats or hard pegs (currency boards or dollarisation) — have been a popular policy choice because they confer instant credibility and high readibility of monetary policy. Coupled with financial liberalisation, however, such corner solutions have often failed as a result of real exchange rate overvaluation, deindustrialisation and low output growth. The dismal outcome of financial opening in the Southern Cone of Latin America in the late 1970s has also been shaped to a large degree by the exchange rate regime. Real exchange rates there became overvalued once attempts were made to stabilise inflationary expectations by announcing future devaluation rates below current inflation rates (*active crawling peg*). Anchoring inflationary expectations to the exchange rate did not work: excessive capital inflows exceeded the sterilisation capacity of the central bank and loosened fiscal and wage discipline, hence eroding the very foundations on which the nominal anchor approach is. New Zealand's bold economic reform in the mid 1980s resulted in macroeconomic disarray which destroyed any net benefits from microeconomic liberalisation for almost a decade. With a *purely floating* New Zealand dollar and with financial opening preceding stabilisation and labour market reform, post–reform monetary tightening was bound to lead to a Dornbusch–style overshooting of the real exchange rate. The appreciation of the currency forced New Zealand's manufactured industry to exit from world markets causing a quasi–permanent loss of exports (Joumard and Reisen, 1992).

These liberalisation experiences illustrate the case for exchange rate management and for its main policy instrument, sterilised intervention of the central bank on the foreign exchange and domestic money markets. During both liberalisation experiences, the monetary authorities failed to supply the appropriate mix of assets: They did nothing in the floating–rate case; they issued money in exchange for foreign assets in the pegged–rate case; they should have issued bonds instead, by engaging in sterilised intervention (Kenen, 1993).

Southeast Asia managed, at least up to the mid 1990s, to reconcile massive capital inflows, low inflation and competitive, stable real exchange rates. This success owed much to the art of central banking, based on fiscal discipline: the pragmatic use of public institutions such as social security funds, state banks and public enterprises as monetary instruments as well as the creation of sterilisation bonds. The use of public–sector savings and of mandatory private savings had to make up for the lack of developed domestic money markets on which in most industrial countries open–market operations are effected (Reisen, 1993a). Additional work, upon request by UN ECLAC, dealt with the many objections which economists have raised against sterilised intervention, such as lack of effectiveness and high fiscal cost. These Development Centre studies gave rise to an academic debate (to which the *Economist* devoted its *Economic Focus Page* in 1993), which has been summarised and advanced by Frankel (1994) who concluded that sterilised intervention is appropriate when there is a temporary rise in external demand for a country' s assets but that the policy is inappropriate when the shock originates in a rise of domestic money demand or an improved trade balance.

The analytical perspective on exchange rate regimes permitted Development Centre research to develop an early–warning system of sorts. Reisen (1993b) warned that Mexico and Argentina — at that time both on a hard peg as advocated by the finance industry and mainstream advice — were vulnerable to a financial crisis as inflows were temporary (rather than permanent), incomes policy too strained and inflation expectations too high to warrant a dollar peg, and the currency in both countries overvalued from a global *Purchasing Power Parity* perspective (a novel approach developed in Reisen's paper). The paper advocated that both countries follow Chile's pragmatic exchange rate management.

On monetary integration, research at the Development Centre has explored the suggestion that Asia's newly industrialising countries form a monetary union jointly with Japan on the pattern of the European Monetary System (Reisen and van Trotsenburg, 1988*b*). The study employed a number of suggestive criteria offered by the fertile theory of optimum currency areas to assess whether the Asian NICs should peg to the yen, as any monetary union in Asia involving Japan is bound to be as asymmetrical as the EMS had been. The answer then was a clear *No*.

After the Asian financial crisis 1997/1998 it had become an almost common view that intermediate exchange regimes were not sustainable in a world of intense capital mobility (Summers, 2000). Countries were advised to the corners of either firm fixing or free floating; there were few efforts to defend the intermediate regimes, such as target zones or basket pegs (Williamson, 2000; Bénassy–Quéré and Cœuré, 2000). Moreover, the introduction of the Euro may have led to a period of higher fluctuations between key currencies, producing risks for unstable competitiveness in many countries facing diverse export markets. Hence the quest for regional monetary integration in the developing world, witness recent initiatives in West Africa, Asia and the Mercosur area. Braga de Macedo *et al.* (2001) warn against instant fixes as these do not provide a fast lane to credibility. Their book makes the case for intermediate regimes for five country groups in Africa, Asia and Latin America and emphasise the importance of reliable and competitive exchange rates. They suggest building institutions in monetary, financial and budgetary matters along the EU Stability and Growth Pact as a way to produce sustainable growth and development.

Reducing Crisis Vulnerability

From the mid–1990s onward, the benfits of financial globalisation became increasingly undermined by a series of intense currency, banking and debt crises in developing countries (Griffith–Jones *et al.*, 2001). These repeated financial crises fed scepticism about the benefits of financial globalisation, the deep slump in the affected crisis countries negated past development achievements and threatened a reversal from globalisation, which would harm industrial and developing countries alike. The causes for financial crises can be found in host country mismanagement as well as in the fickle nature of capital flows (on which see below).

One way to reduce vulnerability to fickle capital flows is the promotion of domestic savings and their efficient allocation (Hausmann and Reisen, 1998). Monetary policy can stimulate savings by opting for money–based rather than exchange rate–based price stability, bringing inflation expectations to a point where the risk of wealth confiscation by bouts of high inflation is minimised without stimulating credit and consumption booms. Supervision of the financial system can help promote savings by keeping the pace of financial reform in line with a country's capacity to monitor and supervise credit risk. Pension reform does likewise if it is tax–financed rather than debt–financed, mandatory with high contribution rates and accompanied by liquidity constraints. Public savings can be stimulated with a minimum of distortions if reasonably low tax rates are combined with a strict enforcement of tax base broadening; in many developing countries, however, this requirement is not easily fulfilled for resistance by powerful lobbies.

Countries receiving large–scale capital inflows are at risk that these flows do not find their way into productive and long–term investment. A joint project between the Development Centre and UN ECLAC (Ffrench–Davis and Reisen, 1998) found that the effects generated by capital inflows vary with the domestic policies adopted. A comprehensive, active policy as practised in Chile has proven effective in influencing the composition of inflows, their volume and spread across time and their allocation into productive investment, while avoiding excessive outlier exchange–rate appreciation and lending booms.

In coping with the macroeconomic risks arising from capital inflows, Asia has been a "latecomer" to problems that Latin America had experienced early on, partly as a result of greater financial openness in the latter region. A paper requested by several Asian authorities (Reisen, 1996) draws five policy lessons from the heavy–inflow episode of the 1990s: identify the origin of rising foreign exchange reserves; identify the limits of foreign debt; discourage above–limit, short–term inflows; observe the trade off between price stability and competitiveness; and design policies to target monetary aggregates and exchange rates, including fiscal policy, sterilised intervention, reserve requirements and exchange rate management. A number of studies (e.g. Reisen, 1998a) recommended that countries resist debt–augmenting flows when they are seen to coincide with unsustainable currency appreciation, excessive risk–taking in the banking system and a sharp drop in private savings and define the size of the current account deficit that should be sustainable in the longer run by emphasising debt–GDP levels, the potential growth rate, import growth, catch–up exchange rate appreciation and the structure of capital inflows that finance such deficit in the current account of the balance of payments.

The 1994/95 Mexico crisis and the 1997/98 Asian crisis hit countries with strong macroeconomic fundamentals but weak domestic financial systems; these proved too weak a conduit for heavy capital inflows, resulting in declining credit quality and financial vulnerability to speculative currency attacks. Calvo and Mendoza (1996) advise developing countries to pay close attention to indicators of financial vulnerability, in particular to short–term debt levels as a fraction of official foreign reserves, as well as to currency and maturity mismatches in the private–sector balance sheets. Reisen (1998b) points to practicable avenues that can be pursued to avoid a rise in the vulnerability indicators above critical levels.

The most recent crises in Argentina and Turkey have brought the prime importance of fiscal discipline in reducing crisis vulnerability back to centre stage. Argentina's currency board arrangement had ceased to confer sufficient fiscal discipline and the consolidated public–sector deficit had been gradually rising from 1995 on. This gradually set in motion a vicious circle of rising country risk premia and depressed growth, in turn fuelling the public deficit through lower tax receipts and higher debt service cost. In a simulation exercise for Argentina, Grandes (2001) demonstrates the strong endogeneity of these variables. In a forecast variance decomposition, he finds that 40 to 60 per cent of the variance of the seasonally–adjusted fiscal deficit, seasonally–adjusted output growth and the sovereign risk premium can be explained by a shock to these very variables. While these findings may confirm the hypothesis of hard–peg supporters that *in theory* super–fixed exchange–rate regimes can trigger off a virtuous cycle of lower deficits, lower yield spreads and higher growth, the cycle has *in practice* turned very vicious indeed.

Towards a New Global Financial Architecture

In the wake of the Asian financial crisis, the international policy community has started to design and gradually build a global financial architecture aimed at preventing and containing financial crises in developing countries. The poorest countries were promised debt relief under the HIPC initiative. The UN initiated a major conference on Financing for Development in March 2002, stimulating debate on the role of global finance to reduce world poverty and raising the awareness for development finance (OECD, 2002).

Access of least developed countries to foreign finance will — apart from their governance performance — depend on the impact of the HIPC initiative signed at the 1999 G–7 Summit and discussed recently at the G–8 Summit in Genoa. Development Centre research (Cohen, 2000) has compared nominal present values of debt relief granted under this initiative and market values approximated by secondary market prices for Latin American debt in the 1980s. The results suggest that the effects of the HIPC initiative on actual resource flows, including debt service, may be less than often suggested. A country–specific impact study of the HIPC initiative was provided for six sub–Saharan countries in Joseph (2000), which reinforces Cohen's warning that the amount of changes in capital transfers achieved by the HIPC initiative has been modest.

The 1997–98 Asian crisis ranks already among the most notable of the many crises in financial history, affecting many key emerging markets beyond the region. The resulting policy challenges have given urgency to the debate on a coherent approach to financial globalisation. Reisen (1999) aims at informing that debate. It evaluates several suggestions for crisis resolution and crisis prevention, both on a global scale and with respect to host–country policies.

Progress towards a less crisis–prone international financial system will hinge on how to correct the excessive risk–taking by banks; regulatory distortions which bias bank lending towards the short–term must be corrected.

It is widely agreed that cross–border lending has faced regulatory distortions through the 1988 Basel Accord. Most importantly, short–term bank lending to the emerging markets has been encouraged by a relatively low 20 per cent risk weight, while bank credit to non–OECD banks with a residual maturity of over one year has been discouraged by a 100 per cent risk weight. This has stimulated cross–border interbank lending, which has been described as the "Achilles' heel" of the international financial system. Hence, a reform of the Basel Accord should be welcome (Basel Committee on Banking Supervision, 2001). Research at the Development Centre, however, warns that reform proposals (Basel II) risk deepening the regulatory divide between investment–grade and many developing–country borrowers; the latter will find it hard to tap debt finance at sustainable cost and at stable terms unless they reach investment–grade status (Reisen, 2001).

Moreover, there is reason for concern that Basel II will raise the volatility of private capital flows to speculative–grade developing countries. The Accord will destabilise private capital flows to the developing countries, if the current proposal to link regulatory bank capital to sovereign ratings is maintained. Assigning fixed minimum capital to bank assets whose risk weights are in turn determined by market–lagging ratings will reinforce the tendency of the capital ratio to work in a pro–cyclical way. The increased importance of rating agencies for emerging–market finance has brought their work to the attention of a wider group of observers – and under criticism. The Mexican crisis of 1994–95 brought out that credit rating agencies, like almost anybody else, were reacting to events rather than anticipating them, an observation reinforced by rating performance before and during the Asian crisis (Larraín et al., 1997; Reisen and von Maltzan, 1999). While the explanatory power of conventional rating determinants has declined since the Asian crisis, recent rating performance for Argentina and Turkey can still be qualified as lagging the markets, as variables of financial–sector strength and the endogenous effects of capital flows on macroeconomic variables seem to remain underemphasised in rating assessments. The market impact of sovereign ratings may decline in the future as agencies have started to modify their country ceiling policy and as market participants try to exploit bond trading opportunities arising from the lagged nature of ratings (Reisen, 2002).

Hausmann and Hiemenz (2000), in the context of the annual Forum on Latin American Perspectives co–organised by the Inter–American Development Bank and the OECD Development Centre since 1990, focuses on evaluating recently suggested changes to the international financial architecture. It debates whether the current reforms of the global financial markets are succeeding in identifying and addressing major distortions to international capital flows between developed and developing countries; essentially, the moral hazard versus sovereign risk question. Particular attention is devoted to bailing the private sector into crisis prevention and resolution, including under the Paris Club framework. Current reforms of the global financial architecture are viewed as containing ever–rising fiscal costs of crisis resolution, while strengthening crisis prevention through (ex ante) private–sector bail–ins. Authorities in developing countries, however, are concerned that current reform efforts will deepen sovereign risk and lower the resource transfer to developing countries. The conference volume concludes that it is urgent for the official community to agree rapidly with private market participants about an ex ante framework for burden sharing (including agreements about seniority claims) in order to end the present uncertainties about the legal investment framework.

The issue is still unresolved, even though the International Monetary Fund has recently advanced discussion on a global bankruptcy framework. Enlisting the private sector in crisis management by introducing rollover clauses into short–term debt contracts and collective–action clauses into long–term debt contracts will be an important step to strengthening the international financial architecture (Kenen, 2001).

Bibliography

ARTETA, C., B. EICHENGREEN AND C. WYPLOSZ (2001), "When Does Capital Account Liberalization Help More than It Hurts?", *NBER Working Paper* No. 8414.

BAILLIU, J. AND H. REISEN (1997*), Do Funded Pensions Contribute to Higher Aggregate Savings? A Cross–Country Analysis*, Technical Papers No. 130, OECD Development Centre, Paris and (1998) *Weltwirtschaftliches Archiv* 134 (4).

BASEL COMMITTEE ON BANKING SUPERVISION (2001), *Overview of the New Basel Capital Accord: Consultative Document*, Basel.

BÉNASSY–QUÉRÉ, A. AND B. CŒURÉ (2000), "Big and Small Currencies: The Regional Connection", *CEPII Working Paper* No. 2000–10.

BERTHÉLEMY, J. AND A. VOURC'H (1991*), Le partage du fardeau entre les creanciers de pays debiteurs defaillants*, Document techniques n° 44, OECD Development Centre, Paris.

BRAGA DE MACEDO, J., D. COHEN AND H. REISEN (2001), *Don't Fix, Don't Float,* Development Centre Studies, OECD, Paris.

CALVO, G. (1988), "Servicing the Public Debt: The Role of Expectations", *American Economic Review* 78 (4).

CALVO, G. AND E. MENDOZA (1996), "Petty Crime and Cruel Punishment: Lessons from the Mexican Debacle", *American Economic Review*, Papers and Proceedings.

CLINE, W. (1995), *International Debt Reexamined*, Institute for International Economics.

COHEN, D. (2000), *The HIPC Initiative: True and False Promises*, Technical Papers No. 166, OECD Development Centre, Paris.

EDWARDS, S. (1990), "The Sequencing of Economic Reform: Analytical Issues and Lessons from Latin American Experience", *The World Economy* 13(1).

FFRENCH–DAVIS, R. AND H. REISEN (1998), *Capital Flows and Investment Performance: Lessons from Latin America*, ECLAC/Development Centre Studies, OECD, Paris.

FISCHER, B. AND H. REISEN (1992), *Towards Capital Account Convertibility*, Policy Brief No. 4, OECD Development Centre, Paris.

FISCHER, B. AND H. REISEN (1995), *Pension Fund Investment: From Ageing to Emerging Markets*, Policy Brief No. 9, OECD Development Centre, Paris.

FRANKEL, J. (1994), " Sterilization of Money Inflows: Difficult (Calvo) or Easy (Reisen)?", *IMF Working Paper* WP/94/159 and (1994) *Estudio de Economia* 24.

GRANDES M. (2001*), External Solvency, Dollarisation and Investment Grade: Towards a Vicious Circle?*, Technical Papers No. 177, OECD Development Centre, Paris.

GRIFFITH–JONES, S., M. MONTES AND A. NASUTION (2001), *Short–Term Capital Flows and Economic Crises*, Oxford University Press, Oxford.

HAUSMANN, R. AND U. HIEMENZ (eds.) (2000), *Global Finance from a Latin American Viewpoint*, Development Centre Seminars, OECD, Paris.

HAUSMANN, R. AND H. REISEN (eds.) (1998), *Promoting Savings in Latin America*, Development Centre Seminars, OECD, Paris.

HOFMAN, B. AND H. REISEN (1990), *Debt Overhang, Liquidity Constraints and Adjustment Incentives*, Technical Papers No. 32, OECD Development Centre, Paris and (1991) *Weltwirtschaftliches Archiv* 127(2).

JOSEPH, A. (2000), *Resoudre le problème de la dette; de l'initiative PPTE a Cologne*, Technical Papers No. 163, OECD Development Centre, Paris.

JOUMARD, I. AND H. REISEN (1992), "Real Exchange Rate Overshooting and Persistent Trade Effects", *The World Economy* 15(3).

KENEN, P. (1993), "Financial Opening and the Exchange Rate Regime", *in* H. REISEN AND B. FISCHER (eds.), *Financial Opening: Policy Issues and Experiences in Developing Countries*, Development Centre Documents, OECD, Paris.

KENEN, P. (2001), *The International Financial Architecture: What's New? What's Missing?*, Institute for International Economics.

KRUGMAN, P. (1988), "Market–Based Debt Reduction Schemes", *NBER Working Paper* No. 2587.

LARRAÍN, G., H. REISEN AND J. VON MALTZAN (1997), *Emerging Market Risk and Sovereign Credit Ratings*, Technical Papers No. 124, OECD Development Centre, Paris.

MACKELLAR, L. AND H. REISEN (1998), *A Simulation Model of Global Pension Fund Investment*, Technical Papers No. 137, OECD Development Centre, Paris.

MCKINNON, R. (1991), *The Order of Economic Liberalization: Financial Control in the Transition to a Market Economy*, Johns Hopkins University Press.

OECD (2002), *2001 Development Co–operation Report – New Impetus, New Challenge*.

OECD (1998a), *Maintaining Prosperity in an Ageing Society*.

OECD (1998b), *Institutional Investors in the New Financial Landscape*.

OECD (1997), *The World Economy in 2020: Towards a New Global Age*.

POLAK, J. (1989), *Financial Policies and Development*, OECD Development Centre Studies.

QUEISSER, M. (1998), *The Second Generation Pension Reforms in Latin America*, Development Centre Studies, OECD, Paris.

REISEN, H. (2002), "Ratings Since the Asian Crisis", *in* R. FFRENCH–DAVIS AND S. GRIFFITH–JONES, *Capital Flows to Emerging Markets Since the Asian Crisis*, UN Wider.

REISEN, H. (2001), "Will Basel II Contribute to Convergence in International Capital Flows?", *in* Oesterreichische Nationalbank, Proceedings of 29th Economics Conference and (2001) *Bankarchiv* 49(August).

185

REISEN, H. (2000), *Pensions, Savings and Capital Flows*, Edward Elgar Publishing Ltd. in association with the OECD.

REISEN, H. (1999), *After the Great Asian Slump: Towards a Coherent Approach to Global Capital Flows*, Policy Brief No. 16, OECD Development Centre, Paris.

REISEN, H. (1998a), *Excessive and Sustainable Current Account Deficits*, and Technical Papers No. 132, OECD Development Centre, Paris and (1998) *Empirica* 25(2),

REISEN, H. (1998b), *Domestic Causes of Currency Crises: Policy Lessons for Crisis Avoidance*, Technical Papers No. 136, OECD Development Centre, Paris and (1998) *IDS Bulletin*.

REISEN, H. (1997), "Liberalising Foreign Investment by Pension Funds: Positive and Normative Aspects", Technical Papers No. 120, OECD Development Centre, Paris and (1997) *World Development* 25(4).

REISEN, H. (1996), "Managing Volatile Capital Inflows: The Experience of the 1990s", *Asian Development Review* 14(1).

REISEN, H. (1994), "On the Wealth of Nations and Retirees", *in* R. O'BRIEN (ed.), *Finance and the International Economy: 8, The Amex Bank Review Prize Essays*, Oxford University Press, Oxford.

REISEN, H (1993a), "Southeast Asia and the 'Impossible Trinity' ", *International Economic Insights 4(3).*

REISEN, H. (1993b), "Integration with Disinflation: Which Way?", *in* R. O'BRIEN (ed.), *Finance and the International Economy: 7, The Amex Bank Review Prize Essays*, Oxford University Press, Oxford.

REISEN, H. (1991), "The Brady Plan and Adjustment Incentives", *Intereconomics*, March/April.

REISEN, H. (1989), "Public Debt, External Competitiveness, and Fiscal Discipline", *Princeton Studies in International Finance* No. 66.

REISEN, H. AND M. SOTO (2001), "Which Types of Capital Inflows Foster Developing–Country Growth?", *International Finance* 4:1.

REISEN, H. AND A. VAN TROTSENBURG (1988a), *Developing Country Debt: The Budgetary and Transfer Problem*, Development Centre Studies, OECD, Paris.

REISEN, H. AND A. VAN TROTSENBURG (1988b), "Should the Asian NICs Peg to the Yen?", *Intereconomics* July/August.

REISEN, H. AND J. VON MALTZAN (1999), *Boom and Bust and Sovereign Ratings*, Technical Papers No. 148, OECD Development Centre, Paris.

REISEN, H. AND J. WILLIAMSON (1994), *Pensions Funds, Capital Controls and Macroeconomic Stability*, Technical Papers No. 98, OECD Development Centre, Paris.

REISEN, H. AND H. YECHES (1991), *Time–Varying Estimates on the Openness of the Capital Account in Korea and Taiwan*, Technical Papers No. 42, OECD Development Centre, Paris, and (1993) *Journal of Development Economics* 41(2).

RODRIK, D. (1998), "Who Needs Capital–Account Convertibility?", *in* P. KENEN (ed.), *Should the IMF Pursue Capital–Account Convertibility?, Princeton Essays in International Finance* No. 207.

SACHS, J. (1988), " Conditionality, Debt Relief, and the Developing Country Debt Crisis", *in* J. SACHS (ed.), *Developing Country Debt and Economic Performance*, Chicago University Press.

SUMMERS, L. (2000), "International Financial Crises: Causes, Prevention and Cures", *American Economic Review, Papers and Proceedings,* Richard T. Ely Lecture.

WEI, S. (2000), *Negative Alchemy? Corruption and Composition of Capital Flows,* Technical Papers No. 165, OECD Development Centre, Paris.

WILLIAMSON, J. (2000), *Exchange Rate Regimes for Emerging Markets: Reviving the Intermediate Option,* Institute for International Economics.

WILLIAMSON, J. AND M. MAHAR (1998), "A Survey of Financial Liberalization ', *Princeton Essays in International Finance* No. 211.

Chapter 11

Civil Society and Development

Ida Mc Donnell and Henri–Bernard Solignac Lecomte

The evolution of non–governmental organisations (NGOs) has been traced and documented by the OECD Development Centre over the past 40 years[1]. Their remarkable rise in numbers and influence, particularly from the 1980s onwards, helped shape international development co–operation, but they were also transformed in the process. At the beginning of the new millennium, NGOs have become so successful that the largest among them contribute to national and international policy debates on development co–operation; public opinion in OECD countries often trusts them better than governments to deliver aid; and as ODA declines, their own budgets keep getting bigger.

However, globalisation has brought with it new development questions, and new actors have appeared. NGOs, heterogenous to start with, eventually find themselves part of a much bigger movement, an emerging "global civil society", which, like them, aims at influencing policy, but unlike them, does not aim exclusively — or at all — to alleviate human suffering in poor countries, and when it does, has little experience of relief and development in practice. As global civil society organisations, in turn, rise in numbers and influence, NGOs must redefine their role and their very identity.

Definitions

"Non–governmental organisation", an umbrella term describing non–state actors in development and humanitarian activities and policy formulation, is often used as a synonym for voluntary, charity, non–profit and civil society organisations:

> There is some confusion about the role of development NGOs in civil society. Sometimes they have been treated as synonymous, and the funding of development NGOs has been rephrased as support for civil society. However, development NGOs only form one group of organisations within civil society (BOND, 1997)[2].

That there is no shortage of definitions merely reflects the heterogeneity of their organisational features — from small close–knit organisations to nationwide federations and international networks — and that of the issues they tackle — which might be anything from the human rights of one particular ethnic group to the entire mosaic of development concerns[3].

While the OECD Development Centre has recently undertaken to broaden the scope of its analysis and dialogue activities to private sector organisations[4], the focus has so far been largely on NGOs in a stricter sense. Thus, in this chapter, "NGOs" are simply defined both by their non–governmental, not–for–profit nature, and their direct, strategic involvement in either *humanitarian* and emergency relief or *development* activities in developing countries[5]. In that, they differ from other groups involved in lobbying for policy change — many of which are labelled as the "global civil society"— to the extent that they originate from involvement in the field. They also differ from NGOs involved in activities other than relief and development in poor countries, such as those working to alleviate suffering and poverty in developed countries. Finally, it should be stressed that civil society organisations *other than NGOs* do have an established tradition of development–related co–operation and training activities, especially trade unions, as documented early on by the Development Centre[6].

How NGOs Changed the World — At Least Shaped International Development Co–operation

Colonisation, slavery and war have been at the root of the modern secular NGO movement. It was preceded in history by *missionary bodies* working in Africa and Asia since the 18th and 19th centuries, and by organisations such as the Foreign Anti–Slavery Society (est. 1839), and the International Committee of the Red Cross (ICRC, est. 1864). Most of today's bigger emergency and development NGOs were established in the 20th century in response to war and related humanitarian crises, first in Europe — the First World War and especially the Second World War, with a "big push" from US–based organisations — and then elsewhere in the world, including in developing countries (e.g. Korea, Nigeria).

From the 1960s, as they turned their attention to disasters and humanitarian crises in the poorer countries, NGOs started to focus mainly on food aid, emergency health treatments and testimony to dramatic events in the "Third World". As their influence grew, and their profiles changed, NGOs gradually established themselves as major actors of development policy formulation. Indeed, they contributed to shaping development co–operation policies of governments too, in at least three ways: by *mainstreaming the humanitarian principles* of the Geneva Convention in governments' foreign and co–operation policies; by taking *an active and growing role* in humanitarian policies, and increasingly in longer–term development policies; finally by intervening directly at the level of policy formulation, in all policy areas that affect distress, poverty and development in the world.

Box 1. **NGOs and War in the 20th Century**

- **Save the Children** was launched at the end of the First World War, in 1919, by a group of volunteers in the United Kingdom to send food to suffering children in blockaded Germany and Austria.

- The **Oxford Committee for Famine Relief** (UK) met for the first time in 1942, during the Second World War, to co–ordinate food to Nazi–occupied territory in Greece.

- The **International Rescue Committee** (US) was formed in 1940 to aid European refugees trapped in occupied France and assist opponents of Hitler.

- The **Catholic Relief Service** (US) was established in 1943 to co–ordinate action by Catholic parishes "outside the country", especially the resettlement of refugees in Europe. The **Church World Service,** established in 1946, did the same for Protestant, Orthodox, and Anglican churches.

- **Co–operation for American Remittances to Europe (CARE)** was created in 1945 as a co-operative by 22 American organisations to rush life–saving packages to survivors of the Second World War.

- **World Vision** was founded in 1950 to help children orphaned in the Korean War.

- **Médecins Sans Frontières** was created in 1971 by doctors who had been involved with the Red Cross in the Biafra secession war.

Mainstreaming Humanitarian Principles in Practice

The first fundamental change brought about by NGOs, as argued by Foy and Helmich (1996), relates to the *renewed vigour* they instilled in humanitarian and development policies. The International Red Cross and Red Crescent Movement, historically the oldest humanitarian actor, founded its work on the principles of independence, impartiality and neutrality. NGOs established since also claim to act upon these principles. With governments of industrialised countries, somehow paralysed in the Cold War context, hesitating in coming to the assistance of the victims of conflicts, independent NGOs began to appear as legitimate and efficient, and enjoyed the support of home publics. In that respect, the Biafra secession war (1967–1970), in the aftermath of decolonisation, arguably was the real point of departure for OECD–based NGOs taking on new roles of intervention (*ingérence*) in poor and/or war–stricken countries, and providing testimony (*témoignage*) in their countries of origin.

The right of intervention *(le droit d'ingérence)* was spelt out by Médecins sans frontières (MSF), which, based on the assumption that all human beings have the right to humanitarian assistance, claimed full and unhindered freedom for NGOs in providing it[7]. It stems from, and is legitimated by, the Geneva Conventions of 1949 and additional Protocols of 1977, as well as the Universal Declaration of Human Rights. This "right and duty of intervention" would later become the justification for state intervention in the sovereign territory of another state on humanitarian grounds[8].

Bearing witness "publicly" in richer countries to the plight of the distressed *(témoignage)* was a second main objective of MSF, in combination with humanitarian intervention. As stressed by Smillie and Helmich (1998), public awareness served to pressurise governments into demonstrating that they were also providing humanitarian relief[9]. By channelling information to the populations of "the West" through their fundraising campaigns and the media, NGOs were instrumental in moulding perceptions of the "Third World" — e.g. by mainstreaming the image of the "starving black baby"[10]. The media, especially television, played a prominent role, which would trigger much criticism — against both NGOs and the media — for creating a long–lasting negative, patronising, charity–dependent image of developing countries[11].

NGOs as Main Actors of Humanitarian, but also Development Policies

The second major change relates to the growing share of humanitarian and development co–operation activities actually carried out by NGOs, as illustrated by the large increase in the number of new relief oriented NGOs from the 1960s until the late 1990s. It gained momentum in the late 1970s and peaked in the 1980s, before slowing down afterwards. Indeed, a study by the Development Centre showed that 40 per cent of the survey population of 2 420 NGOs active in the 1990s had been established in the 1980s (Woods, 2000). It also underlined that the actual volume of resources mobilised by those NGOs may well have been underestimated in official figures (see Box 2).

Box 2. **NGOs in the 1990s**

A snapshot of NGOs from 22 European countries in the 1990s, based on data collected from NGOs themselves rather than official data, challenges several common perceptions.

First, NGOs have most probably been *mobilising far more resources than is commonly assessed* through official figures, with European NGOs alone accounting for some $7.3 billion a year. For all NGOs in OECD countries, the figure could be around $15.5 billion, which amounts to more than one fourth (28 per cent) of total official development assistance (ODA) disbursed by OECD DAC members, roughly twice as much as official figures commonly acknowledge. This is mostly because public money channelled through NGOs for the implementation of development projects is not always easily traceable.

Second, about 57 per cent of their resources on average come from private sources — casting doubts over the reality of their perceived dependence on public funds — and no less than 91 per cent of their staff are volunteers.

Third, resources channelled to NGOs are very concentrated: 20 per cent of European NGOs mobilise 90.5 per cent of financial resources and 95 per cent of human resources in the sector. Among them, Caritas Italiana (Italy), Misereor — Bishop Relief's Fund (Germany) and SOS Children's Village International (Austria) have resources above $1.8 million, followed by Save the Childrens Fund (United Kingdom), Friedrich Ebert Stiftung (Germany) and Caritas France.

A fourth finding was that NGO activities are heavily focused on Africa, and on investment in social infrastructure (education and health).

Finally, in all countries, people increasingly tend to put their trust in NGOs rather than in their own governments for the implementation of development projects[12].

Source: Woods (2000).

Simultaneously, the area of intervention of NGOs expanded, as they gradually moved towards longer term, development–oriented activities, as opposed to shorter–term emergency relief. Experience had revealed how much the "real" impediments to security and well–being were of a structural nature, including economic relations with other countries, reliance on commodities, etc.[13]. By the end of the 1970s, it had become apparent that NGOs had also built *development* skills: they could help to organise and motivate successful and sustainable community self–help efforts in cost–effective and sustainable ways, had special skills in primary health care, non–formal education and other forms of social development. Most importantly, they turned out to be more innovative than governments, quicker to act in certain circumstances, better able to reach the poor and to demonstrate the value of empowerment and participation in practical terms. Humanitarian policy and development policy quickly grew to become two very distinct trades, but it must be recalled that the latter emerged from the former.

From the Field to Influencing the Global Agenda

Third, and finally, the nature of NGOs' contribution to international co–operation changed, as they increasingly expanded the portfolio of their field activities to include policy analysis and lobbying. Indeed, as economic development came to be redefined as poverty reduction within economic growth — with the Non–Aligned Movement and the Group of 77 advocating a New International Economic Order[14] — NGOs increasingly sought to monitor and influence development–related policy making[15]. NGOs started to conduct systematic research and analysis, moving towards more policy–oriented work in the late 1980s and 1990s. Not only did increasingly substantiated reports further their traditional role of supplying information on hard–to–reach areas of humanitarian crisis[16], but they eventually enabled them to become credible opinion makers on global policy issues, such as world trade and its multilateral rules[17].

From the 1980s onwards, therefore, OECD Member governments tended increasingly to recognise NGOs as useful partners, especially for channelling ODA in developing countries. Aid delivery through project implementation thus became their predominant role, as their virtue very much tallied with their perceived independence from Cold War bipolarised tactics[18]. Advocacy and development education, based on field experience and partnerships in developing countries, came to be seen as their second most important role, together with lobbying for policy reform[19].

194

The progressive change in the World Bank's relations with NGOs illustrates this evolution: the 1980s represent a turning point for NGOs, governments and intergovernmental organisations in development thinking, whereby consensus formed around a greater focus on poverty reduction, sustainable development and the involvement of civil society (see Box 3).

Box 3. **NGOs and the World Bank**

The World Bank, which had been working with some NGOs since the early 1970s, formed the NGO/World Bank Committee in 1982. By 1986, NGOs' input was officially sought into policy and project formulation on the debt issue and the impact of structural adjustment programmes. However, their submissions were not well reflected in strategies, which triggered stronger lobbying. NGOs also learnt that their input should be better researched and that they should adopt the language of the World Bank in order to increase their impact. The bigger NGOs added to their grassroots experience by employing development economists, sociologists and other experts to improve their development research. Both sides had to learn how to work together and make compromises, which in some cases backfired[20].

In the early 1990s the World Bank, based on its own research findings, adopted a good governance agenda, which promoted transparency, accountability, efficiency, fairness, participation and ownership. This implied more support for civil society in developing countries, and closer dealings with NGOs as they were best placed to support it. In return, NGOs also argued for democratisation of international institutions — a demand which, in turn, was placed on the NGOs: the Bank, as it opened up to civil society and became more transparent, wanted to know more about its new partners, which opened the debate about legitimacy, representivity, transparency and accountability of NGOs.

The Bank has risen to the challenge of opening up to "civil society", e.g. through consultation with civil society in the Poverty Reduction Strategy Papers (PRSP), or the publication of *Voices of the Poor*. While, for some commentators, what it has learned from ten years of NGO scrutiny and pressure remains to be seen, others think that NGOs themselves have a lot of catching up to do in relation to improving their own transparency and accountability.

Sources: Smillie and Helmich (1993 and 1999); Edwards *et al.* (2000); World Bank (2000, *a, b* and c).

In sum, NGOs from the 1980s got involved in both humanitarian and development work, raised funds from the public and received increasing levels of co–financing from donors[21]. They also made themselves advocates of the developing world, pushing for the reform of international financial and trade systems[22]. They gradually gained access to the works of international organisations such as the various UN agencies, as well as the OECD, alongside the latter's traditional civil society partners, the Business and Industry Advisory Committee (BIAC) and the Trade Union Advisory Committee (TUAC)[23].

The advocacy component of their work, in particular, combined with development education, was successful in pushing agendas such as poverty reduction, sustainable development and the defence of the environment, debt relief, gender equality, food security or banning landmines[24]. Media impact on specific issues, such as the highly publicised opposition of some NGOs to the Multilateral Agreement on Investment (MAI), or exposure of the use of child labour in poor countries by some multinationals, also established them as powerful lobbies. In the 1990s, they had arguably gained an unprecedented prominence in international development[25].

How the World Changed NGOs

In 40 years, NGOs may have contributed to shaping international humanitarian and development policies, but they have undergone some major changes themselves. We take a look at two different sets of factors and their impact: first, the "endogenous" ones, whereby the very success and growth of NGOs resulted in pressure to reform; second, the exogenous ones, whereby changes in the global context in which NGOs operate are questioning their roles.

Maturity or Mid–life Crisis?

Moving into development co–operation, as stressed above, also meant climbing up the ladder of national and global policy–making hierarchies, and managing bigger budgets. This arguably signalled a threat to NGOs' historic independence, the fading away of N in NGO. A decade ago, Smillie and Helmich (1993) already drew attention to that point: success in influencing government and inter–governmental organisations — e.g. on poverty reduction and structural adjustment programmes (SAPs)— and increased public funding exposed NGOs to donors' requirements for greater transparency, accountability and organisational skills, which had eventually showed as their weaker points.

Towards the end of the 1980s there was a lack of focus and of procedures and structures to maintain their (NGOs) work. At the same time donors channelled more resources through them, which in turn resulted in pressure exerted on them to become more rigorous, more professional and more accountable (Wallace, 2000).

Actually, NGOs did not necessarily have the capacity or skills to cope with such a diversification of activities, and dealing with an increasingly complex NGO–government interdependence relationship proved no less of a challenge. The broadening of the development agenda and the emergence of civil society in developing countries only complicated things further[26]. Eventually, the risk of losing sight of their real comparative advantage in addressing basic human needs at the grassroots level and in remote areas often unserved by governments became real[27]. Towards the second half of the 1990s, NGOs found their prominence challenged at several levels[28]:

Legitimacy While hands–on experience has been the main source of NGOs' legitimacy and their primary comparative advantage, their grassroots work is being taken over by NGOs and civil society groups in developing countries, increasingly involved in both development operations and advocacy.

Independence NGO independence from the state and its underpinning political agendas in development co–operation was another comparative advantage, but it is threatened by intensified relations with governments.

Specialisation As activities expanded, larger NGOs have turned into "generalists", losing their focus on their technical comparative advantage.

Credibility The lack of evaluation, transparency and accountability came under the spotlight of academic research[29], donor scrutiny and media publicity, all of which contributed to challenge the right of NGOs to advocate on behalf of developing countries.

Ground–breaker role The "*droit d'ingérence*" so positively pursued in the 1970s was twinned with international military action — e.g. former Yugoslavia, Somalia, Rwanda, Burundi, East Timor, etc. — raising fears of NGOs becoming strategic instruments of governments, allowing the international community to claim it is involved when in truth it has disengaged[30]. NGOs were no longer going where governments would not, but were in fact following them, and "cleaning up the mess".

NGOs did atempt to respond to those challenges, for example by "professionalising" their staff, and adopting standards and financial transparency labels[31]. Despite an obvious need for a more in–depth comparative advantage re–check, though, evidence seemed to hint that reform has been taking place slowly[32].

A Changing Global Context

Turning to the "exogenous" factors which have shaped the evolution of NGOs active in development since the 1980s, we point to three macroeconomic and political events. On the one hand, economic liberalisation policies and the end of the Cold War arguably helped boost their profile. On the other hand, and more recently, the acceleration of the globalisation process seems to question not only the recent prominence of the Northern "generalist" NGOs in international co–operation, but also their very legitimacy.

First, the dominant trend in the 1980s in favour of a larger role for market forces in development, in the form of *economic liberalisation*, privatisation and state downsizing, had two major impacts. The first was that the suspicion of state inefficiency contributed to the observed increase in bilateral and multilateral funding for development channelled through NGOs, rather than governments. Indeed, the post–independence focus on the state for promoting agricultural and industrial change was gradually eroded by the poor economic performance of many countries, giving way to the belief in markets as the mechanism for delivering efficient and effective development. NGOs were seen as an alternative conduit for aid, which could be used to by–pass inefficient, corrupt and overstaffed states[33]. The second was that the implementation of SAPs, and the unfolding of their controversial social impacts, gave a clear focus for NGO advocacy and campaigning, with the World Bank and IMF in the spotlight.

Second, the end of the Cold War at the end of the 1980s provided space for new ideas on development co–operation, in at least two ways. On the one hand, good governance, democratisation and human rights came back to the forefront of recognised prerequisites for effective development assistance and investment, and thus as new donors' conditionalities[34]. Supporting civil society in developing countries — including through "Northern" NGOs — would assist the strengthening of democracy.

On the other hand, greater focus on poverty reduction and pro–poor growth in the 1990s, at a time of declining ODA flows, resulted in even greater focus on aid effectiveness and evaluation, which also applied to the activities of NGOs[35]. Despite the perceived positive influence of the latter on development co–operation, and their popularity among OECD citizens, they were increasingly required by multilateral organisations, bilateral donors and the media[36] to demonstrate their own legitimacy, transparency, organisational skills, accountability, representativity and comparative advantage[37]. Such demands would haunt the NGO sector throughout the 1990s.

Third, *globalisation* arguably makes our understanding of the role of NGOs in international development co–operation more difficult. In OECD Member countries, fears of negative impacts on jobs, welfare, culture, food security, etc., all emerged rapidly in the 1990s as major matters of concern for citizens. This may have partly resulted in a shift from an altruistic to a more self–centered attitude of the public *vis–à–vis* poor countries' fate[38]. Alongside these mostly "domestic" concerns, though, issues of more global relevance, such as the protection of the environment, growing global inequality, human rights violations involving borderless actors, etc., also gained prominence[39]. New aspirations of the public for some form of worldwide, democratic response to these challenges did not merely fuel "traditional" advocacy work of the type of the NGOs described earlier in this chapter, they actually prompted and shaped a larger, very heterogeneous movement of criticism against governmental and inter–governmental institutions and policies, described as unable to provide the sort of global response that global challenges require[40].

New communication technologies allowed cross–border organisations to address those issues, propagating a new breed of non–governmental organisations, which Scholte (2002) defines as the "globalising civil society":

> Global civil society encompasses civic activity that: *a)* addresses transworld issues; *b)* involves transborder communication; *c)* has a global organisation; *d)* works on a premise of supraterritorial solidarity. Often these four attributes go hand in hand, but civic associations can also have a global character in only one or several of these four respects.

These were particularly efficient in making several policy debates spill over onto the internet, and, using "traditional" means of expressing concern, onto the streets[41]. Unlike humanitarian and development NGOs, these organisations rarely have activities in the field other than "soft" ones, such as awareness raising, training, networking or information dissemination. Most of their activities are aimed at influencing the policy debate, to the point where they arguably bridge a gap between charity/humanitarian organisations and outright political activist groups[42].

NGOs at the Crossroads

By the early 1990s the value-added of non-governmental actors had been recognised. However, this comfortable position was quickly challenged. By the mid–1990s changed relations with their Southern counterparts and with Northern governments led to calls for a transformation of their practices. More significantly, by the end of the decade NGOs found themselves radically challenged in terms of their identity and their legitimacy — as the civil society actor, "responsible" for, and experienced in, development. The now find themselves part of a bigger movement of non–governmental, not–for–profit organisations — mostly and erroneously referred to as "anti–globalisation" — whose ambitions and potential influence reach far beyond humanitarian relief and development co–operation. As analysts recognise, though, this movement is here to stay, and may ultimately become an integral part of not only opinion making, but possibly policy making, in domains that affect humanitarian relief and development:

Globalization renders governments and civil society more, not less, important as actors for managing its associated risks and opportunities. The development process in general, and globalization in particular, fundamentally and necessarily changes both civil society and its relations with government [...]. A dynamic civil society is vital for debating the many difficult issues associated with higher levels of integration into the global economy, and for empowering domestic constituencies to press for appropriate institutional and policy reforms. (Woolcock, 2001)

Humanitarian and development NGOs are thus under more pressure to reform their practices and redefine their identity. Some believe they should build on their comparative advantage — in international advocacy, development education and capacity building, support to civil society in developing countries — and move in three main directions[43].

1.   Forging new links. In their more traditional domain of activities, NGOs have witnessed the surge of a range of new actors in humanitarian and development policies, and sometimes they have been instrumental in prompting their involvement. This is the case of UN relief agencies coordinating rapid responses to emergency situations (e.g. UNHCR, peacekeeping forces); the private sector[44]; increasingly skilled civil society organisations in developing countries; and private foundations with large budgets supporting a gamut of development related projects in civil society[45]. Partly for reasons of complementarity, and partly owing to financial constraints, NGOs' work in the future will have to be undertaken in an increasingly collaborative manner with those. In particular, strengthening "Southern" organisations, which donors want to involve as partners in development co–operation, but very often still consider as too weak, should become a priority[46].

2.   Adopting a principled approach to working with governments. Donor funding generates risks of co–option, or of NGOs limiting themselves to what is "publicly popular" work. Merely helping governments speed up the disbursement of rapidly growing ODA budgets may actually result in an impoverished environment for development co–operation in the long run[47]. The safeguard should be clear, internalised and immovable values and principles.

3.   Advocacy at home. In an OECD Development Centre publication, Bernard et al. (1998) have recalled that the NGOs' legitimacy in advocacy stems from experience in the field, as well as from capacity to mobilise private funds, and increasingly public opinion[48]. If they are to improve the latter's understanding of development processes and co–operation policies, NGOs need to develop their relations with the media, and work out more carefully their messages to the public. Besides, new information technologies — the Internet, fax, e–mails — may have boosted the potential impact of their "soft power", and media coverage for major NGOs may have nearly quadrupled since 1996 (Edelman PR Worldwide, 2001), but in a context of information overload, actual impact on populations and target groups will depend on the credibility of information[49]:

> Credibility is the crucial resource in gaining [this] attention, and establishing it means developing a reputation for providing correct information even when it may reflect badly on the information providers.....[T]o be credible, the information must be produced through a process that is in accordance with the professional norms and characterised by transparency and procedural fairness.

A trend seems set in the OECD that will bring non–governmental organisations emanating from groups of citizens gradually closer to the policy process in virtually all areas[50], including of course humanitarian and development policies. In that, NGOs have arguably made a tremendous impact. Under which form this participation will take place remains however unclear. In particular, it is hard to see how the bigger "civil society bubble" in which humanitarian and development NGOs have been caught, could do anything but to burst in the relatively short term: aims, structures and methods differ too much. These differences have been largely glossed over in the last four decades, but the civil society "movement" is most likely to recompose along political and/or functional dividing lines — for instance between those in favour of some form of globalisation vs. the "antis", or poverty–focused vs. environmentalists. It would hardly be a surprise if the very concept of "NGOs" as we know it were then to fall victim to this process. Furthering its work on 20th Century NGOs, the Development Centre is turning to the changing roles of 21st Century global and local "civil society", including that of business organisations, trade unions, human rights organisations, and the multi–faceted Southern civil society organisations.

Notes

1. See Development Centre (various years) and Schneider (1999).

2. BOND is a network of more than 260 UK based voluntary organisations working in international development and development education.

3. Scholte (1999) provides a comprehensive analysis of the concept of "civil society". Not the least contradiction in the definitions he reviews is the fact that most of them may allow for the inclusion of very "uncivil" forms of association, such as criminal networks, groups advocating violence or racism, etc. A few definitions include private sector associations. A critical analysis of the concept can be found in Cassen (2001).

4. For instance, the Centre launched in 2001 a pilot project to support policy dialogue between the government and private investors in Mozambique.

5. "Strategic" means that these activities constitute their core mandate.

6. See OECD Development Centre (1993b), an update of the original directory published in 1967.

7. French NGO Médecins sans Frontières (MSF) was founded upon the "horrific" experience of a few Red Cross workers, during the Biafran famine, which led them to assert that NGOs "could/would take control of a humanitarian situation [in the absence of the international community doing so], crossing a national boundary, without the consent of the international community/law, in the interest of human rights". See www.msf.org.

8. An early example in the post–Cold War era is the armed intervention by Western countries on humanitarian grounds in Kurdish areas of northern Iraq in 1991; see Corten (1999).

9. See also Yankelovich (1991).

10. See also Regan (1996).

11. Winter (1996).

12. This is confirmed by the second *Annual Survey of US and European Opinion Leaders* by Edelman PR Worldwide and Strategy One (2001), which shows that Europeans continue to trust NGOs twice as much as government, and substantially more than corporations or the media.

13. OECD DAC (1988).

14. Lobbying of developing countries through the Non–Aligned Movement (created in Bandung, Indonesia, 1955) and the Group of 77 led to the creation of the United Nations Conference on Trade and Development (UNCTAD) in 1964 where member countries argued for fairer terms of trade and more liberal terms for financing development.

15. Goulet (1995).

16. See for instance the joint report by Oxfam GB, Save The Children and Christian Aid (2001), on the humanitarian crisis in the war–torn Democratic Republic of Congo.

17. See for instance the 2002 report by Oxfam on the global trade system, which received a wide press coverage: Financial Times "Oxfam brands EU bloc as most protectionist", 10 April 2002; WTO press release (press/285) "Moore welcomes Oxfam report but cites omissions and errors", 11 April 2002; Asia Times "WTO hits back at Oxfam critique", 13 April 2002; The Monitor "Oxfam slams rich nations over unfair trade policies", 15 April 2002 (posted on AllAfrica.com on April 15, 2002); Financial Times "EU denies Oxfam criticism" 17 April, 2002. Source: EU–LDC Network (www.eu–ldc.org/src/news.asp?ArticleID = 245).

18. OECD Development Centre (1993a), UNDP (1993).

19. Madon (2000).

20. A World Bank financed workshop in Oxford in 1987 on debt, adjustment and the needs of the poor, contributed to the networking of NGOs for public opinion campaigns that were highly critical of World Bank policies and compromised the World Bank's public image (OECD DAC, 1988).

21. From 1970 to 1985, total development aid disbursed by international NGOs increased ten–fold to 5 per cent of overseas development assistance (ODA). In 1992 International NGOs channelled over $7.6 billion of aid to developing countries. It was estimated in 2001 that over 15 per cent of total overseas development aid is channelled through NGOs (OECD DAC, 1988 and World Bank, 2001).

22. See the reports published by a group of independent NGOs on *The Reality of Aid*, from 1993 to 2001, at www.realityofaid.org.

23. OECD (2001a).

24. OECD Development Centre (1990).

25. Hudson (2001b).

26. Edwards et al. (2000).

27. OECD DAC (1988).

28. Hudson (2001b).

29. See for instance the work of the UK–based Relief and Development Institute, which transferred its activities to the Overseas Development Institute in 1991, of which it is now the Humanitarian Policy Group (www.odi.org.uk/hpg/index.html)

30. Prendergast (1997); Edwards *et al.* (2000).

31. On NGO standards and best practice, see for example "The Sphere Project" (1998): in response to the increasing complexity and incidence of emergency situations in the 1990s, the International Federation of the Red Cross (IFRC), in collaboration with NGOs, developed a "Humanitarian Charter and Minimum Standards in Disaster Response" for the care sectors of water supply and sanitation, nutrition, food aid, shelter and site management, and health services. On financial transparency labels, see for instance the case of the French *Comité de la Charte de Déontologie des organisations sociales et humanitaires* (www.comitecharte.org/), or the pioneering *International Committee of Fundraising Organizations* (est. 1958; www.icfo.de/). See also SCHR (1994).

32. BOND (1997); Fahey and Sutton (2000); Smillie and Helmich (1999). On reform issues identified by NGOs, see BOND (1998).

33. Wallace (2000). See also Powell and Seddon (1997).

34. See Burnside and Dollar (2000); Collier and Dollar (2001); Collier (2002); and the UN Millennium Development Goals, which promote a rights–based approach to development (www.developmentgoals.org).

35. OECD DAC (1996); OECD DAC (1997).

36. See Foy and Helmich (1996); Smillie and Helmich (1998); Edelman PR Worldwide and Strategy One (2001). The 1990s saw the emergence of unfriendly and critical media reporting about foreign aid and the effectiveness of NGOs (Shaw, 1999).

37. Hudson (2001*b*); Edwards *et al.* (2000).

38. According to a 1999 UK opinion poll, over two–thirds of the representative sample think that Third World poverty could have damaging effects on the UK (DFID, 2000).

39. An attempt to conceptualise those lies with the UN concept of "Global public goods", which stems from the idea that "we have entered a new era of public policy, defined by a growing number of concerns that straddle national borders" (Kaul *et al.*, 1999; www.undp.org/globalpublicgoods/; Kaul, 2001).

40. Sixty–five per cent of respondents in a French survey state that they support the so–called "anti–globalisation" movement (Fougier, 2001).

41. Ministerial meeting of the WTO (Nov/Dec 1999, Seattle: 50 000 demonstrators); annual meeting of the World Bank and the IMF (Nov. 2000, Prague: 9 000 demonstrators); G8 meeting (July 2001, Genoa: 200 000); EU summits (December 2000, Nice: 60 000; June 2001, Göteborg: 20 000).

42. Anheier *et al.* (2001); Solagral and UNESCO–MOST (2002).

43. Hudson (2001*a* and *b*); Edwards *et al.* (2000).

44. An illustration of new links between NGOs and the private sector is given by *Business Partners for Development*, a joint initiative by the CARE International, the World Bank, and multinational oil, gas and mining corporations, that was presented to the

OECD at a special Development Centre informal seminar in October, 2001. BPD aims to produce practical examples of how three–way partnerships involving companies, government authorities and civil society organisations can be a more effective means of reducing social risks related to investment in those sectors, and promoting community development. See Warner (2000).

45. For example, the Ford Foundation, Soros Foundation, Bill and Melinda Gates Foundation, etc.

46. Edwards *et al.* (2000).

47. Fahey and Sutton (2000).

48. Hudson (2001*b*) reviewed NGOs' comparative advantages, in their own terms, as *i)* location close to public opinions in the North; *ii)* skills in policy analysis; *iii)* access to resources and information; *iv)* ability to link micro and macro aspects; and *v)* experience of international policy debates.

49. Keohane and Nye (1998) define "soft power" as *"The power to convince others to follow or getting them to agree to norms and institutions that produce desired behaviour, it can rest on the appeal of one's ideas or culture."*

50. OECD (2001*b*).

Bibliography

ANHEIER, H., M. GLASIUS AND M. KALDOR (2001), *Global Civil Society*, Oxford University Press, UK.

BERNARD, A., H. HELMICH AND P.B. LEHNING (eds.) (1998), *Civil Society and International Development*, Development Centre Seminars, OECD, Paris.

BOND (1998), *A Summary of Issues raised at the BOND Directors Workshop on NGO Futures*, www.bond.org.uk/futures/workshop1.html.

BOND (1997), *Civil Society and Southern NGOs*, a working paper on civil society, www.bond.org.uk/wgroups/civils/report.html.

BURNSIDE, C. AND D. DOLLAR (2000), "Aid, Policies, and Growth", *American Economic Review*, September.

CASSEN, B. (2001), "Le piège de la gouvernance", *Le Monde Diplomatique*, June.

COLLIER, P. (2002), "Making Aid Smart: Institutional Incentives Facing Donor Organisations and their Implications for Aid Effectiveness", paper presented at an informal OECD Development Centre seminar on aid effectiveness, Paris, 22 April.

COLLIER, P. AND D. DOLLAR (2001), *Development Effectiveness: What Have We Learnt?*, Development Research Group, World Bank, Washington, D.C.

CORTEN, O. (1999), "Humanitarian intervention: a controversial right", *in The UNESCO Courier*, July/August, http://www.unesco.org/courier/1999_08/uk/ethique/txt1.htm.

DFID (2000), *Public Attitudes on Development; Beliefs and Attitudes Concerning Poverty in Developing Countries*, UK.

DUNNE, T. AND N. WHEELER (eds.) (1999), *Human Rights in Global Politics*, Cambridge University Press, Cambridge, www.sussex.ac.uk/Users/hafa3/voices.htm.

EDELMAN PR WORLDWIDE AND STRATEGY ONE (2001), *The Relationship Among NGOs, Government, Media and Corporate Sector*, www.edelman.com/edelman_newsroom/NGO_1-12–01/ppt0112_files/slide0041.htm.

EDWARDS, M., D. HULME AND T. WALLACE (2000), "Increasing Leverage for Development: Challenges for NGOs in a Global Future", *in* D. LEWIS AND T. WALLACE (eds.) (*op. cit.*).

FAHEY, T. AND M. SUTTON (2000), "An Abundance of Aid — Some Challenges facing the Irish Government and NGOs", *in Trócaire 2000 Development Review*, Dublin.

FOUGIER, E. (2001), "Perceptions de la mondialisation en France et aux États–Unis", *in Politique Étrangère*, Paris, March.

FOY, C. AND H. HELMICH (eds.) (1996), *Public Support for International Development*, Development Centre Document, OECD, Paris.

GOULET, D. (1995), *Development Ethics: A Guide to Theory and Practice*, Zed Books Lt., US.

HUDSON, A. (2002), "Research note: Advocacy by UK–based Development NGOs ", *in Non–Profit and Voluntary Sector Quarterly*, Vol. 31 (3), September.

HUDSON, A. (2001a) "Adding Value? On the Future Roles of Northern Development NGOs", paper available from the author — www.alanhudson.org.uk/publicat.html.

HUDSON, A. (2001b), "NGOs' Transnational Advocacy Networks: From 'Legitimacy' to 'Political Responsibility'?" *in Global Networks: A Journal of Transnational Affairs*, Vol. 1(4), pp.331–352.

HUDSON, A. (2000), "Making the Connection: Legitimacy Claims, Legitimacy Chains and Northern NGOs' International Advocacy", pp. 89–97 *in* LEWIS, D. AND T. WALLACE (eds.), *op. cit.*

KAUL, I. (2001), "Global Public Goods: What Role for Civil Society?" *in Non–profit and Voluntary Sector Quarterly*, Vol. 30 (3), September, pp. 588–602.

KAUL, I., I. GRUNBERG AND M. STERN (eds.) (1999) *Global Public Goods: International Co–operation in the 21st Century*, Oxford University Press, New York.

KEOHANE, R.O. AND J. S. NYE (1998), "Power and Interdependence in the Information Age", *in Foreign Affairs*, Vol. 77 (5), September/October, Council on Foreign Relations, Inc., New York.

LEWIS, D. AND T. WALLACE (2000) (eds.), *New Roles and Relevance: Development NGOs and the Challenge of Change*, Kumarian Press, London.

MADON, S. (2000), *International NGOs: Networking, Information Flows and Learning*, Development Informatics Working Paper Series, Working Paper No. 8, Institute for Development Policy and Management, Manchester, http://idpm.man.ac.uk/idpm/diwpf8.htm.

OECD (2001a), *Civil Society and the OECD*, Policy Brief, October, OECD, Paris, www.oecd.org/pdf/M00018000/M00018283.pdf.

OECD (2001b), *Citizens as Partners: Information, Consultation and Public Participation in Policy–Making*, PUMA, OECD, Paris.

OCDE (1967), *Annuaire OCDE–CIAB, Aide Au Développement, organisations non–gouvernementales sans but lucratif*, Part I and Part II, Paris.

OECD DAC (1996), *Shaping the 21ˢᵗ Century: The Contribution of Development Co–operation*, DAC, OECD, Paris.

OECD DAC (1997), *Final Report of the Ad Hoc Working Group on Participatory Development and Good Governance* Part 1, Development Assistance Committee, DAC, OECD, Paris.

OECD DAC (1988), *Voluntary Aid for Development: The Role of Non–Governmental Organisations*, DAC, OECD, Paris.

OECD DEVELOPMENT CENTRE (1997), *International Co–operation for Habitat and Urban Development: Directory of Non–Governmental Organisations in OECD Countries*, in collaboration with UNCHS-Habitat, UN–NGLS, and GRET, OECD, Paris.

OECD DEVELOPMENT CENTRE (1996), *Directory of Non–Governmental Organisations active in Sustainable Development, Part 1: Europe and Part II: Rest of the World*, in collaboration with EU NGO Liaison Committee, UN–NGLS & The North–South Centre of the Council of Europe, OECD, Paris.

OECD DEVELOPMENT CENTRE (1993a), *Human Rights, Refugees, Migrants and Development: Directory of NGOs in OECD Countries*, in collaboration with UNHCR & HURIDOCS, with assistance from IOM, OECD, Paris.

OECD DEVELOPMENT CENTRE (1993b), *Directory of the Development Activities of Trade Unions based in OECD Countries*, OECD, Paris.

OECD DEVELOPMENT CENTRE (1990), *Directory of Non–Governmental Organisations in OECD Member Countries*, OECD, Paris.

OECD DEVELOPMENT CENTRE (1981), *Directory of Non–Governmental Organisations in OECD Member Countries Active in Development Co–operation*, Vols. 1 and 2, OECD, Paris.

OXFAM (2002), *Rigged Rules and Double Standards – Trade, Globalisation, and the Fight Against Poverty*, Oxfam report, March, www.maketradefair.org/assets/english/Report_English.pdf.

OXFAM GB / Save The Children / Christian Aid (2001), *No End in Sight – The Human Tragedy of the Conflict in the Democratic Republic of Congo*, Oxfam Briefing, August, www.oxfam.org.uk/policy/papers/drc2.htm.

POWELL, M. AND D. SEDDON (1997), "NGOS and the Development Industry" *in Review of African Political Economy*, No. 71, pp 3–10, Roape Publications, UK.

PRENDERGAST, J. (1997), *Crisis Response: Humanitarian Aid and Conflict in Africa*, Boulder, Colorado; Lynne Rienner, London.

REGAN, C. (1996), *Images and Impact: Media and Voluntary Agency Images, Messages and their Impact*, Comhlámh, Dublin.

SCHNEIDER, H. (1999), "Participatory Governance: The Missing Link for Poverty Reduction", Policy Brief No. 17, OECD Development Centre, Paris.

SCHR (1994) *Code of Conduct for the International Red Cross and Red Crescent Movement and NGOs in Disaster Relief*. RRN Network Paper 7, London: Relief and Rehabilitation Network, Overseas Development Institute, London.

Scholte, J.A. (2002), in "Global Civil Society: Its Rise to Power", in *Courrier de la Planète*, No. 63, Solagral et Unesco–Most, Montpellier.

Scholte, J.A. (1999), "Global Civil Society: Changing the World?", CSGR Working Paper No. 31/99. www.warwick.ac.uk/fac/soc/CSGR/wpapers/wp3199.PDF

Shaw, M. (1999), "Global Voices: Civil Society and Media in Global Crises", *in* T. Dunne and N. Wheeler (eds.), *op.cit.*

Smillie, I. and H. Helmich (eds.) (1993), *Non–Governmental Organisations and Governments: Stakeholders for Development,* OECD Development Centre, Paris.

Smillie, I. and H. Helmich (eds.) (1998), *Public Attitudes and International Development Co–operation*, in collaboration with The North–South Centre of the Council of Europe, OECD, Paris.

Smillie, I. and H. Helmich (eds.) (1999), in collaboration with T. German and J. Randel, *Stakeholders: Government–NGO Partnerships for International Development,* OECD Development Centre Studies, OECD Development Centre, Paris; Earthscan, London.

Solagral and UNESCO–MOST (2002), "Global Civil Society: Its Rise to Power", *Courrier de la Planète,* No. 63, Solagral, Montpellier.

The Sphere Project (1998), *Humanitarian Charter and Minimum Standards in Disaster Response*, The Sphere Project, Geneva.

UNDP (1993), *Human Development Report*, Oxford University Press, New York.

Wallace, T. (2000), "Development Management and the Aid Chain: the Case of NGOs", *in Development and Management — Experiences in Value–Based Conflict,* co-edited by D. Eade, T. Hewitt and H. Johnson, *A Development in Practice Reader*, in association with The Open University, UK.

Warner, M. (2000), *Tri–Sector Partnerships for Social Investment within the Oil, Gas and Mining sectors: an Analytical Framework*, Working Paper No. 2, Business Partners for Development — Natural Resources Cluster, BPD, London. www.bpd-naturalresources.org/media/pdf/working/work2.pdf

Winter, A. (1996), *Is Anyone Listening?*, Development Dossier, United Nations Non–Governmental Liaison Service, Switzerland, http://ngls.tad.ch

Woods, A. (2000), *Facts About European NGOs Active in International Development*, Development Centre Studies, OECD, Paris.

Woolcock, M. (2001) "Globalization, Governance, and Civil Society" background paper for DECRG Policy Research Report on *Globalization, Growth, and Poverty: Facts, Fears, and an Agenda for Action.* http://econ.worldbank.org/files/2871_governance_woolcock.pdf.

World Bank (2001), The World Bank and Civil Society, http://wbln0018.worldbank.org/essd/essd.nsf/NGOs/home.

World Bank (2000a), *Voices of the Poor, Can Anyone Hear Us?*, D. Narayan with R. Patel, K. Schafft, A. Rademacher and S. Koch–Schulte, World Bank, Oxford University Press, New York.

WORLD BANK (2000b), *Voices of the Poor, Crying out for Change,* D. NARAYAN, R. CHAMBERS, M.K. SHAH, P. PETESCH, World Bank, Oxford University Press, New York.

WORLD BANK (2000c), "Involving Nongovernmental Organisations in Bank–Supported Activities", *in Good Practices: The World Bank Operational Manual,* GP 14.70, World Bank, February, http://wbln0018.worldbank.org/Institutional/Manuals/OpManual.nsf.

YANKELOVICH, D. (1991), *Coming to Public Judgement: Making Democracy Work in a Complex World,* Syracuse University Press, New York.

Chapter 12

The Development Challenge[1]

Jorge Braga de Macedo, Colm Foy and Charles P. Oman

Development is ultimately about people's enhancing their capacity to realise their individual and collective human potential. While societies may differ on the relative importance they attach to its individual and collective dimensions, development (national and international) is always a societal process.

Economists, who focus on the material bases of development, are concerned with the way a society organises itself to produce, and distribute, the tangible and intangible goods and services it requires to survive, reproduce itself, and eventually develop. Development, they believe, requires the building or evolution of institutions that create an environment in which people are able and motivated to engage in complex forms of co–operation.

Even the most primitive society, of course, requires co–operation among its members for survival. The key difference between primitive and more developed societies is the latter's achievement of considerably more complex and impersonal forms of co–operation. Impersonal and complex forms of co–operation make it possible for the members of society collectively to capture more of the significant potential gains to be derived from specialisation and economies of scale in their productive efforts. Those gains show up in more developed societies' significantly higher level of resource productivity (independently of whether that enhanced productivity is used to produce, say, more or better health care, weapons, consumer products, cultural activity or leisure time). Economists therefore tend to regard a country's level of productivity and ability to achieve sustained productivity growth as important indicators of development achievement.

The problem is, however, that alternative approaches to development policy have failed to deliver precise recipes for inducing a sustained improvement in people's standard of living. Reliance on both market institutions and liberal democracy has not systematically brought prosperity. Neoclassical economic theory does not explain either why the currently industrialised countries developed or how to respond to the challenges faced by developing countries. Building on

211

the other contributions to the volume (referred to by Chapter number), this Chapter summarises three interdisciplinary issues — institutional change, international peer pressure and proximity to the citizen — which have a bearing on the challenge faced by the international development community. They are presented against the background of the work of the OECD Development Centre surveyed in Chapter 1 — and in particular the current programme of work on globalisation and governance. Also important are the Millennium Development Goals set by the United Nations in September 2000 ("an ambitious agenda for reducing poverty, its causes and manifestations", see also OECD, 1996): halve extreme poverty and hunger; achieve universal primary education; promote gender equality and empower women; reduce under–five mortality and maternal mortality by two–thirds and three–quarters respectively; reverse the spread of HIV/AIDS, malaria and other diseases; halve the proportion of people without access to safe drinking water; ensure environmental sustainability; and develop a global partnership for development with targets for aid, trade and debt relief.

In March 2002, the UN Conference on Financing for Development in Monterrey, Mexico produced a declaration — known as "Monterrey Consensus" — reinforcing the role of developing countries' policies in meeting the challenge of this global partnership for development.

Institutional Change

Institutions, needed for co–operation, can be understood as any form of constraint, such as property rights, that people devise to shape their interactions — society's procedures and "rules of the game". Institutions may be consciously created (e.g. a nation's constitution, statutory laws, a contractual agreement) or may simply evolve (e.g. common law, social norms and conventions). They comprise both formal rules (e.g. written laws, written contracts) and informal ones (e.g. cultural values and norms). They can be violated, yet the constraints they impose on individual choices are pervasive. They serve greatly to reduce uncertainty in everyday life by establishing a stable — though not necessarily efficient — structure to human interactions. They structure incentives and determine the costs of human exchange in social, economic and political activity[2].

Together with the constraints imposed by resource scarcities (the standard constraints of economic theory), institutions determine the opportunities for economic and political entrepreneurs in society. Entrepreneurs create or modify organisations (e.g. firms, political parties, government bodies, civil society organisations) to take advantage of those opportunities, and, in some cases, to seek to modify institutions. The actions of organisations, and the interactions between them and institutions, thus drive and shape the path of institutional change.

The fact that key informal institutions (culture, norms, customs) are embedded or deeply rooted in society also means that institutional change remains incremental, slow, relatively impervious to deliberate political or judicial decisions that seek to impose or induce major institutional change. When such decisions or actions to change formal institutions create new tension between formal and informal institutions, the latter tend to prevail, and change only slowly[3].

A society's institutions, notably including such crucial informal ones as cultural values and norms, connect its past with its present and future. They provide a key to understanding the path–dependence of change, and go far to explain why history matters a great deal for development. Not only do they set limits at any given point in time on a society's capacity to adapt, they condition or determine the effectiveness of government policies and regulations, and of attempts to reform these policies and regulations.

Revolutionary political changes can of course translate into sustained economic and social development, but they often hinder adaptive capacity, and therefore do not induce enough institutional change to foster convergence towards OECD countries' standards of living. Moreover, the expectations generated by the sudden change are often unrealistic and therefore bring perceptions of divergence rather than convergence. Institutional change is more likely to be reversed when growth expectations are frustrated in this way, turning the institutional "lock–in" effect into an important development challenge.

This is empirically visible in the "convergence clubs" discussed in Chapter 4. It stems from the symbiotic relationship that develops between the institutions and organisations that have evolved in a country as a consequence of the incentive structure provided by the institutions. In addition to the incremental and path–dependent nature of institutional change, the importance of network externalities in a country's institutional framework means that organisations that are well adapted to and evolve in that framework will often capture increasing returns from it. The lock–in effect comes from the dependence of the resultant organisations — political, economic, social — on that particular set of institutions for the success or profitability of their actions. The result of a "high" (pro–development as opposed to anti–development) institutional equilibrium is the convergence of living standards and development policies.

Incremental change in a country's institutional framework can come from expectations about the future. Political, economic and social entrepreneurs and organisations perceive that they could do better by altering the existing framework, depending on the information they can acquire, its cost, and on how they process it. If, as much of economic theory assumed for many years, information and transaction costs are negligible (notably those of specifying, monitoring and enforcing contracts and property rights), then the choices and actions of entrepreneurs and organisations should produce a set of institutions and transactions that is socially efficient and pro–development. In no society, however, whether in economic or in political activity, are those costs negligible[4].

Throughout history, and in much of the "developing" world today, institutions and the opportunities they create for political and economic actors have overwhelmingly tended to favour actions that promote the redistribution of existing wealth and income (actions that also consume and sometimes destroy resources) rather than the creation of new wealth. Even in today's more developed countries, institutions remain a mixed bag of those that induce productivity growth and those that do not. Only in the last few centuries, moreover, have these countries managed to achieve an institutional framework that induces the development of organisations whose combined actions have produced significant long–term productivity growth.

Particularly relevant, for example, has been the widespread development since the late 19th century of the corporate form of business enterprise to capture major economies of scale and scope — brought about by wider and deeper national and global markets. Even more important has been the development of sets of institutions and organisations of public, i.e. political, governance capable, however imperfectly, of creating a polity endowed with enough coercive power to enforce contracts and property rights, but enough accountability not to engage in predatory redistributive behaviour.

Generally, and in many developing countries, predatory actions by such agents and (with the advent of corporate capitalism) powerful corporate "insiders" in both the private and public sectors have been, and remain, an overwhelming obstacle to long–term productivity growth[5].

The "convergence problem" (relative failure of many of today's developing countries to reduce the gap between their per capita income level and that of today's more developed countries), is documented and discussed in Chapters 2, 3 and 4. It can thus be understood as reflecting the difficulty or failure of many developing countries to develop a matrix of institutions and organisations (and thus policies) conducive to sustained productivity growth. The key to achieving such growth is to develop a set of institutions that more closely aligns the private rewards to political and economic actors with the societal benefits of their actions. This would serve to channel (motivate and constrain) them much more, on balance, into new wealth–creating, as opposed to mere redistributive and destructive, activity. Policy reform in the absence of such an institutional framework is likely to prove difficult or ineffective. And institutional change, as explained, is inherently incremental.

International Peer Pressure

Our focus must therefore turn squarely to the question of how to address the great dilemma of achieving pro–development governance, and institutions that promote co–operation and sustained productivity growth by adequately enforcing property rights and voluntary contractual agreements while restraining predatory actions by powerful government and corporate "insiders". It is not a new challenge, as the persistence of reflections on the importance of separating powers and including checks and balances in the construction of a modern state and democratic governance testifies. The complexity of the challenge is illustrated well by the case of India — initially cited in Chapter 3 to illustrate the convergence problem. Chapter 8 on the transition from state to regulatory capitalism illustrates the challenge as well.

As the per capita income figures for India and the United States cited in Chapter 3 suggest, there is no simple or easily explainable relationship between democratic governance and development. Yet the importance of governance for development is clear. It reflects the importance, noted earlier, of the expectations of the political, economic and social entrepreneurs and organisations whose actions collectively drive and shape change in a country's institutional framework.

In a world of increasing returns (to institutions and, more and more, to knowledge and technology) the relative weight of history in determining those expectations can be understood as depending on the interaction of three key variables. One is people's (entrepreneurs' and organisations') collective degree of patience, or what economists call their rate of discount of the future; the more they discount the future, i.e. the greater their impatience, the more they will be prisoners of history. A second variable is the strength of increasing returns, i.e. the size of external economies, which determines the degree of interdependence of people's decisions. Third is people's collective flexibility, which determines both their ability and the speed with which they are able to adapt to changing circumstances. The more adaptive they are the less will be the weight of history; conversely, if they adapt slowly, history becomes decisive and it is difficult or impossible to break out of a "low" institutional equilibrium. Expectations of development rather than stagnation can thus prevail over the weight of history and produce movement from a "low" to a "high" institutional equilibrium, only insofar as people's rate of discount is lower than the strength of increasing returns relative to adaptive capacity, measured by the speed of adjustment[6].

Not only are we reminded that patience is a virtue. We see that, as the size of external economies and therefore the strength of increasing returns grows, then it becomes vitally important to increase flexibility and lower adjustment costs. This importance is visible at the microeconomic level (i.e. in the organisation of activity within and among firms) in the move, driven by competition, to the more flexible post–taylorist forms of organisation that is discussed in Chapter 7. But what about the governance challenge? And is there an international dimension to this challenge beyond the fact that through greater competition and accountability, more open societies tend to be less corrupt[7]?

The Marshall Plan provides important lessons on the potential value of international peer pressure among governments and policy makers, who worked together in the Organisation for European Economic Co–operation (OEEC) collectively to achieve reconstruction and development in a framework of mutual surveillance and institutionalised international interdependence. Successor organisation to the OEEC, the OECD has kept peer pressure among Member countries and public managers and policy makers as its driving force, to the point that they have developed forms of complex interdependence among themselves which depart from standard international relations[8].

The success of the Euro, and before it of the European Monetary System's Exchange Rate Mechanism, have similarly benefited from peer–pressure and management practices that originated in the Marshall Plan. Such international "benchmarking" practices encourage institutional change by promoting better monitoring and enhanced accountability of public managers and policy makers[9]. Indeed, among developing countries, such regional organisations and arrangements as Mercosul's Macroeconomic Monitoring Group and the Chiang Mai Initiative (among ASEAN members plus China, Japan and Korea) could benefit from similar procedures. As mentioned at the outset, the Monterrey Consensus explicitly recognises the role of peer pressure and good governance. And the New Partnership for Africa's Development (NEPAD) may soon illustrate the scope for peer pressure to play a key role in poorer countries that face serious trade–offs between complying with international agreements and investing in such basic development infrastructure as education, health and social security.

Proximity to the Citizen

The Monterrey Consensus constitutes an important example of global co–operation among organisations (the UN, IMF, World Bank, WTO), their member governments, business and civil society organisations. Whether or not the democratic accountability of the international organisations is sufficient (arguably it is not), those organisations cannot contribute to the common good without relying on national and local polities; national legitimacy remains the source of their accountability. Yet institutional changes at the global level are not prerequisites for most needed policy reforms. The principle of proximity to the citizen (also called the principle of subsidiarity) in fact suggests rather the opposite, i.e. that governance responses at the local level, through the combined action of elected officials and civil society, are central. While the European experience shows that regional institutions and organisations can contribute to the common good, the quality of governance can be improved by solving problems closer to the citizen than the often–cumbersome regional or national administration allows. This is why the 1992 Treaty on European Union explicitly recognises the principle of proximity.

Improving governance does however call for international policy co-operation on many issues, as discussed in Chapters 5, 9 and 10. The quest for appropriate regional arrangements or organisations reflects this need, and in this regard the EU and OECD deserve close attention because both are built on the understanding, based on experience, that peer pressure can produce better policies. The quest for protection of the environment and thus "sustainable" development, both nationally and internationally, as explained in Chapter 5, is an important illustration.

International development calls for international dialogue about policies, as development has become a two–way street rather than some sort of "institutional technology transfer". Such dialogue, building on sound comparative analysis, naturally involves mutual feedback and peer pressure. Globalisation has partially blurred the analytical distinction between "North" and "South" and exacerbated perceptions that the problems of income and skills inequality are global. The perception that globalisation, not poor governance, has reinforced inequality is behind many of the recent confrontations around the international trade and investment agenda. Yet, as Chapters 6 and 9 clarify, domestic policies are needed to ensure the poor benefit from trade.

If the main responsibility for change were global, citizens and policy makers in developing countries could in effect only wait for a better global order — perhaps even in the form of a legitimate world government that provides for global public goods. If, on the contrary, main responsibility rests with individual citizens and policy makers then the focus shifts from global to national, regional and local governance and accountability. Greater proximity to decision making brings hope, but also calls for deeper and more immediate institutional change[10].

The context of debate on the nature of the relationship between democracy and development has changed. Four decades ago the context was one of a divided world where the choice of political system by developing countries was frequently based upon strategic alliances among political and economic elites. To gain access to financial and military aid, regimes aligned themselves with one of the international blocs. Those who chose the Soviet bloc eventually found themselves abandoned, but more because of a realignment of the international political order than a genuine difference in political institutions compared to those aligned with the "West".

With the end of the Soviet Union, new efforts have been made to achieve pluralist democracy in the developing world. Virtually all developing countries now enjoy at least nominally democratic regimes, defined as those with universal adult suffrage. Yet this definition neglects the importance of the quality of governance for promoting long–term productivity growth as well, in many cases, as for the individual citizen.

Parliamentary government does not ensure accountable economic policy or policy–making procedures. Governments sometimes even use democracy as an excuse for their absence. Nor do multiparty elections ensure participation in the policy–making process by functionally relevant groups. There is only a weak correlation between participation in elections and the transparency of economic policy.

Yet lack of democracy is not a solution. Authoritarian governments often stand on narrow coalition foundations and cannot risk alienating key supporters. If their social foundations are weak they generally do not have the coalition support they need to sustain reforms and often cater to narrow but volatile and highly mobilised special interest groups[11].

Research also shows that the persistence of severe famines in many of the sub–Saharan African countries — both with "left–wing" and "right–wing" governments — relates closely to the lack of democratic political systems and practice and that even if democratic countries have more trouble avoiding malnutrition they have managed to avoid famines. History reminds us that there has been no war between liberal democracies for over a 100 years. Recent empirical analysis suggests a positive correlation between democratic political systems and the levels of income, investment, human capital, economic openness and shared income growth in society[12]. There is no causal link, however, rather a balancing between the tendency for democracies to achieve lower savings and investment, which does not promote growth, and their promotion of growth through higher education and human capital formation.

It has also been observed that exclusive, divisive and intolerant societies are antithetical to development. Here again Europe's experience is revealing. Though the great social movements for reform were born in the injustices and misery of the 18th and 19th centuries, they were also the result of growing education, information and national awareness. They occurred in the midst of rising, not falling, wealth. Growth and development preceded and led to the transfer of power from an historical elite to a growing proportion of the population, rising standards of living and longer life expectancy.

It would thus be a mistake simply to equate good governance and democracy. Democracies that do not have the means to supply the needs of their people through economic growth risk being replaced by regimes that favour a particular group (e.g. ethnic group) whose wealth comes at the expense of development. Where growth slows or fails to occur, investment in people, through education and better health care, or in roads and modern means of communication, is reduced concomitantly.

Good corporate and political governance are also inseparable, and accountability is needed to guarantee political, as well as financial, freedom. Corrupt governments and corrupt corporations misallocate resources. The scarcer those resources, the greater the cost to the economy and the more harm done to development. Regulators must effectively be protected from both the pressure of politics and politicians and the threat of "capture" by powerful corporate insiders and other "market" actors. They must be accountable to all.

Transparency is vital for accountability[13]. The media, too, have a central role to play. Much more cross–border than in the past, they make access to information much harder to control. While press freedom cannot guarantee democracy, democracy cannot exist without press freedom. In this respect, international agreements on media freedom can contribute to open debate, transparency and accountability, and facilitate international peer pressure.

Governance can, and should, prepare the ground for successful democratic reform. The concept is analogous to the sequencing of reforms in the policy context. The possibility of successful implementation is increased and improved with each step, and there can be "test periods" wherein time itself tests feasibility. Yet progress in the construction of democracy should not be neglected because of governance reforms.

The particular governance institutions most conducive to growth, stability and democracy will be specific to each country. This is true because of the importance of history and culture and the path–dependent nature of institutional change, but also because of the newly enterprising role of "civil society" organisations, as discussed in Chapter 11. Though these organisations are rarely fully democratic themselves, and are by definition not fully representative, they can perform invaluable surveillance and lobby functions that reinforce transparency and accountability of polities and corporations. They strengthen democracy.

Conclusion

Development implies a sustained improvement in people's welfare. As the history of mature democracies reveals, the linchpin of progress is governance. Institutions promoting the rule of law and the role of civil society underpin the co–operation and social cohesion necessary for development.

From its creation in the wake of the Marshall Plan, the OECD serves as a yardstick for development. This is because its Members, despite their heterogeneity, constitute a group of successful reformers who share well–developed institutions of governance. Those institutions make possible and benefit from the depth and success of their international peer–pressure practices. OECD Members, like those of the European Union, have created a new culture of policy interdependence and mutual respect.

This gives the lie to the idea that cultures are deterministic, backward–looking realities that prevent some countries from developing and help others to do so. International policy dialogue and co–operation shaped and strengthened by peer pressure can be appropriate not only for the OECD's membership but for others, especially if they share, at least among themselves, reasonably similar values on governance. Dialogue between cultures is possible and can be very effective in the quest for inclusive globalisation described in Chapter 1 in connection with the OECD Development Centre's current programme of work (see also World Bank 2002).

Local, national and international organisations all have a role to play in development, good governance and the drive for democracy. They can help developing countries to leapfrog the centuries that many OECD Members took to construct liberal democratic societies and achieve high levels of development. More than that, they can demonstrate that governance is the cement that binds growth and democracy together.

Belonging to regional arrangements which combine external and peer pressure is only one example of direct ways in which national governance may be improved. Clearly, each national development strategy has its specificity and the portability of the European experience to a development context cannot be assumed. The NEPAD illustrates, however, that international peer pressure can be a concept of interest to poorer countries.

Establishing the institutions and structures required by good governance represents a formidable problem, especially in societies which lack a tradition of good governance — the case with many developing economies. While socio–political and economic devices can be found theoretically to underpin the development process, their implantation requires political will based on the interests of a multitude of competing constituencies, each of which will have to be persuaded, in some cases, to learn to adapt. This is the new development challenge.

Notes

1. Earlier versions of this Chapter were presented as a keynote address at the annual conference of the European Society for the History of Economic Thought (ESHET) held in Rethymnon (Crete) on 14–17 March, 2002 and at the International Forum on National Visions and Strategies, co–hosted by the KDI School of Public Policy and Management, OECD and World Bank in Seoul (Korea), on May 20–22, 2002. Comments from Centre colleagues, especially Ulrich Hiemenz and the authors in this volume are gratefully acknowledged, but we are solely responsible for the final product.

2. Given the importance of property rights in predicting convergence of living standards, De Soto (2000) shows how difficult those might be to enforce in practice, a point also emphasised by Tommasi (2002).

3. In the context of the gains from international trade, Kindleberger (1962) has stressed that the capacity to transform — what might also be called "adaptive capacity" — determines whether or not a national economy will develop. North's institutional lock–in effect discussed below in the text also reflects adaptive capacity, or lack thereof.

4. Indeed, in the field of policy reform (Williamson, 1994), attention has been drawn to the uncertainty attached to benefits from reform for particular groups (Fernandez and Rodrik, 1991) and to the associated need for "institutions to compensate losers from reform" (Rodrik, 1996). Borrowing from Coase's theorem, the massive "political transactions costs" prevailing in some institutional settings have also been noted (Tommasi, 2002).

5. Following the tradition of what Olson called distributive cartels, work on the "voracity" of special interests in developing countries has confirmed the harmful effect on both equity and growth prospects (Tornell and Lane, 1996, 1998, 1999). Azam (2002) sees a triangular predation game among the state, the elite and the village as common in Africa.

6. This is illustrated in a series of models due to Krugman (1981, 1987, 1991). Harris and Yoannides (2000) show that the effect of expectations was less than that of history in explaining land values in the United States.

7.   In Bonaglia, Braga de Macedo and Bussolo (2001), a causal relation is found between greater import openness and lower apparent corruption.

8.   Keohane and Nye (1977) proposed the notion of complex interdependence to illustrate relations among OECD Member states. In the monetary and exchange rate field this is discussed in Braga de Macedo, Cohen and Reisen (2001) and Eichengreen and Braga de Macedo (2001).

9.   Besley and Case (1995) call it "yardstick competition", a term introduced by Shleifer (1985) in industrial organisation.

10.   On global public goods, Kaul et al. (1999). On the importance of regional governance in promoting institutional change, Braga de Macedo (2001).

11.   The East and Southeast Asian experience, among others, shows that authoritarian governments often fail to gain confidence in the business sector, and to make the tough economic decisions needed to sustain growth. The best performing economies in that region have undergone a transition in recent years from rule by moral authority vested in persons to rule by impersonal institutions. They have moved to develop rules to replace favouritism with merit, political leaders' personal preferences with impersonal codes, and seen their economies evolve from largely network–based to more contract–based relationships and family–based to rule–based trust (Root, 1994).

12.   Drèze and Sen (1990); Bardhan (2002) have comparisons between India and China in regard to famines and malnutrition. The devastating effect of conflict on growth has been documented in Azam and Morrisson (1999); Goudie and Neyapti (1999); and Klugman, Neyapti and Stewart (1999). The results on democracy and growth are from Tavares and Wacziarg (2001). See also United Nations Human Development Report 2002 : Deepening Democracy in a Fragmented World.

13.   Keohane and Nye (1999); Persson, Roland and Tabellini (1997); Collier (2000). Experiments in citizen mobilisation, such as "participatory budgeting", first refined in the Brazilian municipality of Porto Alegre, can contribute: Hiemans (2002); see also Abraham and Plateau (2000). Besley and Prat (2001) find a positive relationship between accountability and press freedom.

Bibliography

ABRAHAM, A. AND J.–P. PLATEAU (2000), *The Dilemma of Participation with Endogenous Community Imperfections,* CRED, University of Namur, August.

AZAM, J.–P. (2002), "Statecraft in the Shadow of Civil Conflict", unpublished paper presented to the Second International Forum on African Perspectves, February, Paris.

AZAM, J.–P. AND C. MORRISSON (1999), *Conflict and Growth in Africa: Vol. 1: The Sahel,* Development Centre Studies, Paris.

BARDHAN, P. (2002), *Relative Capture of Local and Central Governments: An Essay in the Political Economy of Decentralization,* Department of Economics, University of California, Berkeley.

BESLEY, T. AND A. CASE (1995), "Incumbent Behavior: Vote–seeking, Tax–Setting and Yardstick Competition", *American Economic Review,* March, pp. 25–45.

BESLEY, T. AND A. PRAT (2001), *Handcuffs for the Grabbing Hand? Media Capture and Government Accountability,* London School of Economics, October.

BONAGLIA, F., J. BRAGA DE MACEDO AND M. BUSSOLO (2001), "How Globalisation Improves Governance", CEPR Discussion Paper n°2992, October.

BRAGA DE MACEDO, J. (2001), "Globalisation and Institutional Change: a Development Perspective", *in* E. MALINVAUD AND L. SABOURIN (eds.), pp. 223–267.

BRAGA DE MACEDO, J., D. COHEN AND H. REISEN (eds.) (2001), *Don't Fix, Don't Float,* Development Centre Studies, OECD, Paris.

COASE, R.H. (1960), "The Problem of Social Cost", *Journal of Law and Economics.*

COLLIER, P. (2000), *Consensus Building, Knowledge and Conditionality,* World Bank, Washington,D.C., April.

DE SOTO, H. (2000), *The Mystery of Capital: Why Capitalism Triumphs in the West and Fails Everywhere Else,* Bantan Press, London.

DREZE, J. AND A. SEN (1990), Hunger and Public Action, Oxford University Press, Oxford.

EICHENGREEN, B. AND J. BRAGA DE MACEDO (2001), "The European Payments Union and the Evolution of International Financial Architecture", *in* A. LAMFALUSSY, B. SNOY AND J. WILSON (eds.).

FERNANDEZ, R. AND D. RODRIK (1991), "Resistance to Reform Status Quo in the Presence of Individual Specific Uncertainty", *American Economic Review* 81, pp. 1146–1155.

GOUDIE, A. AND B. NEYAPTI (1999), *Conflict and Growth in Africa: Vol. 3: Southern Africa,* Development Centre Studies, OECD Development Centre, Paris.

HARRIS, T.F. AND Y.M. IOANNIDES (2000), "History versus Expectations: An Empirical Investigation", Discussion paper 2000–14, Department of Economics, Tufts University.

HIEMANS, J. (2002), *Strenghening Participation in Public Expenditure Management: Policy Recommendations for Key Stakeholders,* Policy Brief No. 22, OECD Development Centre, Paris.

KAUL, I., I. GRUNBERG AND M.A. STERN (eds.) (1999), *Global Public Goods,* UNDP, New York.

KEOHANE, R. AND J. NYE (1999), "Power and Interdependence in the Information Age", *in* E. CIULLA KAMARCK AND J. NYE (eds.), *Democracy.com? Governance in a Networked World,* Hollis Publishing Company, NH.

KEOHANE, R. AND J. NYE (1977), *Power and Interdependence,* Little Brown, MS.

KINDLEBERGER, C. (1962), *Foreign Trade and the National Economy,* Yale University Press, Hew Haven.

KLUGMAN, J., B. NEYAPTI AND F. STEWART (1999), Conflict and Growth in Africa: Vol. 2: Kenya, Tanzania and Uganda, Development Centre Studies, OECD Development Centre, Paris.

KRUGMAN, P. (1991) "History vs Expectations", *Quarterly Journal of Economics* n°2, May, pp 651–667.

KRUGMAN, P. (1987), "The Narrow Moving Band, the Dutch Disease and the Competitive Consequences of Mrs. Thatcher: Notes on Trade in the Presence of Dynamic Economies of Scale", *Journal of Development Economics* XXVII pp. 41–55.

KRUGMAN, P. (1981), "Trade, Accumulation and Uneven Development", *Journal of Development Economics* VIII 149–61.

LAMFALUSSY, A., B. SNOY AND J. WILSON (eds.) (2001), *Fragility of the International Financial System,* PIE Peter Lang, pp. 25–41.

MALINVAUD, E. AND L. SABOURIN (2001), *Globalization, Ethical and Institutional Concerns,* proceedings of the Pontifical Academy of Social Sciences, Vatican City.

NORTH, D.C. (1994), "Economic Performance Through Time", Vol. 84, N° 3, *American Economic Review.*

OECD (1996), *Shaping the 21st Century: the Contribution of Development Co–operation,* OECD/DAC, Paris.

OLSON, M. (1982), *The Rise and Decline of Nations : Economic Growth, Stagflation, and Social Rigidities,* Yale University, New Haven, Conn.

PERSSON, T., G. ROLAND AND G. TABELLINI (1997), "Separation of Powers and Political Accountability", *The Quarterly Journal of Economics,* Vol. CXII, for Harvard University by the MIT Press, Cambridge, Mass.

RODRIK D. (1996), "Understanding Economic Policy Reform", Vol. XXXIV, pp. 9–41, *Journal of Economic Literature.*

ROOT, H. (1994), *The Fountain of Privilege : Political Foundations of Markets in Old Regime France and England,* University of California Press, Berkeley, Calif.

SHLEIFER, A. (1985), "A Theory of Yardstick Competition", *Rand Journal of Economics,* 16(3), pp. 319–27.

TAVARES, J. AND R. WACZIARG (2001), "How Democracy Affects Growth", No. 45, pp. 1341–1378, *European Economic Review.*

TOMMASI, M. (2002), *Crisis, Political Institutions, and Policy Reform: It is not the Policy, it is the Polity, Stupid,* Annual World Bank Conference on Development Economics — Europe, June.

TORNELL, A. AND P. LANE (1999), "The Voracity Effect", *The American Economic Review,* March, 22–46.

TORNELL, A. AND P. LANE (1998), "Are Windfalls a Curse? A Non–representative Model of the Current Account", *Journal of International Economics,* February, pp. 83–112.

TORNELL, A. AND P. LANE (1996), "Power, Growth and the Voracity Effect", *Journal of Economic Growth,* June, 213–241.

UNDP (2002), *United Nations Development Report 2002: Deepening Democracy in a Fragmented World,* Oxford University Press, New York, Oxford.

WILLIAMSON, J. (1994), *The Political Economy of Policy Reform,* Institute of International Economics, Washington, D.C.

WORLD BANK (2002), *Globalisation, Growth and Poverty, Building an Inclusive World Economy,* Washington, D.C.

225

PART TWO

PERSONAL PERSPECTIVES

Chapter 13

Origins of the OECD Development Centre

Carl Kaysen[1]

The Development Centre, whose 40th anniversary we are observing this month (October 2002) was created on the initiative of the United States. In what follows, I will say something about what the US government was trying to do, where the underlying idea came from and the bureaucratic and political processes within the government that led to the final result. I was at the centre of internal government discussion almost from its beginning until the final vote in the OECD. The idea of a Development Centre in OECD was first given public expression in a speech by President Kennedy to the Canadian Parliament in Ottawa on May 17, 1961. Speaking of OECD and the Development Advisory Group, he said: "I propose further that the OECD establish a Development Centre, where citizens, officials, students and professional men of the Atlantic areas and the less developed countries can meet to study the problems of economic development."

Where the idea came from remains something of puzzle. The Kennedy archives show that the first draft, written by presidential speech–writer, Ted Sorenson, did not contain that sentence. A later draft showed it was an insert, but with no indication of where the suggestion came from[2]. We also know that Thorkil Kristensen, the first Secretary General of OECD, met briefly with the President at the end of February, the occasion being the US ratification of the Convention that transformed OEEC into OECD, but there appears no record of whether it was more than a courtesy call.

The broader context of Kennedy's Ottawa speech is worth noting. It was a recital to the Canadians of the tasks in which they and the US — and by implication the rest of NATO and the "West" in general — needed to cooperate. First, was strengthening our military power and commitment to containing the Communist bloc; second, promoting our own economic growth; third, assisting the spread of freedom by helping promote economic growth in the less–developed world. All this reflected the Cold War context of the time, and, indeed, the themes of Kennedy's presidential campaign.

During the early summer of 1961, the concept of the Development Centre was further elaborated by me and Kenneth Hansen, Assistant Director of the Bureau of the Budget for International Affairs. We added a new element to the purposes of the Centre, not mentioned in the Ottawa speech: the Centre should assist the process of economic and social planning and policy making in the developing countries. Such assistance would take the form of securing experts who would spend substantial periods of time in these countries, helping them formulate their development plans, training the relevant officials in their governments, setting up continuing training programmes and advising them in particular in their negotiations with the IBRD and the IMF as well as bilateral aid donors.

The new element reflected the ideas and experience of Edward S. Mason, Professor of Economics at Harvard and his colleagues. Mason had organised a Development Advisory Service at Harvard with both foundation and US government support. DAS teams had operated in Pakistan, Iran, and Greece, beginning in Pakistan in 1954. Two former leaders of such teams had joined the new administration in Washington: David Bell (Pakistan) as Budget Director and Kenneth Hansen (Iran) as Assistant Director for International Affairs. While I had not served in any of these teams, I had discussed their work with Mason and some of them, particularly with respect to Greece. After going to Washington, I continued these discussions by correspondence and by telephone.

The next step in the summer of 1961 was to discuss the ideas for the Centre with the officials concerned in the State and Treasury Departments, the International Cooperation Administration (ICA — predecessor to the Agency for International Development), and the Development Loan Fund (soon to be absorbed into AID). These discussions addressed the fact that a somewhat similar institution was being proposed within the World Bank, and also, independently, as a part of a proposed UN Development Authority. The discussion within the US bureaucracy led to the conclusion that creating the Centre under OECD auspices was the better choice. It would be more likely to sustain autonomy and independent judgement there than in the Bank, where it would be seen as another instrument of Bank policy, subordinate to its operating activities. The more ambitious proposal for a UN development authority was also rejected; there was strong scepticism about the UN's capacity to create an effective operation.

The United States presented its proposal for an OECD Development Centre to the Development Advisory Group meeting in Tokyo, on February 1961. In the document circulated to DAG members, two paragraphs characterised the purposes of the Centre as follows:

The main purpose of the OECD Development Centre would be to stimulate contracts and the exchanges of information and ideas among the industrialized and less–developed countries, and to increase knowledge about and help achieve economic growth in the less–developed countries.

In pursuit of these purposes, the OECD Development Centre could hold seminars and conferences, sponsor research projects, provide research grants to individuals and groups in the industrialized and less–developed countries, publish studies and proceedings, make available library and other facilities, and provide professional assistance in the preparation of development plans. As appropriate, it might include on a continuing basis programs already under study or proposed by the Development Assistance Committee of the OECD. It would also be free to initiate programs on its own and respond to requests for professional advice and assistance from the less–developed countries.

The Members of DAG responded favourably to the US presentation, requesting that it be studied further. Thorkil Kristensen, Secretary General of OECD, subsequently appointed an expert Advisory Committee to report on the proposal consisting of Roger Gregoire (France), Palamadai S. Lokanathan (India), Edward S. Mason (United States) and Jan Tinbergen (Netherlands). The Committee reported in February 1962, recommending the creation of the Centre, sketched its functions and discussed its initial scale and costs[3]. The report lists six functions for the proposed Centre, the third of which was "to provide and arrange for the provision of advisory services to less–developed countries...." Observing that there are efforts by others in this area, three reasons for the proposed Centre are offered: some less–developed countries may prefer the Centre to existing sources; the Centre may have a particularly effective group of personnel for this work, especially Europeans; the needs are great and growing and the abilities of other organisations to meet them are limited. The report also recommends that the Centre not solicit requests for adversary services but wait for requests, perhaps arising from suggestions by DAC or the Secretary General in the course of their normal work with developing countries.

The other five tasks listed are: *1)* providing training instruction for professional and technical personnel involved in development planning and economic and social policy making; *2)* arranging seminars and study conferences for people in both member countries and developing countries; *3)* promoting the creation of facilities for training persons in developed Member countries to work in less–developed countries; *4)* promoting research activities in relevant subjects; *5)* advise about training facilities for people from less–developed countries.

The report does not make clear whether these tasks are listed in priority order. In an appendix to their report, the experts discussed two possible scales for the Centre, and their costs (including some overhead and support costs that it expected OECD to provide): either a scale of six senior and six junior members, or one senior and ten junior, and two large conferences and six smaller meetings each year; at costs of $420 000 (1962) and $620 000 respectively.

At its meeting in Paris in March 1962, the Development Advisory Committee (DAC) (DAG renamed after OEEC became OECD) further discussed the proposal for a Development Centre in OECD and the experts' reports and recommended to OECD that it go forward with the Centre[4]. In the next meeting of OECD, in October 1962, the Centre was created, and began to function early in 1963.

In between the two Paris meetings, I initiated efforts to secure funding for the Centre in addition to what the regular OECD budget would provide. I approached the Ford Foundation for the possibility of its providing $100 000 a year for five years, and also discussed with US officials in the State Department, the Agency for International Development (AID) and the Bureau of the Budget the possibility of providing funds directly to the Centre in addition to the US contribution to OECD. I do not know the outcome of these efforts.

Looking back over the four decades of the Centre's life, it is clear that one of the purposes featured in the US proposal was never taken up — the provision of advisory services on development planning and economic policy to developing country governments. Its research efforts, beginning with the fundamental work of Goldsmith and Maddison on organising a consistent statistical record of basic economic measurements for the developing countries, have flourished. So have the programmes of seminars and conferences in which officials, experts, and wider groups from developing and developed countries can exchange and compare experiences.

Having had only intermittent contact with OECD over this period and none directly with the Centre, I have no idea why that particular function was never developed. But given the checkered history of government policies in the developing countries, and shifts of focus and changes in the scale of development efforts and other kinds of assistance to undeveloped countries in the OECD countries, I continue to believe that this was an opportunity lost, and for some parts of the world, one still worth taking up.

Notes

1. I went to Washington from the Harvard Economics department in May 1961, to become a senior member of the NSC staff, promoted in November to Deputy Special Assistant to the President for National Security Affairs, and remained to the end of the Kennedy administration. In writing this note, I have relied on the documentation in the Kennedy Library archive to stimulate, reinforce, and supplement my memory. Most of the material comes from the National Security Files, Box 374, Carl Kaysen file on a Development Centre.

2. David Bell, Director of the Budget, and Walt Rostow of the White House NSC staff are the likeliest possibilities for having suggested the idea.

3. The report is OECD document CES/62.19

4. I had the pleasure of being the US delegate to the DAC meeting, and formally moving the proposal.

Chapter 14

A Personal Account

Edmond Malinvaud

In the context of closer relations between the Centre and research institutions of the host country, Professor Malinvaud came to the Centre on 15 June 2001. During his visit, he became aware of the work underway which resulted in the chapters making up the first part of this book and he expressed a wish to be associated with the project through a personal contribution.

* * *

For France, where the OECD Development Centre is located, 1962 marked a turning point in relations with the Third World: the independence of the countries of the former colonial empire was becoming a reality, confirmed by that of Algeria. This obliged us to rethink our activities aimed at promoting the economic development of French–speaking Africa. There were many such activities, concerned in particular with the training of the new elite classes and with advice on development strategies.

In the context of our educational responsibilities, Eugène Morice — my predecessor as director of the Ecole nationale de la statistique et de l'administration économique (ENSAE) — and I were clearly aware of the challenge facing us: to train the many official statisticians who were to serve the new states, and to do so by modifying our recruitment methods, which were too selective for the purpose at hand, and our curricula, which were short of material on the developing–country context, but maintaining our standards as to the effort required of students. Thanks to the immediate interest shown by the EEC Commission in our project, we founded the Centre européen de formation des statisticiens–économistes des pays en voie de développement (CESD). The programmes of study offered by the Centre, which initially were closely interwoven with those of the ENSAE, were subsequently transferred in stages to Africa.

This period saw the beginning of a substantial shift in our thinking as to the economic strategies to be recommended to developing countries. In the immediate aftermath of the Second World War, many experts had believed that the remedy for under–development lay primarily in good planning, which would guide the development of an autonomous industrial sector. By 1962, the most realistic of them had grasped that the matter was not so simple: planning techniques proved to be of only limited help; industrialisation itself could not succeed in countries where productivity was still too low; neglecting agriculture and craft industries was a serious error, and so forth. It was necessary to rethink development economics in all its many aspects.

The OECD, for its part, had very rightly recognised that all of its Member countries had a duty to assist developing countries. The Organisation also knew from experience that to conduct its missions properly, it needed to be able systematically to provide countries with high–quality economic expertise. As the staff at OECD headquarters in the rue André Pascal would always be too occupied with its main agenda, it made good sense to form a Centre specialising in development problems. Since that time, the Development Centre has participated in an immense global network of expertise, involving not only economists but also specialists in the various fields on which development depends, not only academic researchers but also Third World decision makers and the countries that provide them with aid.

The time has indeed come to take stock, giving consideration first and foremost to the topics where development economics is developing fresh insights to face the challenges of the coming decades.

Chapter 15

The Origins and Early Years of the Centre: A Personal Perspective

Angus Maddison[1]

The creation of an OECD Development Centre was proposed by President Kennedy in an address to the Canadian Senate and House of Commons in May 1961. It was approved by the OECD Council in October 1962, and started to function in mid–1963. It was a significant element in the transition from OEEC to OECD. The old organisation was a co–operative endeavour by 16 West European countries to promote the recovery and expansion of their economies between 1948 and 1961. The new organisation added a commitment to foster growth in the "less developed" countries of Asia, Africa and Latin America by stimulating a bigger flow of financial resources (the responsibility of the Development Directorate), and providing advice on the formulation and implementation of economic policy (responsibility of the Centre). The membership of the new organisation was enlarged to include Canada, Japan and the United States (though the United States and Canada had been associate members of OEEC).

There were three main reasons for the changes. One was the realisation that European growth had been much faster in the 1950s than in the rest of the world. The already wide income gap between the rich countries and the rest was widening. The US government (which had provided a massive flow of aid to Europe in 1948–52) nudged the West European countries to increase or initiate aid to the Third World. It was also felt that OEEC experience in liberalising trade, promoting growth and allocating Marshall Aid was relevant to poorer countries. A second reason was that decolonisation of Asian and African countries was nearing completion. They wanted to broaden their international links, and it was felt that OECD member countries should encourage this process. A third consideration was the intensification of rivalry between Western nations and what was then called the Sino–Soviet bloc. There was increasing competition from the USSR and China to win friends and allies in the Third World by providing technical assistance, financial and military aid. Many newly independent countries joined the non–aligned group (led by Egypt, India, Indonesia, Mexico and Yugoslavia), which wanted to maintain a neutral posture between East and West.

At that time, private capital flows were small and NGOs were of marginal significance. This explains the heavy emphasis on government finance. At the initiative of the Eisenhower administration, a Development Assistance Group (DAG) was created to prepare the ground for the DAC (Development Assistance Committee) of the new organisation.

The DAG consisted of 12 European countries, Canada, Japan and the United States and held five meetings in Washington (March and October 1960), Bonn (July 1960), London (March 1961) and Tokyo (July 1961). I was the secretary of the DAG. The first task was to set up a comprehensive statistical reporting system to monitor the flow of different categories of financial resources to developing countries (official loans and grants, private credits, bond purchases, equity and direct investment, export credit guarantees etc.) from each of the countries which were deemed to be developed. Most countries had no comprehensive view of such flows. We could get a rough aggregate cross–check from balance of payments statistics but we had to go to central banks, finance ministries, export credit agencies, the World Bank and IMF to break down the different categories. The results were often unexpected, e.g. the flow from France was very much bigger proportionately than in the United States, but as expected the flows were relatively small from Germany, Japan and Scandinavia. The first survey, *The Flow of Financial Resources to Countries in the Course of Economic Development*, was carried out at breakneck speed and published in April 1961. It set the main guidelines which the Development Assistance Committee still uses for collecting data from its Member countries.

A second survey was submitted to the fifth DAG meeting in Tokyo in July 1961. This showed the various types of financial flows to 60 individual recipient countries together with indicators of their GDP growth and levels, domestic capital formation and saving, the burden of foreign public debt, export earnings, literacy rates and population. It was a major tool for analysing the role of aid and capital flows in economic development, though it obviously needed to be followed up by more detailed analysis of the efficiency of economic policy in allocating resources — a job which the founding fathers expected the Development Centre to undertake.

The third task of the DAG was to design a review procedure for assessing the adequacy and efficacy of the aid effort of donor countries.

The Development Centre was created in order better to understand the policies of developing countries and to act as an intellectual intermediary between them and OECD. Its mandate was "to bring together the knowledge and experience available in participating countries of both economic development and of the formulation and execution of general economic policies; to adapt them to the needs of countries or regions in the process of economic development and to place the results by appropriate means at the disposal of the countries concerned".

The Kennedy administration's proposal to create the Centre was put to the DAG at its Tokyo meeting by Carl Kaysen from the White House staff. It originated with Edward Mason (1899–1992) who had created the Harvard advisory service and David Bell (1919-2000) who headed the first Harvard Group in Pakistan before becoming chief of AID (Aid for International Development) in Washington. The Secretary-General of OECD, Thorkil Kristensen (1899-1989), was very keen on the idea and set up an expert group (Roger Gregoire, Dr. P.S. Lokanathan, Edward Mason and Jan Tinbergen) to advise on the staff structure and research topics. Kristensen wanted a distinguished academic as president.

The first President was Robert Buron (1910–72), an MRP (Christian Democrat) politician with wide connections in the Third World. He held nine ministerial posts between 1950 and 1962 in the Fourth and Fifth Republics — notably Minister of Colonies (d'Outre Mer) for Mendès France (1954–55) and Minister of Transport 1958–62. He participated in the negotiations for the French withdrawals from Viet Nam and Algeria. His friends included Presidents Eduardo Frei of Chile, Felix Houphouet–Boigny of Côte d'Ivoire, Sekou Touré of Guinea, and Prime Minister Hoveida of Iran. Buron's main personal interest was in "mobile" seminars for ministers and senior officials in countries (Cameroon, Côte d'Ivoire, Guinea, Ecuador, Peru, Iran, Chile and Sri Lanka) where he had contacts and there was scope for a dialogue on development problems and policies. He was also keen to promote operational activities of a kind with which he was familiar as a result of long experience as President of the French National Productivity Centre. There were three main activities of this kind: a) creation of a pragmatic question and answer service "so designed that the authorities of each developing country will regard it as their own library, with a staff able to understand their needs and find the right answer quickly"; b) provision of advice to small and medium business on ways of increasing productivity; c) transfer of OECD experience on educational planning (in the Mediterranean Regional Project). Buron appointed Rostislaw Donn to run these operational activities. Rostislaw had worked (1945–56) in the French Embassy in Washington transferring American know–how to France and in the European Productivity Agency from 1957 onwards. He was in charge of these activities in the Centre until 1971.

Raymond Goldsmith (1904–88) was Vice–President for the first two years. He was a professor at Yale who had made pioneering theoretical contributions to the study of capital and wealth, analysis of savings and financial flows and produced a massive flow of comparative empirical studies in these fields. He was very much a loner. He did not create a research team but got on with his own work, and let the fellows pick their own topics, insisting only that they be related in some way to foreign aid. He was an ardent bibliophile and helped ensure that the Centre's library played an active role in serving the needs of officials and economists in the Third World. Our librarian, Billie Salter, did an excellent job in facilitating our research and that of many others throughout the world. She left in 1967 to be librarian of the Yale Growth Centre. Goldsmith's two studies for the Centre were published in 1966 — *The Determinants of Financial Structure*, and *The Financial Development of Mexico*.

Goldsmith was responsible for creating the Research Division. It established contact with statistical offices throughout the Third World to produce standardised national accounts. These were an essential tool of research on comparative economic performance. The first large volume, *National Accounts of Less Developed Countries, 1950–66*, appeared in 1968[2]. It was followed by 23 annual volumes until 1991. In the course of my travels for the Centre I made a habit of visiting national statistical offices to explain what we were doing, discussing adjustments necessary for international comparability of GDP and investment rates, and bringing back as much documentation as I could get. I did this in Iran, Japan, Pakistan, the Philippines, Thailand, Argentina, Brazil, Mexico and the USSR. In April 1965, I organised a Development Centre workshop on international comparison of real income levels and variations in the purchasing power of currencies. This was a field which OEEC had pioneered (Gilbert and Kravis, 1954; Paige and Bombach, 1959) and Irving Kravis wanted to extend the analysis to lower income countries. Wilfred Beckerman prepared a paper on short–cut methods which might be used pending the results of more fundamental studies (*International Comparisons of Real Incomes*, 1966), but we failed to rekindle OECD interest. Kravis eventually got a large grant from the Ford Foundation, set up his project in the University of Pennsylvania in co–operation with the UN statistical office, and produced three fundamental studies. His colleagues, Alan Heston and Robert Summers created the Penn World Tables and OECD restarted its work in this field in 1982. As a result it is now possible to measure real income levels on a comparable basis, more or less worldwide.

There were five "fellows" who constituted the senior staff of the Centre. Herbert Giersch was a distiguished liberal economist, who in 1948–51 had been head of the OEEC division dealing with liberalisation of European trade and payments and a professor in the University of the Saar. He was later President of the Kiel Institut fur Weltwirtschaft for many years, an advisor on economic policy to the German government and a prominent member of the Mont Pelerin Society. His research project was a comparison of the efficiency of three Indian steel plants. Two were government–owned and supported by foreign aid and technical assistance. Rourkela got help from Germany, Durgapur from the United Kingdom. The third was the privately owned Tata plant at Jamshedpur. Giersch went to India in April 1964 to start the project but was unable to complete it as he was appointed to the Wissenschaftliches Beirat (the German government's Council of Economic Advisors).

Edmond Janssens was a Belgian economist, also trained in law and philology, who had worked for the United Nations in New York, Turkey, Mexico, Guinea and Ruanda–Burundi on technical assistance assignments. His linguistic ability was astounding. He could speak most West European languages, Chinese, Russian and Turkish. He had operational responsibility for some of the mobile seminars and compiled a *Global Directory of Development Finance Institutions,* 1967.

Nino Novacco was a regional planner who was executive secretary of SVIMEZ. This was a brains trust of the Italian government agency promoting economic development in southern Italy (Cassa per il Mezzogiorno). He participated in the preparation of Italy's first five year plan (1956–61) and did a similar job (with Professor Saraceno) for the Karamanlis government in Greece.

Göran Ohlin (1926–97) was an economic historian of great distinction. He had translated Hecksher's *Economic History of Sweden* into English in 1954, and had written a brilliant Harvard PhD thesis in 1955 on European demographic experience from the middle ages to the 18th century. This was widely cited but not published until 1981. Göran was a meticulous scholar, and had great literary talent, but he applied such exacting standards to himself that he had published very little. Being in the Centre was good for Göran. The pressure to publish unleashed his talent, and inspired a life–long commitment to development issues. He wrote three studies for the Centre: *Foreign Aid Policies Reconsidered, Aid and Indebtedness,* and *Population Control and Economic Development.* After he left, he joined the staff of the Pearson Commission on International Development 1967–69, was secretary to a similar commission headed by Willy Brandt in the 1980s, and after a period as professor in Uppsala became Assistant Secretary General of the United Nations.

I became a fellow in January 1964 and stayed three years[3]. I had already been in OEEC for 11 years. From January 1953 I worked in the Economics directorate where I was head of the division responsible for writing the annual economic survey of the Western economies and servicing the Group of Economic Experts (chief policy advisors of the five biggest European countries and the United States). In these 11 years, I learned a great deal about economic policy analysis. My boss was Milton Gilbert, an economist and statistician of the highest calibre. When we prepared discussion papers for the experts we would spend hours over the draft trying to get a document that was lucid and creatively pungent with regard to policy options. Milton had an eagle eye for tables, making sure they were the most appropriate we could produce, and elegantly presented. He had organised and defined the scope of the official US national accounts in the 1940s and played a major role in standardising the macroeconomic accounts of OEEC countries in the 1950s. He also inaugurated a series of pathbreaking comparisons of the purchasing power of currencies and comparability of real product levels. As a result we had a steel frame for our assessments of policy effectiveness over time and across countries. The discussions in the Expert Group were a great educational experience because of the wide range of views. Tinbergen was a social engineer and model builder. Etienne Hirsch, the head of the French Plan, was very flexible and free of etatist prejudice. Otmar Emminger, the chief economist of the Bundesbank, was the most articulate. He was primarily concerned with financial stability and payments equilibrium. He was not interested in microeconomic questions which were to be solved by market mechanisms set in train by macro–policy. Arthur Burns was the least concerned with employment and growth. He pushed the US government away from Keynesian activism in favour of price stability and budget balance. Nevertheless he was interested in close monitoring of the performance of the leading economies and their mutual interaction. Sir Robert Hall was a pragmatic Keynesian of great wisdom and professional competence. He was an excellent chairman, judicious, slow–speaking and master of the meaningful grunt. He kept the proceedings articulate and effective. The quality of these confrontations on policy issues, and the fact that the European economy had shown such extraordinary growth, gave me the exhilarating impression that OEEC was largely responsible for making capitalism work[4].

From the beginning of 1960 to mid–1962 our workload increased tremendously and Milton left. The Kennedy administration added new excitement to our economic policy work by sending a wave of brilliant economists to our meetings (Walter Heller, Jim Tobin, Bob Solow, Robert Roosa and Richard Cooper). We also had the main responsibility for servicing the new development initiatives. My main colleagues in the development work were Bill Parsons and Helmut Führer (who became directors of the Development Department in 1966–69 and 1975–93 respectively) and Friedrich Kahnert (later director in the Development Centre).

The pressure eased in mid–1962, so I took leave of absence for six months to write *Economic Growth in the West* (1964) where I tried to explain the postwar acceleration of growth in Western Europe, and the greater stability of the growth path. I pushed the historical perspective back to 1870, using the same type of quantitative national accounting evidence we had been using in OEEC for the postwar period.

At the end of 1962 I was a member of a United Nations Expert group on techniques of long–term economic projection, which met in Bangkok. The group included leading Asian economists associated with policy problems (Mahbub ul Haq, K.S. Krishnaswamy, Tsunehiko Watanabe), as well as Raymond Goldsmith and myself. This was a useful introduction to a wide array of policy concerns very different from those which OEEC countries faced.

When I came back in January 1963, I moved to the Development Directorate for a year as Director of Technical Co–operation. The main job was to provide technical assistance (including advice on economic policy analysis) to Greece, Portugal, Spain, Turkey and Yugoslavia plus a number of activities carried over from the European Productivity Agency. One of these was to help support the Mediterranean Regional Project on Educational Planning in Greece, Italy, Portugal, Spain, Turkey and Yugoslavia[5]. Another was the annual meeting of Directors of Development Research and Training Institutes. The last meeting, prior to its transfer to the Centre, was in Berlin in September 1963. The programme reflected what I hoped would be a significant activity in the Centre. It was an exchange of views on macroeconomic policy problems in Africa, Brazil, France, India, Japan, Pakistan, Yugoslavia between top policy officials (including Roberto Campos, François Leguay, Hari Krishna Paranjape, Saburo Okita and Branko Horvat). It also included an illuminating exchange between these experts and Buron and Goldsmith who outlined their hopes for the Centre[6].

My initial research for the Centre was concentrated on the role of skills and education in development. In the early 1960s, the role of education in economic growth attracted wide attention amongst economists thanks to the pioneering work of Ted Schultz and Ed Denison. When I was running OECD's aid programmes for Southern Europe it was very clear that skill shortages and poor education were a significant obstacle to faster economic growth. I had already started a review of the Greek case. This was a very detailed survey of foreign aid received in the postwar period, the characteristics of the education system, and an analysis of the strategy of Greek development (*Foreign Skills and Technical Assistance in Greek Development, 1966*). A second comparative survey of human capital and the transfer of skills covered Brazil, Mexico, Pakistan and Guinea (*Foreign Skills in Economic Development, 1965*).

I finished writing these books in mid–1965, at which stage Goldsmith, Giersch and Novacco left. The new Vice President, Ian Little, and the two new fellows, Maurice Scott and Tibor Scitovsky, decided to work as a team on industrialisation and trade. Ian also published a major study on industrial project analysis (with Jim Mirrlees), and brought in two Indian economists, Jagdish Bhagwati and Padma Desai which added welcome variety to our overly Western profile.

I also redirected my research. My first instinct was to make a general survey of development experience in quantitative and historical perspective as I had done in *Economic Growth in the West* for the advanced capitalist countries, but the developing world was much more heterogeneous than OECD countries in institutions, ideologies, policy objectives and weaponry, cultural and political heritage, social structure and level of real income. Given the huge range of these countries and my relative ignorance of them, it seemed sensible to postpone this ambitious project and concentrate on a case study of Japanese and Soviet development experience[7]. Both these countries had attempted with some degree of success to catch up with the advanced countries, so it seemed worthwhile to scrutinise their policies and performance, looking at their history and institutions as well as the more proximate causality one can measure with growth accounts.

In 1964 I visited Moscow and Leningrad to see what material I could collect on Soviet growth. I contacted IMEMO (the Institute for World Politics and Economics) in Moscow (which was the main institute of the Academy of Sciences for studying western economies), and found myself unexpectedly welcome as their Deputy Director, Manoukian, had just translated *Economic Growth in the West*. The most outspoken and interesting of their economists was Stanislav

Menshikov. It was more difficult to meet economists working on the Soviet economy, but with some difficulty I got the telephone number of Gosplan and contacted Valentin Kudrov who had translated the OEEC real income studies into Russian and made comparative studies of Soviet/US performance. Kudrov came, with a minder, to meet me at the Metropole Hotel. In his halting English and my very limited Russian, we discussed the work of leading US Kremlinologists and Soviet Americanologists, and exchanged views on problems of measuring real product and growth which we still continue. I also managed to take in something of the flavour of Soviet society, looking at museums, being accosted by people wanting Beatles records, watching the May Day parade in Red Square, with Kruschev, Ben Bella and Oginga Odinga on Lenin's tomb.

In 1965, I made a second visit to Japan for a few weeks to collect material on Japanese growth. Here it was possible to have a much deeper dialogue than in Moscow, and most government statistical information was available with headings in English as well as Japanese. I already had friends in Hitotsubashi University, particularly Kazushi Ohkawa, who was starting to publish 13 volumes on Japanese quantitative economic history. Saburo Okita opened the doors of government agencies such as the Bank of Japan, the Economic Planning Agency, the Ministry of Agriculture, and the Ministry of Education where one could often find ten economists in a room all fresh and eager to talk after their morning callisthenics. Apart from the sophistication of these people I was struck by the strong discipline and an organisation that operated like clockwork. I had had the same impression about Japanese industry on my first trip in 1961 when I had visited the Sony radio factory, and found the foremen had Ph.Ds and all the operatives had high school education. On the way back, I spent two weeks in China, but did not manage to contact any Chinese economists, and there were no believable statistics, so my impressions were based almost entirely on visual inspection with all the risks that flow from lack of documentation. In terms of clothing, bicycles, cameras, watches and housing, living standards in Canton and Peking were better than I had expected and were certainly higher than in India. The people's commune I visited specialised in raising ducks and had some industrial activity, but was clearly an official showcase. I went with a young Englishman who had inherited a large farm in East Anglia which he ran with seven people. The Chinese farm was not much bigger in area, but had hundreds of people working on it.

During 1966, when I was writing the Japan–Russia study, I was fortunate in having fairly frequent contact with Arthur Lewis. He spent six weeks in the Centre in the summer of 1966 writing *Reflections on Nigeria's Economic Growth* (1967) Arthur (1915–1991) was probably the brightest economist to work on development and as a West Indian, had a lifetime familiarity with the problems. He had been economic advisor to Nkrumah in Ghana when it first gained independence, and to Sekou Touré in Guinea. I profited greatly from contact with him, both in our daily luncheon sessions in Paris, and from his written comments on my drafts which were always forthright, penetrating and enlightening. In fact, they were so persuasive that I rewrote the book completely. *Economic Growth in Japan and the USSR* was published in 1969, by Norton, New York.

It is perhaps worthwhile to give an impression of the situation I found in countries I visited for the Centre. Intercountry differences in policy and institutions were very wide and often neglected by economists who tried to make general models of development.

Greece

The study on Greece was done in co–operation with Ben Higgins (1912–2001), one of the pioneers of development economics, and Alexander Stavrianopoulos, the chief civil servant in the Greek Ministry of Co–ordination (the economics ministry). At that time Andreas Papandreou was the minister and his father, George, was Prime Minister. I already knew him and Ben Higgins was an old colleague of his, so our project had political blessing. We also had a good rapport with the Bank of Greece where my friend from Cambridge days, John Pezmazoglou, was Deputy Governor. Xenophon Zolotas, the Governor, was also interested and very helpful in what we were doing. Other people involved were Constantine Doxiadis, an urban planner and architect with great breadth of vision and powers of organisation, who had founded his Institute of Ekistics in Athens, and Ingvar Svennilson who was an OECD consultant on Greek education.

It did not seem to me that human capital had been a constraint on Greek development, as there was a huge range of skills and entrepreneurship in the worldwide Greek diaspora to supplement domestic resources. Nevertheless there was a large inflow of technical assistance and a large outflow of students to foreign universities because of weaknesses in Greek higher education. A major recommendation of our report was to reduce dependence on technical assistance by creating a third, new–style university. Doxiadis pressed strongly for a private university in Sounion, as he feared political interference if it was a state institution. In fact the new university was a state institution in Patras, and Doxiadis' fears turned out to have some foundation, but a private university did not seem a practical proposition.

Brazil

Brazil was the country where I developed the widest range of contacts and saw most of the policy–making process. I went to Rio in October 1964 at the invitation of Roberto Campos, Minister of Planning in the military regime which had just overthrown the populist government of Goulart. Campos (1917–2001) was an economist–diplomat with a very wide range of experience. He was born in a monastery in the backwoods of Mato Grosso and was a seminarist before he joined the Foreign Ministry in 1939 as a junior consul. On his way up, he got a Ph.D in economics from Columbia University, was one of the Brazilian delegates to Bretton Woods and helped make the development plan of President Kubitschek. He became head of the Brazilian Development Bank and Ambassador to the United States. Campos was by far the most powerful minister, strongly supported by Octavio Bulhões as Minister of Finance. Campos had a team of outstanding young economists in his ministry, including Mario Simenson and João Paulo dos Reis Velloso who later became ministers. The mentor of both Campos and Bulhões was Eugenio Gudin (1886–1986), a *laisser–faire* liberal, who had founded the academic study of economics in Brazil after a career as an engineer.

The main preoccupation of the economic team was a stabilisation exercise to put a halt to hyperinflation, reduce the budget deficit, reform the tax system, get rid of a distorted set of price controls and subsidies, liberalise foreign trade, create a new exchange rate mechanism and reform financial institutions. The stabilisation exercise was an outstanding success in laying the foundations for a subsequent decade of very fast economic growth and it was carried out in gradualist fashion in 1964–67, without pushing Brazil into recession. I was able to observe this operation at close quarters in the research department of the Planning Ministry where I was a consultant on education. I also had contact with the research group in the Vargas Foundation, which performed some of the functions of a statistical office, producing both the national accounts and the price indices as well as providing short term business cycle analysis in its journal *Conjuntura*. I went to Brazil four times in 1964–66, visited a good many parts of the country, acquired some modest competence in Portuguese, as well as learning the samba and bossa nova.

A striking feature of Brazil is the vigour and originality of its intellectual life. The population has cosmopolitan roots, with significant immigration of Italians, Germans, Japanese, Lebanese as well as the original mix of Portuguese settlers and African slaves. It is a big country with several very large cities, so its intellectual life is multipolar. It has been blessed with much gentler political transitions than most of Latin America, so the tone of intellectual life was less bitter than in some other places. It was a frontier country with a high degree of self confidence without a chip–on–the–shoulder feeling of exploitation by powerful neighbours. Added to this was the fascination of the economic problems they were tackling, because I had had no previous experience of such an inflationary economy, such boldness in institutional innovation, or such an elaborate set of institutions for coexistence with inflation. The approach to these problems was basically liberal and (except for its gradualism) not too different from that of the World Bank and IMF in the 1980s, but at that time it went counter to the prevailing policy views in other Latin American countries.

The most disconcerting thing about Brazil was the very high degree of inequality. Regional variance in per capita income in the 20 states ranged from nine to one, and the horizontal variation of income was also very sharp and noticeable, particularly in Rio with its impoverished ramshackle *favelas* poised on slippery hillsides behind luxurious beachfront apartments. It was also very noticeable that the black population was completely absent from the seats of power or any well–paid activity except sport and entertainment[8].

Guinea

In January 1965, four of the Development Centre fellows, Edmond Janssens, Nino Novacco, Göran Ohlin and I, went to Conakry for a month with Buron and Goldsmith. In the first week, we talked to Sekou Touré, the President, Ismael Touré his brother, who was Economic Development Minister, Siafoulaye Diallo, the Minister of Finance and Planning, who appeared to be second man in the regime, and Keita Fodeba, a professional dancer and founder of the national ballet, who had become a highly original Minister of Defence. Buron made a speech to the national assembly and then we had all the senior economic officials and the Director of Planning (a veterinarian) in a seminar for three weeks.

In the colonial period, Sekou Touré, who started life as a postal worker, had been a Communist (CGT) trade union leader and a member of the French parliament. He was a great grandson of a warrior chief, Samory, who fought the French between 1879 and 1898. In the 1950s, he went to Czechoslovakia to a school for party cadres. In Guinea he had organised political life on a single party basis. Virtually all adults were expected to join. The party had nearly 8 000 committees and when we visited outlying regions we found roomfuls of villagers who had come to palaver — often with very searching questions. One of the functions of the party was to reduce the significance of ethnic divisions which were physically very marked. Sekou was a very dark skinned stocky Malinke, whereas Saifoulaye was a tall lanky Peul with light brown skin and semitic features.

The Guinean situation was unique in Africa as the French had abandoned the country when it opted for independence in 1958. There was no neocolonial apprenticeship as there was elsewhere in French Africa which became independent in 1960. In a population of 3 million, there were less than 50 Guineans with higher education. There had been 600 Frenchmen in government service, several thousand French soldiers, and about 2 500 expatriates in productive and service enterprises who all left abruptly. As a result, the administration, health services and modern economy had collapsed. The country was excluded from the franc area to which its neighbours belonged. Ministers (virtually all without higher education) had had to improvise an administration from scratch, getting technical assistance from wherever they could. The radio, (La Voix de la Révolution) was run by a beautiful Hungarian lady. The only newspaper, *Horoya*, had a circulation of 8 000 every two or three days but the East Germans had built the Patrice Lumumba printing plant with a capacity of several hundred thousand newspapers a day. Military advice and incompatible equipment came from China, Czechoslovakia, and the German Democratic Republic. The military effectiveness of the army seemed doubtful, but they did useful work on development projects. They made shoes, clothing and suitcases, mended roads and trained rural *animateurs*. The Defence Minister was also responsible for security and police. There was a crack unit of glamorous ladies who served as traffic police in Conakry and doubled as a night club orchestra. Before we came, the army had had a visit from Franz Joseph Strauss, the German Defence Minister, and when we were there they had another from Che Guevara, the Cuban specialist on guerilla warfare.

The Guinean ministers and civil servants were friendly, without guile, ready to answer all questions, and several of them dressed in traditional Muslim robes. We visited the big bauxite and aluminium operation in Fria, a banana and pineapple plantation, a matchstick factory and a model state farm run by a group of ministers. The farm was littered with Soviet tractors and other machinery, but had no visible output. When I asked the Minister of Planning about the output, he replied "Tu sais, j'ai pas la tête pour les chiffres" (I have no head for figures). The state trading organisation had taken over French shops, which were almost completely empty, and plantation agriculture was faltering. In spite of the chaos, it was a lively and interesting place. It survived by virtue of a robust subsistence economy, widespread smuggling by ethnic groups with relatives in neighbouring countries, and rich deposits of bauxite and iron ore which attracted foreign investment. The mixed bag of foreign aid was quite sizeable, and, on balance, was probably helpful but some of the projects seemed very dubious, e.g. the Chinese matchstick factory imported huge Chinese trees to provide its raw material.

Iran

In July 1965 there was a seminar on supposedly similar lines in Teheran, but it was totally different from Guinea. We met elegant officials and junior ministers with sleeked hair and expensive suits, who listened politely and said little. Hoveida (later executed by Khomeini) was the only interesting one, but we did not learn much about the country. When I tried to discuss the oppressive atmosphere of the place with Buron, he shut me up, as he suspected that his chauffeur might understand and report our conversation.

Pakistan

In May 1965, I went to Pakistan for a month to advise on manpower budgeting (education and use of foreign skills) for the third five–year plan. The visit to Karachi and Lahore was financed by the Harvard Advisory Service, at the initiative of Mahbub ul Haq (1934–98), the chief economist to the Planning Commission.

The Planning Commission was the central agency co–ordinating economic policy and foreign aid. It was part of the Presidential Secretariat, as the President was also head of the Commission.

The 1965 visit was rather brief, but I returned for a year in 1969–70, with the Harvard Advisory Group to work on the social chapters of the fourth five–year plan.

From 1958 to 1969, the military government of Ayub Khan had a strategy of functional inequality. In Mahbub's words, "the underdeveloped countries must consciously accept a philosophy of growth and shelve for the distant future all ideas of equitable distribution and welfare state. It should be recognised that these are luxuries which only developed countries can afford".

Ayub was toppled in March 1969 by workers and students in a climate of social unrest. Political opposition was gathering strength in East Pakistan because of the uneven allocation of foreign aid and the fruits of development. The new military dictator, Yahya Khan, took a number of measures to appease discontent, suspending 15 per cent of high level civil servants for corruption, raising the minimum wage, chastising business tax evaders, promising more resources to education and to East Pakistan. There was also greater emphasis on social policy in the fourth plan than there had been earlier.

In the Planning Commission my main job was to scrutinise policy proposals for education, health, housing, urban water supply, and family planning that came to the Commission from the relevant ministries and the regional planning agencies in Dacca and Karachi. I had to get a perspective of what was feasible from whatever documentary evidence I could collect, cross–examining my colleagues, and occasional visits to hospitals or public works projects.

Pakistan's social structure was still strongly influenced by the heritage of the British raj. The nationalist forces which created the country had no commitment to social reform as in India, nor were they particularly religious. At that time, the religious content was primarily anti–Hindu and certainly not Islamic in any fundamentalist sense. The Pakistan Jinnah created was Vice–regal and the primary locus of power was the bureaucratic–military elite. The organisational framework of this group was still the one created by the British and their working language was English. Their houses, clubs, cantonments, life style and idioms were British colonial. The group was much bigger than in colonial days. The armed forces numbered 300 000 with 7 000 officers compared with 100 Muslim officers in the smaller Indian army of the British period. There were 500 members in the elite civil service (CSP) and about 1 150 Class I officers under them. This was more than ten times the number of top Muslim officials under the British. These people got the major benefits of government housing expenditure. Urban improvements were concentrated in their cantonment areas. They benefited substantially from expenditure on secondary and higher education. The new class of businessmen got subsidised loans, licences to import scarce goods and other perquisites. The traditional landlord elite was virtually untouched by land reform except in East Pakistan where most landlords had been Hindus. Landlords in West Pakistan were major beneficiaries of government expenditure on irrigation, particularly the new waters that became available after the construction of the Tarbela dam on the Indus river — a World Bank project intended to replace potential water losses to the Indian Punjab.

The bulk of the population was extremely poor. The average weight of an adult Pakistani was 120 lbs, i.e. about 30 lbs less than the average European. Their average haemoglobin count was two–thirds of that in Europe, and in this anaemic state they were readily prone to tuberculosis, pneumonia and influenza. At any one time, a third of the population suffered from intestinal disorders, the rural population was infected by hookworm, and prone to typhoid. Eighty-five per cent of the population were illiterate and most women had a very low status, hidden behind veils with very few opportunities to get a job.

Most social policy action bypassed these people, i.e. major expansions in secondary and higher education, medical training for doctors who emigrated on graduation, housing and urban facilities for the bureaucracy and military. There had been progress in areas where welfare gains were cheap. Malaria, dysentery, and smallpox eradication programmes, together with access to simple drugs had prolonged average life expectation from 30 to 50 years in the two decades since independence, and there was plenty of scope for further cheap gains by expanding and improving primary education, better water and sewerage, birth control programmes, better trained teachers and nurses, better rural health centres.

By the beginning of 1970, it was clear that the government was incapable of bringing any significant social change, political unrest increased, particularly in East Pakistan, and it seemed likely that the country would break up. In mid-1970, the Harvard Advisory Group's work was discontinued.

Mongolia

On my terminal leave from the Centre in January and early February 1967 I undertook a bizarre and picaresque mission for my friend Herbert Philips in UNESCO. I visited Outer Mongolia and Cambodia to investigate the role of science in economic development. I was mainly interested in the Mongol part of the trip, as I had taken a course on Mongol history at Johns Hopkins, where Owen Lattimore had a project including the exiled head of the Mongolian buddhists, the Gegen Dilowa Hutuktu, and two Mongol princes. My companion on the trip was Ratchik Avakov, a Soviet Armenian who had worked in IMEMO in Moscow and who was then working in UNESCO. At first he was a bit suspicious of me but after a month together and 30 000 miles of travel in climates ranging from 30 degrees below zero to about 80 above, we ended up like brothers.

I began to realise Ratchik's value in Moscow when he got the Mongol ambassador out of bed early in the morning and demanded that he give me a visa. That way we got an Aeroflot plane the same day that landed at Omsk and Tomsk and finally deposited us in Irkutsk, where we waited a long time for the two–engined Antonov of Mongol Air. By mistake I picked up what I thought was the only British passport in Irkutsk and met its owner, the wife of the British ambassador to Mongolia, who was on the same plane.

There was only one hotel in Ulan Bataar, a city where a large proportion of the population still lived in *yurts* (felt tents). Most of the adult inhabitants had deeply lined faces from constant exposure to the extreme climate. A large proportion were bow–legged — they spent a good deal of their lives in the saddle in a country with two and a half million horses and only a million people. They drank fermented mare's milk (*kumiss*) which they boiled with tea, and they ate a good deal of horsemeat, often steaks sliced off the haunch of a living animal. The food in the hotel was abysmal. The Yugoslav cook had gone insane trying to improve the local diet. There had been a big expansion in cereal output, so he had put bread on the menu, but it came in damp, heavy, unsliceable chunks. Fortunately, Heath Mason, the British Ambassador, invited me to dinner a couple of times. The Embassy was in the hotel, and he got a regular monthly supply of tinned Yorkshire steak and kidney puddings, delivered in the diplomatic pouch by two Queen's messengers who helped eat them. Mason seemed to me a very good ambassador. He spoke Russian (as all Mongol officials did), went hunting with the locals, and idiosyncratically, wore tropical khaki shorts indoors, amortising an outfit from his previous posting in the Congo!

The country had broken away from Chinese rule in the early 20th century and had been in the Soviet sphere of influence since the 1920s as a buffer state. The old princely class, and the large population of Lamaistic Buddhist monks had been obliterated. The old cursive script, written in vertical columns was replaced by a cyrillic script, written horizontally. The political system was reorganised on the Soviet model, and there were large amounts of Soviet aid and technical assistance. In particular there was a large Soviet military input. In the Summer of 1939 a Japanese invasion had been repulsed by the Soviet army in the battle of Khalkhin–Gol.

Chirendev, the head of the Academy of Sciences, was an atomic physicist and told us about its major research projects. The biggest was on agriculture, a second on mathematical and natural sciences, with a much smaller commitment to social sciences. There was also research activity in the University of Ulan Bataar and in the geological institute. In all, there were 9 000 people with higher education (540 times the Guinean ratio to population) and 1 000 of these were in research institutes. We also talked to the ministers of labour and education, the rector of the university, the planning ministry and the statistical office. It was difficult to assess the impact of science and technical change on growth, but there had clearly been large changes over the previous 40 years. Communication was sometimes a bit difficult. I asked Mrs. Lchamsoryn, the president of the State Commission on Labour and Wages, how many people were unemployed. The interpreter told me it was a silly question. I persisted, and was told that "under socialism there can be no unemployment".

We made a field trip about 30 kilometres out of Ulan Bataar to a collective farm where yurts were huddled together and surrounded by wooden fences to mitigate the cold wind. Here as elsewhere, there were hundreds of horses. We went to an outlying brigade, a kilometre or so from the farm headquarters, to have boiled tea and interview an old peasant. I asked him what difference socialism had brought, and he said, echoing Lenin, that socialism meant electricity. It was only then that I noticed an electric wire from the main camp to his yurt. As Mongols move their herds and yurts around to different pasture in the course of the year, I wondered if the electricity moved with them.

What Might Have Been

Before I went to the Centre, I spent more than a decade on the policy problems of advanced capitalist countries, assessing their growth potential. Generally the results exceeded my expectations. I felt that OEEC's efforts in reducing trade barriers and promoting articulate exchange of views on policy options contributed greatly to the euphoric performance of the 1950s and 1960s.

The Centre's activities were devoted to a "Third" world which then had a population of 1.5 billion compared with 650 million in OECD countries and a billion in the communist world. This Third World was much more heterogeneous in institutions and levels of income than OECD countries, with different policy problems and predilections and no experience of the type of co–operation which OEEC had developed. From my point of view the Development Centre was the ideal place to get to know this world, of which I was fairly ignorant. I was able to visit a wide range of countries, develop a new network of contacts and get some understanding of their problems. I enjoyed a great deal of freedom in my research topics and choice of countries I worked on. What worked for me was true for many others in the Centre.

In retrospect, there are two ways in which it might have been better:

a)   the senior staff of the Centre were all from OECD countries. Our work would have been enriched if some of them had been from the Third World. It was clear from my experience in Brazil, Mexico and Pakistan that there were extremely sophisticated people engaged in policy analysis in those countries. Their experience, insight and judgements would have been very useful to the Centre, and they would also have become more familiar with OECD. We did, of course have visits of a few weeks by Arthur Lewis and Jagdish Bhagwati, and some junior staff like Arjun Sengupta, But the Centre should have been able to invite a senior visiting fellow at least six months every year;

b)   the Centre could have played a bigger role in familiarising OECD with the macroeconomic performance, problems and policy weaponry of the Third World. This was not for want of trying. We did prepare a paper on these lines in the autumn of 1965, which we proposed to present to the Economic Policy Committee, but were rebuffed by its Secretariat. I think we should have persisted and produced an annual report on these lines for publication. Apart from its substantive value in analysing interactions between two major parts of the world economy, it would have been useful in orienting the Centre's research programme, which, in the early days, was kaleidoscopic in its range, and it would have been a public declaration of the Centre's role as an intermediary link between these two worlds. It could have been done by a handful of people, as was the case with the annual OEEC reports on the European economy, and the Centre had a better macroeconomic database at that time than the World Bank.

Notes

1. I am grateful for comments from Derek Blades, Michel Debeauvais, Rostislaw Donn, Giulio Fossi, Colm Foy, Ron Gass, Carl Kaysen, Ian Little, Helen Schneider, and Margaret Wolfson and for documentary material from Carl Kaysen and the OECD Archives Service.

2. The first head of the research division was Gerry Arsenis (later governor of the Bank of Greece and Finance Minister). Friedrich Kahnert (1929–2002) took over in July 1966 and stayed until 1977. He played a major role in reorienting the research activities of the Centre when it was restructured. In 1967 it was decided to discontinue the appointment of fellows and use the resources to create a much larger research division. In 1972, the post of vice president was abolished and Friedrich became the chief staff member under the President. Within the research division, systematic assembly of developing country national accounts was a major commitment. The work was started by Witold Marczewski (also from OEEC), who left in the 1980s and was succeeded by Michèle Fleury. In the 1970s the national accounts work intensified with the arrival of Derek Blades, who had been chief statistician in Malawi for eight years, and David Roberts who had had a similar appointment in Gambia. The Centre held a number of seminars for statisticians from Asia, Africa and Latin America, and published two large volumes, *National Accounts in Developing Countries of Asia*, 1972, and *National Accounts and Development Planning in Low Income Countries*, 1974. Derek Blades and David Roberts moved to the OECD Statistics Directorate and played a major role from 1982 onwards in reviving its former research on the purchasing power of currencies and comparative levels of real product. In the 1990s they were active in helping the successor states of the former USSR to create Western style national accounts.

3. When I came to the Centre, several people came with me from the Technical Co-operation directorate. They included Frank van Hoek, who organised the Centre's relations with Development Institutes; Giulio Fossi, who worked in the Question and Answer Service and acted as an aide to Novacco. Gisela Schade became Goldsmith's research assistant. George Fessou and Christiane Guymer came as administrators. Solange Bernadou worked as a statistical aide in the research division. Valerie di Giacomo and Hilary Georgeson had been my secretaries and also came to the Centre. The cheerful ambiance was further enhanced by the arrival of Ohlin's research assistant, Ardie Stoutjesdijk (later a Director in the World Bank and the

Bank's man in Moscow), and my research assistants, Arjun Sengupta (later economic advisor to Mrs. Gandhi, and Executive Director of the IMF), and Taky Thomopoulos (now Deputy Director of the Bank of Greece).

4.   For a more detailed assessment of OEEC work on economic policy, see my autobiographical essay "Confessions of a Chiffrephile", *Banca Nazionale del Lavoro Quarterly Review,* June 1994.

5.   The Mediterranean Regional Project (MRP) was probably the most successful operational activity of OECD. It was intended to help the six participating governments to improve educational resource allocation and analysis and to provide training opportunities and work experience to a large number of young "fellows in human resource development" (20 each year). Apart from the six country reports in 1965, there were several other publications on the role of education in growth and development. Most notable were the lectures given at the first training course at Frascati (*Planning Education for Economic and Social Development,* 1963) and seminal papers in *The Residual Factor in Economic Growth,* 1964 (by Ed Denison, Trygve Haavelmo, Harry Johnson, Nicholas Kaldor, John Kendrick, Eric Lundberg, Tibor Scitovsky, Amartya Sen, Jan Tinbergen and John Vaizey). The MRP approach was extended to Latin America and the Middle East in 1964–68 in a project financed by the Ford Foundation, and Michel Debeauvais came to the Development Centre in 1968 to follow up these activities. The MRP and most subsequent OECD educational activities were initiated by Ron Gass, the head of the Science and Technical Personnel Division in the European Productivity Agency and Director of Social Affairs, Manpower and Education in OECD. His imagination, vitality and organising ability were a major reason for their success

6.   See *Development Plans and Programmes,* Development Centre, 1964.

7.   I did this study after I left the Centre, see *Economic Progress and Policy in Developing Countries,* Allen and Unwin, London, and Norton. New York.

8.   See Maddison, A. (1992), *The Political Economy of Poverty, Equity and Growth: Brazil and Mexico,* Oxford University Press.

Chapter 16

The Centre since the 1960s

Ian Little

I am happy to be able to reminisce briefly over the first 40 years of the life of the Development Centre. I was not in at the beginning, but not long after. I succeeded Raymond Goldsmith, the first vice president, in September 1965, and immediately set about designing a research programme which would, I thought, achieve a critical mass. The President, Robert Buron, gave me a free hand as far as research was concerned: his main interest was in the travelling seminars, which were supposed to transfer appropriate knowledge from OECD to developing countries. I recall Goran Ohlin's description of Goldsmith's efforts to teach the quantity theory of money to officials in Guinea.

I was able to recruit two fellows who agreed to work on the programme I planned, Tibor Scitovsky and Maurice Scott. I also recruited David Turnham as chief assistant. We all survive, and David Turnham since resumed an active association with the Centre. The same is true of Angus Maddison, who was already a fellow when I arrived, but preferred to do his own thing. He has gone from strength to strength, becoming the globe's leading creator of world historical statistics.

The research comprised a comparative study of seven developing countries each with a single country consultant, except for India where there were two. This formula was innovative, but has since been repeated many times, e.g. by Jagdish Bhagwati and Anne Krueger's NBER Studies of Liberalisation in the late 1970s, and by numerous World Bank multi–county studies in the 1980s promoted by Anne Krueger.

The culminating comparative OECD volume Industry and Trade in Some Developing Countries (hereafter referred to as LSS) became probably the most quoted book in the development literature; and I believe it was influential in the move by many developing countries to more open policies in the 1980s and 1990s . But the six country studies should not be forgotten. In particular, Bhagwati and Desai's (1970) India, Planning for Industrialisation, was I believe, the first major analytical empirical study of the Indian economy. I attended a Development Centre seminar in India a few years ago, and was shocked that the then President of the Centre seemed to be unaware of this publication.

The other notable study of the Development Centre in my time was the *Manual of Industrial Project Analysis for Developing Countries,* which later evolved into Little and Mirrlees' (1974) *Project Appraisal and Planning for Developing Countries.* I believe the latter is still in print, selling one or two copies a year! It fitted in well with LSS, but this was chance. The Manual was conceived before my time as a rival to the projected UNIDO Guidelines for Project Evaluation, and had been entrusted to a French consultancy firm. I disliked the social cost–benefit part of the resulting draft, and after a fierce battle succeeded in getting it suppressed, thereby incurring the responsibility of creating an alternative[1]. This work on cost–benefit analysis has been influential, spawning other manuals and a number of studies of investments in developing countries.

The latter included Little and Tipping's study of the Kulai oil plantation (1972), which was the first published cost–benefit study of a developing country investment; and the first published work by Deepak Lal (1972), both published by the Centre. However, the effective use of cost–benefit analysis by developing countries themselves has been disappointingly scarce.

It is worth comparing the OECD study of trade and industrialisation with the IBRD study of macroeconomic policy 1974–89, which I was engaged on in the 1980s, and which culminated in the comparative volume *Boom, Crisis and Adjustment* (1993) by four authors — Little, Cooper, Corden and Rajapatirana. I, together with Max Corden, was responsible for the original intellectual design of the project; but we were far from having a free hand in its implementation. Eighteen countries were included, usually with two or more consultants per country. From start to publication of the comparative volume, it took nine years (12 to the appearance of the last of the country studies that were published). This compares with five years for the OECD study. Its cost in real terms must have been many times that of the OECD study. I believe its influence will prove to have been much less.

Part of the reason for the lesser presumed influence of the IBRD study is that research on developing countries and knowledge of them, especially their macroeconomic and sectoral policies, have become much more widespread in the 30 years since the OECD study. But there were other reasons. The research took too long, so that results and policy suggestions were outdated. Also, the quality of dissemination was inferior. Only one country study (India), by Vijay Joshi and myself, was published by the OUP: the others were produced only in soft covers by the IBRD itself (one hesitates to use the word "published"). On the cost side, the management was both excessive, and expenditure tolerant. The central direction was also confused. I found myself supposedly responsible for the quality of the project, but unable to take decisions closely affecting that quality. The mixture of interested departments, bank staff, consultants, and the flock of external and internal advisers, was not always a happy one.

But above all the project was too big. However, I must at this point insist that I am not opposed to multi–country comparative studies. Such comparisons of policies and institutions can be very valuable, especially perhaps when the issues are fairly narrowly defined. But the countries must be carefully selected for potential interest. Some pre–study may be needed to decide whether a country should be included in a study.

I have indicated that the OECD base was for me more research friendly than the IBRD, although access to information on the constituent countries came more readily to hand at the IBRD. I hope that the Development Centre retains at least some of the advantages that I found in 1965; to wit, the possibility of forming a small team of high–quality to work on a well defined subject, and the ability to take decisions without excessive clearance and consultation.

After I left in 1967, I kept in contact for a year of two when Monty Yudelman was Vice President, and employment became a focus of research. Then Yudelman and Turnham left to join the IBRD, and I lost touch for 30 years with the Centre's activities, although I continued to be a development economist. This absent–mindedness may be a personal characteristic, but I think it would not have been possible if the Centre's research had been more focused. It can be argued that the best way to run a research institute is to collect first–class people without regard to their particular interests and then let them do what they want. I doubt this because there are areas of economics where knowledge can be best advanced when several people collaborate, albeit maybe adopting different approaches to the same problem. Moreover, a small institute may lose support if it does not acquire the prestige which is impossible if its output is very fragmented, however good each fragment is.

I was shocked when the post of vice president was abolished. It will not surprise anyone to know that I thought that it was the post of president that should have gone. The President had been concerned with politics, public relations and the supposed transfer of existing knowledge; and the vice president with economic research. I thought research was more important, and likely to suffer. But now after many years there is a President who is an economist of world status, and also not unacquainted with politics. So my objections to the amalgamation of the offices of president and vice president vanish for the time being.

It would be presumptuous of me to criticise the work programme for 2001/2002 because I do not know the constraints of money or organisation under which the President operates. By "organisation" I primarily mean the terms and conditions governing appointments and tenure. I also do not know the advice of the Advisory Board, nor the extent to which some of the activities discussed in the Note of April 2000 by the President have been discontinued.

The document Globalisation and Governance (henceforth G&G) clearly intends to provide the focus which, I feel, may have been lacking. I also like the references to co-ordination with other development research institutes. There is a large number of such institutes, some large but many very small. I guess almost everything is being studied somewhere, but often with inadequate resources. I also note with approval that where inter-country comparisons are involved the number of countries is manageably small.

I am less happy with the actual headline concepts. Sometimes new concepts are very valuable, bringing together features of situations or processes whose commodity was not previously obvious, thus facilitating and deepening discussion. Examples are "pareto optimum", the "second best", and "rent seeking". They are precisely definable. But "globalisation" is the very opposite. I believe it originated in an article in The Spectator in 1962, and cannot I think have been coined by an economist. It tends to bring together matters which should be firmly kept separate. It tends to confuse discussion and create dissention. It is too fuzzy to be definable. Is the formation of the European Union "globalisation" or "de-globalisation" ? I expect that unnecessary books will continue to be written about it, whatever it is.

"Governance" is not a neologism. It refers to methods of governing, but had long been replaced by "government", until its recent revival, when it seems first to have been used in "corporate governance". This concept seems to include company law and labour laws, and other regulations regarding the behaviour of corporations, and also the market in corporate ownership. In other words it is about all the external factors governing corporate behaviour, not management itself or how corporations or firms are governed by their owners. However, it now seems to be used even more widely including the way in which national governments manage the economy. Good governance is necessary for development. Why not good government? Perhaps the IBRD and other development pundits felt that it sounded too neo-colonial to preach good government.

I think I understand the main point of connecting globalisation and governance. If limitations on transactions with foreigners are reduced, then new opportunities are created. The extent to which these are seized may be called the general elasticity of supply of tradables. I suppose this in turn may be said to depend on good governance. But it is hardly an advantage that almost any feature of an economy could be studied under this heading.

The document G&G does single out some elements affecting the elasticity of supply. But I myself would like to see a closer connection made with poverty reduction. I believe that the best way of reducing poverty is to increase the demand for relatively unskilled labour. There is no doubt that increasing the openness of an economy permits production to be more labour demanding than otherwise. This is as important as any effect of greater openness on growth. Unfortunately it is usually offset by other policies which discourage employment. There is plenty to study here. Ultimately, of course, the skills of the labour force need enhancing. But, in the meantime, there are any many millions who must be employed despite their lack of skill.

It is unfortunate that the structural reforms which may be required to make an economy more labour demanding have often been, for reasons of political economy, associated with a crisis that demands stabilisation; that is, a reduction of demand which reduces the demand for labour. The vested interests which oppose reform may deliberately confuse stabilisation and reform.

I must not go on grinding an axe, although it is never as sharp as I would like. Let me stop and simply finish by hoping that the Development Centre will, during the next 40 years, have some success in improving the prospects of the poor in the poorer countries of the world.

Note

1.   I have told the history of the Manual at greater length in my Collection and Recollections (1999), Clarendon Press, Oxford.

Bibliography

BHAGWATI, J.N. AND P. DESAI *(1970), India: Planning for Industrialization: Industrialization and Trade Policies since 1951,* Oxford University Press, London.

LAL, D. (1972), *Wells and Welfare: An Exploratory Cost–Benefit Study of the Economics of Small–Trade Irrigation in Maharashtra,* Development Centre Studies, Series on Cost–Benefit Analysis: Case Study 1, OECD, Paris.

LITTLE, I.M.D, R.N. COOPER, W.M. CORDEN AND S. RAJAPATIRANA (1993), *Boom, Crisis, and Adjustment: The Macroeconomic Experience of Developing Countries,* Oxford University Press, New York, NY.

LITTLE, I.M.D. AND J.A. MIRRLEES (1974), *Project Appraisal and Planning for Developing Countries,* Heinemann Educational Books, London.

LITTLE, I.M.D. AND D.G. TIPPING (1972), A Social Cost Benefit Analysis of the Kulai Oil Palm Estate, West Malaysia, Development Centre Studies, Series on Cost–Benefit Analysis: Case Study 3, OECD, Paris.

TURNHAM, D. (assisted by I. JAEGER) (1971), *The Employment Problem in Less Developed Countries: A Review of Evidence,* Development Centre Studies, Employment Series: 1, OECD, Paris.

Chapter 17

Remarks on the Occasion of the 40th Anniversary

Louis Sabourin

Some people will see the 40th anniversary of the OECD Development Centre as an occasion to assess the Centre's past activities and outline its future prospects, while paying homage to those who have provided inspiration and leadership. Others will probably wish to take another look at its special status within the Organisation and its constant efforts to make the most of its role as an interface between the Member states and developing countries.

While fully agreeing with both, I will emphasise three points. The first relates to the objective of the founders of the Centre, the second outlines the policy stance defined at the time of the Centre's 15th anniversary and the third relates to two considerations that occur to me 25 years later. These points correspond to three stages in the evolution of the development community.

The "Four Wise Men" — Ian Tinbergen, Edward Mason, Polamadai Lokanathan and Roger Grégoire — appointed by Secretary–General Thorkil Kristensen to determine the basic rationale, goals and nature of the Centre wanted to give it a very broad mandate, comprising activities of research, provision of information and sharing of experience. This was the period when the Member countries of the OECD were becoming aware of their responsibility to support the Third World. In addition to specifying the structure and mandate of the Centre — adopted by the OECD Council in November 1962 — the "Four Wise Men" aimed to grant it a special autonomous status within the Organisation. It would thus become a forum for scientific thought, communication and information and be able to establish relations with experts, academics and organisations interested in development. While research and dissemination of information have always been central to its activity, exchanges of experience also enabled the Centre to form ties with many developing–country nationals who subsequently played leading roles in their respective countries. To take the case of Latin America alone, Enrique Cardoso, Ricardo Lagos and Ernesto Zedillo all worked at the Centre before rising to hold the presidencies of their countries. This "third dimension" of the Centre's activity should not be forgotten.

After its first 15 years of activity, the Centre was confronted with not only a complex internal situation but also a different international environment.

Facing demands for the creation of a New International Economic Order and the establishment of the North–South Dialogue in the mid–1970s, the Centre decided to investigate new forms of interdependence in the relations between industrialised and developing countries.

Subsequently, for a colloquium on "Interdependence and Development", held in December 1978 to mark its 15th anniversary and inaugurated by Raul Prebisch, a former director of UNCTAD, the Centre conducted studies that involved active participation by many academics from Latin America, Asia, Africa and the Middle East. These led to the publication of analyses that also entailed sustained contacts with researchers working for other international economic institutions.

These years also saw the consolidation of the Centre's relationships with the continental and regional associations that bring together associations of non–governmental organisations. A special effort was made to build on the collaboration of academics working in a number of different disciplines. Of the Centre's fields of research — investment in new technologies, food requirements, policies to cope with external shocks etc. — those relating to the use and management of knowledge and to the negotiations over foreign investment in developing countries aroused a great deal of interest among those concerned with gaining better control over the effects of interdependence.

The Centre's initiatives in the early 1980s to encourage trade with China and the Eastern European countries met with reservations in some circles, but subsequently proved to be very helpful.

Is it surprising that, 25 years later, the Centre is once again facing a "complex internal situation" and a "different international environment"? Not at all — in fact, it would be surprising if this were not the case. Conceptions of development have not grown any simpler over the last few decades, and although globalisation is bringing greater uniformity in some respects, the world is becoming more and more complex.

Analyses of development require consideration of many dimensions: economic, financial, political, demographic, ecological, scientific, technological, strategic, cultural, social, ethical and so on. Studies in the field are increasingly obliged to take account of multidisciplinary approaches and to ensure more harmonious treatment of the various dimensions. Such studies also require more prominent involvement of developing–country academics and experts.

The Development Centre, drawing on its wealth of experience in these two respects, and aware of its role as a recognised intermediary, has much to contribute to the development debate in the era of globalisation. I wish President Braga de Macedo and his staff all possible success in taking up this challenge.

Chapter 18

The Development Centre in the World of Ideas

Just Faaland

This personal perspective is drawn from the statement made to the Advisory Board upon the author's departure from the presidency [extracted from document CD/AB/M(85)1].

* * *

Ideas do have consequences. Intellectual fashions move as powerful currents through development thinking: indeed they may have to, if policy makers are to act with the decisiveness and conviction which is often required. But, at the very least, conditions change over time and refinements and new insights are constantly needed. The fostering of a pluralist intellectual community in the development field greatly facilitates the constant process of reflection and renewal in our thinking.

This brings me to the suggestion that OECD Member States might like the Development Centre to put more emphasis on a role which it so far has fulfilled somewhat irregularly and accidentally, but which it is uniquely situated to fulfil. That is to put currently powerful ideas or contentious issues into a context: to, in effect, provide commentaries on, for example, policy prescriptions for sub–Saharan Africa or, to give another example, strategies for the debt crisis, by reviewing and contrasting the contending analyses and solutions, bringing out the intellectual traditions on which they are based, and drawing out the lessons (if any) of historical parallels. In this way the Development Centre could add quickly accessible depth to a discourse which is often, by necessity, conducted in catch–phrases or generalisations (...).

When the Council established the Advisory Board on the Development Centre in 1971, it stipulated that the Board was to be kept regularly informed of future trends in the Centre's work and that its role was to advise the Centre and the Council on the Centre's programmes and activities. As you know, Delegations are — and indeed should be — very much involved in the process of decision–making on future programmes and activities. It is usually in the course of our regular meetings with all Delegations present, but also in bilateral discussions, that they make proposals for work in general or on specific areas of particular interest to our Member governments. This is very helpful and, to the extent that the Centre is able to do so, we have sought to respond to and follow up on these proposals. In addition, the views of Delegations on the general orientation and balance of the Centre's programme, though they may differ, are heavy inputs in drawing up the Centre's profile.

The process of interaction with Delegations and other parts of the OECD notwithstanding, to preside over the Centre is at times a lonely occupation. Fortunately we have begun to build up more professional interaction within the Centre through internal seminars and through joint research planning and execution. This is only beginning to take hold and needs to be pushed further and harder in coming years. The three regional seminars we have conducted, particularly the one on Africa last year, provided a special opportunity for Centre staff, immersed as they are most of the time in their individual pieces of research, to focus their research on a common set of development challenges. For this reason, as well as for the intrinsic value of regional seminars, I suggest they should be continued for Latin America and Africa, and the tentative plans for one or several Asia seminars might well be further explored and, I hope, realised.

My experience over the last three years has led me to the conclusion that with respect to the research programme in particular, considerable benefit could be derived from also seeking the views of a group of outside experts on development issues. These could include colleagues from academic circles in both OECD and developing countries who would be invited to review the Centre's programme outline, identify priorities and exchange ideas on research objectives. It is my belief that periodic consultations of this nature in one form or another could contribute to making the Centre's research effort more relevant to current and upcoming concerns in the field of development. Such a group might also help ensure quality control of our activities.

Since I came here nearly three years ago I have had the opportunity to observe at close quarters how constrained we are — politically and psychologically — in OECD countries in coming to grips with the problems of management of the world economy. At this point, when I am about to leave the Centre, I naturally reflect quite a bit on what I have seen and where it is all going. Let me make only three points — or if you like, assertions.

First, I must confess that my reluctant conclusion from lifelong involvement in this field has been confirmed: namely, that the rich nations are capable of, at most and at best, a limited response to the central, life–and–death challenges of development throughout the world. Coming to grips with world poverty is not high on the agenda of action for Member countries. Not yet.

Second, the fact of growing interdependence is increasingly recognised in our countries. However, this has not found much expression in our policies *vis-à-vis* developing countries — except in an atmosphere of crisis — and then mainly where and when OECD country interests are directly threatened. So far.

Third, the work of the OECD directed to support members' felt needs for consultation and co-ordination, must reflect these realities. The Organisation may be a funnel for leadership, at times it may itself provide leadership, but only selectively and not too far ahead. The Organisation is primarily and necessarily an instrument of policy of Member countries, collectively and individually. And so is the OECD Development Centre.

Given these realities, the Centre is a good place to devote one's energies to comprehend better what development and world poverty are all about. And the Centre provides a constant challenge to ingenuity and imagination to orient one's efforts so that they become at least relevant if not decisive for formulation and implementation of policies for development by our Member governments, as well as by our partners in developing countries.

It is the challenge to all of us, to the President of the Centre and indeed to this Advisory Board, to so inspire and manage, so organise and orient the Centre that it can — in ever fuller measure — realise these aspirations.

Chapter 19

Thoughts on the Role of the Development Centre within the OECD

Jean Bonvin

Extract from the talk given to the Centre's Advisory Board on 10 March 1999 [CD/AB/M(1999)1].

* * *

If one thing characterised the 20th century, it was the state. It even made a tragic mark in the form of the many totalitarian states, of both left and right, that sprang up on every continent. This century of statism is now behind us. It is clear that in the 21st century the state will be less powerful and will have to be more efficient. It will be less powerful because decentralised decision–making structures will proliferate, while varieties of regional co–operation will grow. The domain of the state will be cut back from the top and the bottom at the same time, but this does not mean it will disappear, because it will retain responsibility for promoting economic growth.

With this new version of the state in mind, the Centre did a number of analyses of decentralisation and regional co–operation. How, for example, to reconcile financial decentralisation and balancing budgets in big countries such as Brazil, China and India? In Brasilia in 1997, with Brazilian Finance Minister Pedro Malan and other top officials, we organised a conference on federal financing that drew more than 200 experts from all over Latin America and from the Bretton Woods institutions.

In the same spirit, we searched for ways to implement decentralised education and development initiatives, aware of how hard it is to push grassroots development but also in the knowledge that empowering poor people is the most efficient path, whatever elites in developing countries sometimes think.

269

Regional co-operation will increase in coming years. This is why the Centre has analysed relations between new regional bodies — such as Mercosur, APEC, ASEAN and the SARC — and the growth of big powers such as China and Brazil that are members of them.

It was also after the fall of the Berlin Wall, and because of it, that with General Obasanjo, president of the Africa Leadership Forum, we organised a conference in 1990 on the implications for Africa of changes in Eastern Europe. The event attracted some 50 political leaders and decision makers from Europe and Africa, including two former prime ministers, Jacques Chaban-Delmas of France and Maria de Lourdes Pintasilgo of Portugal.

The conference dealt with the great concern of African countries at that time that the flow of aid and capital would be diverted from them to Central and Eastern Europe. They needed encouragement to be more coherent in their policies. The result was an "Agenda for Africa" addressed to political leaders of North and South, urging those of the South to step up their efforts to develop the continent and stressing the principle that what a society does not do for itself, no-one else will do.

The Centre has always been involved in seeking economic policies that might be suitable for Africa and has kept in contact with researchers and political leaders there. We were aware that, with the big movement towards globalisation, some political leaders were tempted to draw a line under past efforts and leave the continent to its fate. The Centre has always refused to abandon such efforts however difficult they might be.

To meet this challenge and guide our work on Africa, we have sought to listen to Africans. A meeting in Paris in 1994 with the continent's political leaders and experts resulted in the launch of several projects directly addressing African realities, such as conflict prevention, rent-seeking linked to weak institutions and the feasibility of reforms.

The Centre had accumulated knowledge about the feasibility of reforms through its work on structural adjustment programmes. The unhappy experiences of countries where such programmes sparked riots and dozens (sometimes hundreds) of deaths made us investigate the political feasibility of structural adjustment. The studies we did provided a real service because they showed clearly for the first time that the risk of disturbances was very different according to what measures were taken. So if a government chose a suitable mix of measures it could achieve the same stabilisation as others but without serious civil disturbances.

The most common form of rent-seeking in Africa is unfortunately corruption and we all know how large-scale corruption is often the main obstacle to development. This is why, rightly, we have tackled this problem head-on as shown by the success of the conference on Corruption, in Washington in 1999, attended by the then US Commerce Secretary, William Daley, and Under-secretary of State, Stuart Eizenstat.

The main goal of the 21st Century Partnership Strategy, launched by the Development Assistance Committee (DAC), is long-term poverty reduction. The Centre contributes to this with an extensive programme on emerging Africa.

The project's initial idea was that poverty could not be reduced in African countries without economic take off, in other words faster growth. The history of Latin America and East Asia shows that starting from a situation of extreme poverty, such take off can occur and poverty gradually be reduced through sound economic policies. This obviously cannot be a uniform process. There will be those who lead and those who follow. In today's sub-Saharan Africa, half a dozen "leader" countries pull the rest along.

The end of the Cold War has also given the international community a unique opportunity to cut excessive spending on armaments and war. The Centre has tackled this key question because excessive military spending jeopardises the future of developing countries.

It was important to make both aid donors and decision makers in developing countries aware of this and to find new resources for productive investment. Encouraged by the Japanese government, we organised a conference in Paris attended by political leaders from various OECD Member states and developing countries, including Robert McNamara and Michel Jobert.

At the conference, Takao Kawakami, president of the Japan International Cooperation Agency, suggested that I take a look at how China was converting its old military industries. Germany and Japan followed this up by staging two major conferences — in Berlin and Tokyo — on reducing military spending. Also, at the request of Heng Gaoding, the head of China's Commission of Science, Technology and Industry for National Defence (COSTIND), and the vice-minister for the State Planning Commission, Gan Zeyu, the Centre began a huge project for converting military industries employing some 3 million workers into civil ones.

We organised a conference in China, attended by more than 140 delegates and industrialists from all major arms-producing countries, the G-7 nations and, in a special success, three representatives from Chinese Taipei. At the end of the conference, I was invited to meet Vice-Premier Qian Qichen, along with several figures from OECD Member and non-member states, to describe the work of the OECD and the Development Centre and to present the conclusions of the conference and the follow-up. The Vice-Premier immediately stressed the special role of the Centre and its intellectual independence, which for the Chinese made it a body worth dealing with.

Why such a project? China maintained a powerful military machine that was a threat to regional peace. Our aim was to help the country transform it. Chinese leaders, including those in the army, supported transformation but to bolster their position, they had to show they could carry out economically viable conversion schemes, to contribute to implementation of the reform of state firms decided on by Deng Xiaoping. We were touching on extremely delicate political matters, impossible to handle without a solid relationship of trust.

The resulting study caused a big stir not just among Chinese politicians but also among intellectuals. It set off a stream of requests to work with us from bodies such as the Chinese Academy of Social Sciences (CASS) and from the People's Bank of China, for which we did a study of modernising the country's banking sector.

There was also strong demand for our studies to be translated into Chinese. Ten policy briefs were translated by a private publisher, along with recent publications such as The World Economy 1820–1992 and The Chinese Economy: a Historical Perspective.

We analysed the dynamic Asian economies, as well as those of Indonesia, Viet Nam, India, Pakistan and Bangladesh, and organised conferences, including a large one in Vietnam about managing the country's environment.

We chose Viet Nam because, like its neighbours, it has very serious problems protecting its environment, especially its forests. The meeting enabled an open dialogue to take place among 80 or so national, regional and local level environmental managers from Southeast and Northeast Asia. At the end of the conference, the country's Vice–President, Mrs Nguyen Thi Binh, asked us to help Viet Nam draft an environmental protection law. Once again, the Development Centre paved the way for work that was done by others, in this case the OECD's Environment Directorate.

Several studies have also been done of India, especially on poverty, the environment and economic reforms. In 1995, at the request of Finance Minister Manmohan Singh, we organised a seminar in New Delhi on economic reforms, structural adjustment and competitiveness in India. The first day was spent behind closed doors with Indian political leaders, who asked the Development Centre to make a critical analysis of the reforms implemented since 1991.

The Indian participants, including Commerce Minister P. Chidambaram and Central Bank governor C. Rangarajan, did not seem at all persuaded of the advantages of short or medium–term opening–up of financial markets. On the last day of the seminar, we organised a wide debate with the Confederation of Indian Industries about privatisation, attended by more than 200 businessmen, government members and Indian journalists. We discussed the experiments carried out in Brazil (presented by Winston Fritsch, former personal adviser to President Henrique Cardoso) and in Korea, Mexico and Europe.

There were also many meetings with the Korea Development Institute (KDI) in Seoul, the Chung–Hua Institute in Taipei, the Thailand Development Research Institute in Bangkok, the Colombo Plan Bureau in Colombo and the Institute of Southeast Asia Studies in Singapore.

At regional level, the Centre has worked with regional development banks such as the Inter–American Development Bank (IDB), the Asian Development Bank and, more recently, the African Development Bank.

Since 1990, the Centre has organised a yearly Forum with the IDB to deal with, and often to anticipate, in–depth economic policy issues in Latin America. There too, we bring together Latin American government ministers, invited by the French economy and finance ministry, to meet industrialists, businessmen and journalists during the conference.

Since 1995, with Japan's support, a similar forum has been held with the Asian Development Bank. Like the IDB conference, it is a unique meeting place between the political and business world, this time of Asia and Europe. In 1994, the Forum discussed financial liberalisation in Asia, then a very hot subject.

The Centre reacted swiftly to the challenges of the economic crises themselves, with an informal seminar in March 1998, two studies, one analysing the causes of current account deficits, the other capital flows and investment performance, and Policy Brief No. 16, *After the Great Asian Slump: towards a Coherent Approach to Global Capital Flows.*

The Centre has not just responded swiftly to crises, it has anticipated them. In the early 1990s, the Centre warned the international community about the dangers of an uncontrolled opening–up of capital markets and recommended consolidating local financial institutions before doing so, a view now shared by the OECD.

The Centre was also a source of proposals for policies aimed at solving problems of over–indebtedness. The point of departure was to show that the Brady Plan, for all its merits, would not solve Latin America's financial problems, since the reduction of debt would not alone trigger new investment and growth. It was also a source of policy proposals in showing the urgent need in Africa for determination to reduce excessive debt, through dialogue with member countries of the Paris Club and the multilateral institutions.

In 1994, the Centre's proposals on the need to reduce African debt were presented to a meeting organised in Abidjan with the African Development Bank and with the help of the World Bank, the IMF and funding agencies.

In 1996, we were glad to note there had been total convergence between our Abidjan conference proposals and the Highly–Indebted Poor Countries Initiative (HIPC) decided on by the Bretton Woods institutions and the Paris Club. Progress had been made, even if the G–7 countries now admit this progress is too slow and not enough.

This source of policy proposals exists because of the quality and seriousness of the analyses but also because of the Centre's neutrality. Because it is not involved in the preparation or funding of policies, it is neither judge nor judged.

The Centre has done a lot of work on Africa and Asia, but Latin America is probably the region where it has best worked with partners, as shown by a study by Professor Abreu (of Rio de Janeiro's famous Pontifical Catholic University) on Growth in Brazil since 1930. It goes with a similar study on Argentina in the 20th century, presented last year in Buenos Aires with Ambassador Lañus, whose book A World Without Shores: State, Nation and Globalisation was perhaps inspired by the Centre's work, at least I like to think so.

We have forged close working relationships with several Latin American countries, obviously including Argentina, Brazil and Chile, which have honoured us by becoming full Members of the Development Centre.

The personal conclusion I draw from all this is that even if the world has changed, the basic mission of the Centre, as spelled out nearly 40 years ago, is still valid. However, its activities and its relationship with developing countries and with Member states were bound to change. The Centre has changed them so as to remain true to its mission. A turning point came in 1993, when the Centre moved significantly towards greater integration with the work of the OECD. The leadership role it played in Linkages 1 and its close involvement with Linkages 2 showed this.

There too the Centre has been a pioneer, starting out as the part of the OECD most involved in horizontal activities, such as population ageing, policy cohesion and sustainable development. Moreover, the Centre has authored many studies with other Directorates, in areas such as corporate governance, pension funds, anti–corruption and participatory development.

To ensure it remains effective in the future, I think the Centre must continue to be as flexible as it is now.

More than once, the Centre's researchers have shown their ability to react quickly to new problems in new fields. The Centre has even acted as a "scout" for major problems in developing countries and in the oft–contentious relations between North and South. Here is just one example:

In 1992, when the Uruguay Round negotiations were deadlocked, I learned from the director–general of GATT that US President George Bush and Jacques Delors, President of the European Commission, were going to meet in six weeks' time to discuss how to get the talks restarted. So I asked two researchers to work out the details of the net benefits of a partial reform of trade policies that would result if the negotiations succeeded.

They concluded that, by 2002, the annual gain would be $195 billion, more than $90 billion of it going to developing countries. This would be double the amount of public aid to development. This "policy brief," published a week before the Bush–Delors meeting, got wide press coverage and British Prime Minister John Major quoted the figures at a G–7 meeting in Munich and then in the House of Commons in London.

After taking the liberty of making these suggestions to you, allow me to end on the following note.

As I leave the Development Centre, I leave behind a staff with unequalled experience, know–how and commitment to analysis and dialogue with emerging economies and developing countries. I am proud of my colleagues and what they do.

More than ever, I think the OECD will need a unit that plays the role of guide, always on the look–out. The Centre has this role through its statutes and its special position within the OECD. It has the capacity to tackle new subjects, to go to the cutting–edge of ideas, to engage in dialogue with this or that country without committing the OECD.

It is also a platform of dialogue for NGOs and civil society, thanks to its remarkable network of contacts. It is not at all like a university research centre. It is a true "think–tank" inside the OECD, at the service of governments of Member countries and non–members.

I think that, more than ever, the OECD will need a unit that has the freedom to think and speak out so as to ensure its credibility among non–member states and has a certain freedom of movement. But my vision of the future is also one of a Development Centre that works constantly in partnership with other Directorates and Committees and in complete harmony with the OECD's strategic goals.

In the interests of the OECD and Member countries, I think we ought to preserve this fund of credibility and thus the possibilities of dialogue with all interested parties, government and non–government, in non–member countries. The Centre can be an instrument to open up the OECD. It remains for its Member countries to make best use of the resources that have been built up over nearly 40 years.

Chapter 20

On "The West and the Rest"

Peter Jankowitsch

It has now been more than 50 years since — with the end of the Second World War and the birth of new global institutions such as the United Nations — the idea of international co–operation, not least co–operation for development, gained universal acceptance and entered the international agenda.

The massive wave of decolonisation that took place shortly afterwards gave this new international objective a special degree of urgency as well as a strong political significance. The moment, however, that provided the real test for the willingness of the developed world (now totally identical to the "West") to raise international development to the top of any international agenda was the end of the Cold War. As the menace of deadly confrontation finally disappeared, it seemed legitimate to ask what the new economic and political priorities should be. There was much talk about "peace dividends" available to fight some of the most ancient and persistent scourges of mankind such as hunger, poverty and illness.

Yet still, it would have been hard to anticipate that international development would be the single issue to figure most prominently on international agendas in the 1990s and the early 21st century. While the end of the Cold War has certainly unified the world within one dominant economic and political system to a degree hardly imaginable only a short time ago, the responsibility of the West as the core group of this new universe has also increased. Yet, this new and hopeful advance in the world structure has not resulted in the strength to eliminate or at least reduce existing or new inequalities or imbalances.

Thus neither the 1990s nor the beginnings of a new millennium produced new and more efficient strategies for economic development to replace a string of development policies and theories which had failed to turn the tide.

The Washington Consensus principles such as rapid opening to international trade and financial flows, privatising publicly owned industries and a wide degree of deregulation are often cited as policy prescriptions that did not fare well in many cases and led to numerous economic disasters, particularly where they replaced more tailor–made, country–specific development strategies. Parts of these policies — apart from elements that were more home–made — could certainly be seen in the Asian economic crisis of 1998, but also in the concurrent or later economic and financial crises that shook Mexico, Russia, Brazil and today Argentina.

If the West finds it even more difficult to deal effectively and equitably with the "rest" through new and more comprehensive development policies today another reason is certainly the all invading phenomenon of globalisation. For Western governments in particular, globalisation seems to offer an excuse to relinquish previous responsibilities for the design and execution of workable development policies and leave much of the work to the pure influence of market forces. Massive reductions in ODA that happened throughout the 1990s thus seemed much more acceptable as the level of private investment, particularly FDI, began to increase. In addition to the fact that these latter flows were highly erratic and responded to the same impulses as the movements of the major stock exchanges, they were largely limited to a small number of more prosperous emerging market countries like China, India and some others and could never fully replace the indispensable functions of genuine ODA .

Tendencies in this direction, however, continue strongly and many critics have noted that even the European Union, the largest and most generous donor among Western actors, is beginning to adopt strategies that depart dramatically from past models: thus the new Cotonou Agreement (2000), that will govern relations of Europe (as well as an enlarged Europe) with African, Caribbean and Pacific (ACP) countries for the next 20 years, is seen by some development economists as a successful effort by the European Union to roll back concessions that were made since the Lome convention including such important innovations as the Stabex arrangements — the single, workable alternative to Southern demands for commodity price stabilisation.

The picture of present relations between the "West" and the "Rest" as it emerges from even a superficial balance as the one above offers little comfort, despite brave words still spoken when leaders of the West (now complete with a new friend from the former East) meet selected leaders of the South to discuss such ambitious projects as the NEPAD.

Western actors that deny any need for drastic changes often forget, however, that the West's relations with the rest of the world, not least the developing nations of Africa, Asia, Latin America, the Caribbean and the Pacific have always been highly political. This political element seemed to have disappeared with the fall of the Berlin Wall, when all the world, a few negligible exceptions apart, seemed to be a happy family united by a catalogue of common values and beliefs. While on occasion "rogue states" might come to disturb this peaceful and friendly atmosphere there seemed to be no serious cause for alarm, no serious need to address a growing divide between rich and poor in the world that seemed to grow together more rapidly than ever through the benign consequences of globalisation and modern wonder techniques like the Internet.

September 11 has shattered these cosy beliefs and offered a cruel and dramatic reminder of the prevalence of conflicting forces emerging from unexpected quarters — unexpected only to those who had forgotten "how the other half lives".

While, fortunately, only small, desperate and fanaticised minorities will choose the language of terrorism as their means of expressing their grief towards the West, the West needs fundamentally to reconsider its approach to the "Rest". It will have to start from the idea that the overall responsibility remains great and that it cannot be delegated to the prevailing "zeitgeist" be it neo–liberal or something else. It is only in this way that the West will be able to influence the way in which the "Rest" will, inescapably, shape our future.

Chapter 21

Development with a Big D:
A 21st Century Mission for the OECD?

Kimon Valaskakis[1]

The Contemporary Challenge: Harmonious Global Development

When the OECD Development Centre was created in 1962 the world was neatly divided in blocs. The OECD represented the First World with its democratic tradition and free market philosophy. Opposing that bloc was the Second World centred around Soviet Russia and espousing a socialist–communist system. Then of course, came the Third World, an assembly of poorer countries in need of rapid economic growth. One of the OECD Development Centre's tasks was to create and maintain an interface with that Third World and help it further its "development" by learning from the successes of the OECD countries.

The World in 2002 is vastly different in at least five respects.

— First and foremost, Planet Earth is a much smaller place than in 1962 because of globalisation. Although this historical process is not new and could be traced all the way back to the Voyages of Discovery or even to Alexander the Great, late 20th century globalisation has proved itself to be quite different from earlier forms. It has been characterised by increased cross–border factor mobility (labour, capital, technology and ideas) and has made the world a single competitive arena featuring the integration of global production. In addition it has led to mounting (and largely unwanted) global interdependence which has meant that there is no place to hide, so to speak. We are all in the same boat.

— Second, the division into neat blocs has disappeared. The stable bipolarity of the Cold War has been replaced by a breakdown in global governance. There is one reigning superpower — the United States, strong enough to brook no rivals but insufficiently powerful (or unwilling) to govern the world.

This has led to a crisis in global governance which was dramatised by sectoral seismic shocks such as September 11th (terrorism), the possibility of a nuclear duel between India and Pakistan, talk of pre–emptive war against Iraq, and a breakdown in corporate governance (Enron, etc.). At the global level, no–one seems to be in charge, which makes some observers look back nostalgically at the stability of the Cold War where the two superpowers enforced a condominium on the world.

— Third, at the socio–economic level. whereas in 1962 there was a rich "North" and a poor "South", in 2002 there are now both pockets of extreme poverty in the "North" and islands of extreme wealth in the "South". The division between rich and poor is no longer exclusively geographical. Forty years ago, there were few if any beggars in the OECD capitals. Today it is almost impossible to take the Paris metro or its equivalent in other OECD capitals without being accosted by beggars or desperate individuals requesting help. Meanwhile, the lavish lifestyle of the moneyed elite in some developing countries is sometimes shocking as opulence amidst misery exposes grave inequalities.

— Fourth, official and private aid from "developed" to "developing" areas is now under increasing scrutiny. Both the efficiency and legitimacy of aid are being subjected to mounting criticism. Many feel that international aid has not succeeded in its primary purpose of promoting the rapid and balanced development of the recipient countries. The World Bank and the IMF are sometimes perceived as aggravating the problem. In a general sense, given the ubiquity of unequal income distribution both between and within countries there are those who fear that we may be falling into a trap. Under the guise of international aid we may end up, as one observer put it, taking money from the poor of the rich countries to give to the rich of the poor countries, money which could end up in numbered accounts in Switzerland instead of promoting human progress.

— Fifth, and most important of all, the Development Models of successful countries, once considered the ultimate reference points, are now falling one by one in the garbage heap of history. In 1962 a developing country could choose between a menu à la carte of a dozen or so models to try and emulate. There were a number of variants of Western capitalism (US, Japanese, French, German, Swedish, etc.) There were different socialist models (Soviet, Chinese, Cuban and even a Yugoslav model) and individual Third World experimentations (Arab Socialism, Asian and Latin American models, etc.) Today, almost all these models have collapsed. The Soviet Union no longer exists, Japan has experienced stagnation for a decade, the Asian and Latin American bubbles have collapsed, China is switching to some form of capitalism, etc. The only surviving model by default is US capitalism. During the Clinton boom, it was toted as the exemplar of success. But today, it is under severe strain following the burst of the stock market bubble and the recent escalating crisis in corporate governance (Enron, WorldCom, etc.). It is quite possible that the next decade will see the collapse of even that model. There is another emerging model in experimental stage: European integration which is a fascinating attempt at building a convivial and synergistic supranational entity by revising and updating the concept of state sovereignty. The next few years will demonstrate how successful that model will be and we wish it great success, but for the moment it has to deal with severe growing pains and will have successfully to survive the difficult test of enlargement.

Development with a Big D and the OECD's Potential Contribution

In the face of this new world picture what emerges is a fundamental proposition: no one country or group of countries is in a position to offer lessons which are applicable to the others. Development, if it is to happen at all, must be global in nature and must take full account of the mounting interdependencies. The old adage of "think globally act locally", a key mantra of the 1970s and 1980s is now being replaced by the idea that in many areas we must both think and act globally. Most of the contemporary policy challenges can no longer be dealt with at the national level. Financial crises, the fight against terrorism, conserving the supply of fresh water, adjusting to climate change, battling AIDS and mad cow disease or regulating cloning and the Internet are challenges that must be met at the global level or not at all. The nation–state has, to paraphrase a well–known saying, become too big for the small issues and too small for the big issues.

Big D development is a proposed answer to all these emerging questions and it could be characterised by a number of features.

First, it must be increasingly interdisciplinary in nature, as economic, social, technological, political and ecological issues are so intertwined that they cannot really be dealt with separately. The present policy making structures tend to be sectoral and fragmented. An integrated global approach to problem solving is needed.

Second, global interdependence requires that national and sub–national policies be viewed in a much larger context of globalisation. The illusion that the 195–odd national governments in the world have the degree of freedom necessary to choose their own socio–economic future in isolation must be resisted in favour of more collective and synergistic strategies. Policy formulation must be globalisation–proof. At this stage most national policies are not and they significantly overestimate the regulating power of national governments which has been severely clipped by globalisation.

Third, we must get away from the idea that the OECD or any one country within or without it has all the answers. New answers have to be discovered because the old answers are unsatisfactory. Development, balanced growth and good governance are not subjects to be "exported" from the "advanced" countries to the "developing" ones. We are all developing together. If we succeed then we will have global harmonious development. The keywords here should be "balance" and "symmetry" as opposed to the unbalanced and asymmetrical pattern that development has taken so far. The idea is to promote true development and avoid the maldevelopment which masquerades for progress not only in the former Third World but also in the former Second and First Worlds.

The OECD can play a leading role in the construction of a number of Big D development models. As the premier intergovernmental think–tank and as representative of the Westernised and rich industrial world, it has enormous power and credibility. Within the OECD is the Development Centre which can enhance its traditional role as a bridge with the former Third World and in harmony with other sister institutions throughout the world, offer major contributions to the intellectual design of alternative Big D development models along the parameters discussed.

Looking back to my years at the OECD augmented by the experience of the last three spent outside OECD, I can now confirm that in my view, this Big D Development mission is not currently implemented elsewhere. There is a serious gap in normative policy thinking about what to do about the world and how to achieve the J.S. Mill ideal of the greatest happiness of the greatest number. Most intergovernmental organisations are muddling through, belatedly adjusting to new challenges by pouring old wine into new bottles. We need new wine and new bottles.

Note

1. Kimon Valaskakis was Ambassador of Canada to the OECD from 1995 to 1999 and a former chairman of the OECD Development Centre Advisory Board. He is at present President of the Club of Athens Global–Governance–Group, an international initiative involving world leaders intent on improving global governance. He is also professeur–honoraire de sciences économiques at the University of Montreal and a senior fellow at Groupe Futuribles, Paris, France.

Postscriptum

Jorge Braga de Macedo

In the interval since this book was begun and its publication on 23 October 2002, a number of significant changes took place within the OECD family. The process of increased integration in the world economy, frequently referred to as globalisation, has implied that the Organisation's relationships with non–Members have diversified and intensified. Indeed, the very concept of "development" has become much more intricate and wide–reaching.

The pages of this book reinforce the notion that approaches to economic development are both manifold and evolutive. In Part One we examined policy approaches which have changed along with circumstances and experience; in Part Two we have reflected on the specific role of the Development Centre in all this, with some reference to the way in which that role has itself been modified. We are justly proud of the Centre's record and that of the OECD in helping developing countries seek economic growth that is sustainable and just.

We have been effective, however, because we have been able to adapt.

On 12 September 2002, the OECD Council decided to reinforce its emphasis on development issues by forming a cluster of bodies with a common strategy and co–ordinated work programme. Alongside the Centre for Co–operation with Non–Members (CCNM), the Development Co–operation Directorate, and the Sahel and West Africa Club, the Development Centre will play an equal role in driving the OECD's work on development issues. Its task will be to feed into the Organisation's processes, working with the other units through the Deputy Secretary–General responsible for the development cluster.

For the anniversary of the creation of the Centre, this represents a new challenge, but is also a logical step in its own evolution. Some things will stay the same: the Centre will retain its intellectual independence; it will still be funded separately by its Member countries; and, most importantly, it will continue to interact dynamically and flexibly with developing countries at all levels. The changes will bring the Centre closer to the OECD, reinforcing its influence on the Organisation's thinking and attitudes, and integrating itself more closely in the OECD work programme.

For the OECD to be effective and efficient in translating its own Members' experience of economic development into the requirements of other countries, it needs to have an integrated and co-ordinated approach to non–Member issues. This is one of the goals towards which the Development Centre has been working since its creation.

Over the recent past, as development questions came to figure more and more frequently on the agendas of OECD work programmes and as the work of the specifically development–related bodies expanded, it became clear that the same "constituencies" in developing countries were being reached by diverse parts of the Organisation. This led to a perception of conflicting messages and blurred signals both inside and outside the OECD, something I have contrived to combat in defence of the OECD brand as a reformers' club and the Development Centre's contribution to this brand name.

Thus, the Development Centre wholly supported the reform that has now been put in place by the OECD Council in the interests of reinforcing and rationalising co–operation with developing countries. The Development Centre thus finds itself injected with new vigour and fresh energy to continue its task with the support of the entire OECD and in co–operation with partners within the development cluster: the unity with diversity mentioned in the Preface.

That it brings hope in development is a fitting note of optimism on which to conclude this commemorative volume.

Contributors

(and others mentioned in this volume)

General Secretariat of the OECD

Secretary–General   Donald J. Johnston

Deputy Secretary–General Seiichi Kondo

Development Centre Staff and Former Staff or Associates

Jean–Claude Berthélemy   Special Advisor

Maurizio Bussolo   Economist

Daniel Cohen   Special Advisor

Catherine Duport   Head of Administration and Support Services

Giulio Fossi   Former Head of External Co–operation

Colm Foy   Head of Communication

Kiichiro Fukasaku   Head of Division

Andrea Goldstein   Senior Economist

Ulrich Hiemenz   Director for Co–ordination

Carl Kaysen   Emeritus Professor of Political Economy and Senior Lecturer at the Massachusetts Institute of Technology (MIT); Deputy Special Assistant for National Security Affairs to President Kennedy (1961–1963)

Ian Little   Emeritus Professor, Oxford University; Former Vice President

287

Angus Maddison	Emeritus Professor, Faculty of Economics, University of Groningen, Former Fellow
Edmond Malinvaud	Emeritus Professor, Collège de France and former Inspector General of the Institut National de la Statistique et des Études Économiques *(INSEE)* (1946–1987)
Ida McDonnell	Visiting Expert
Christian Morrisson	Special Advisor
David O'Connor	Senior Economist
Charles P. Oman	Senior Economist
Helmut Reisen	Head of Division
Véronique Sauvat	Editor/Communication
Henri–Bernard Solignac Lecomte	Economic Analyst of Civil Society
Morag Soranna	Administrative Officer

Chairs of the Advisory Board on the Development Centre (Ambassadors, Permanent Representatives to the OECD)

Joëlle Bourgois	France	January 2001– present
Soogil Young	Korea	July 1999–December 2000
Kimon Valaskakis	Canada	February 1999–July 1999
Peter Jankowitsch	Austria	November 1994–December 1998
Eric Roethlisberger	Switzerland	1991–October 1994
Wilhelm Breitenstein	Finland	1998–January 1991
Emile Cazimajou	France	1984 –1987
A. Randolph Gherson	Canada	1983–1984
W.F. Pelt	Netherlands	1977–1982
C. Bobleter	Austria	1975–1976
J. Kaufmann	Netherlands	1972–1974

Presidents of the Development Centre

Jorge Braga de Macedo	Portugal	December 1999–
Jean Bonvin	Switzerland	October 1993–March 1999
Louis Emmerij	Netherlands	January 1986–December 1992
Just Faaland	Norway	February 1983–December 1985
Louis Sabourin	Canada	December 1977–November 1981
Paul–Marc Henry	France	March 1972–April 1977
André Philip	France	September 1967–October 1970
Robert Buron	France	April 1963–September 1967